A Brief History of
American Sports

A Brief History of American Sports

. . . .

Elliott Gorn and Warren Goldstein

Consulting Editor: Eric Foner

AMERICAN CENTURY SERIES

 HILL AND WANG

A division of Farrar, Straus & Giroux

Copyright © 1993 by Elliott J. Gorn and Warren Goldstein
All rights reserved
Printed in the United States of America
Published simultaneously in Canada by HarperCollins*CanadaLtd*
Designed by Fritz Metsch
This edition first published in 1993

LIBRARY OF CONGRESS CATALOGING-IN-PUBLICATION DATA

Goldstein, Warren Jay.
A brief history of American sports / Warren Goldstein, Elliott J.
Gorn ; consulting editor, Eric Foner.
p.   cm.
Includes bibliographical references and index.
1. Sports—United States—History.   I. Gorn, Elliott J.
II. Title.
GV583.G66   1993   796'0973—dc20   93-12628   CIP

Contents

List of Illustrations

ix

Preface

In *A Fan's Notes*, a brilliant fictional memoir of "that long malaise, my life," Frederick Exley described his Sunday afternoons in fall 1954 at New York City's Polo Grounds. He stood in the cold with his friends—an Italian bread-truck driver, an Irish patrolman, a garage mechanic, two or three burly longshoremen—and hollered, laughed, and cheered for the Giants. But sometimes, he remembered, "when the play on the field seemed astonishingly perfect, we just fell quiet. That was the most memorable picture of all . . . Though we may not have had the background, or education, to weep at Prince Hamlet's death, we had all tried enough times to pass and kick a ball, we had on our separate rock-strewn sandlots taken enough lumps and bruises, to know that we were viewing something truly fine, something that only comes with years of toil, something very like art."

Exley's intense devotion to football focused above all on Giants' wide receiver Frank Gifford: "It was very simple really. Where I could not, with syntax, give shape to my fantasies, Gifford could, with his superb timing, his great hands, his uncanny faking, give shape to his." Gifford, the golden-boy athlete, had outrun "life's bleak anonymity," whereas Exley—struggling writer, alcoholic, erstwhile mental patient—could only dream of the fame he craved. If not through his own deeds, then in the vicarious world of fandom, Exley clutched at the glory that always receded from his grasp.

A Fan's Notes reminds us of the entanglements of sports with life, and of how confused the real accomplishments of players on the field become with American culture's giddy dreams. Sports arenas are America's living galleries, where we witness all the beauty and grace and passion of which humans are capable. They are also our asylums, filled with delusional fantasies, misogyny, misplaced loyalties, racism, homophobia, and unclear boundaries between self and others.

A Brief History of American Sports is not a jeremiad, not a call to return to the true and clean ways of our fathers. Sports have always been Janus-faced. The strange mixture of sordidness and transcendence, crudity and refinement, venality and selflessness are part of sports' appeal, the source of their drama, integral to their history. Moreover, our goal as authors has not been simply to describe the rise of sports; we do not merely "call the plays." This is a work of interpretive history, of speculation on the changing place of sports in American life. Chronicles of particular games and compendia of seasons past are available in countless other volumes. Here we do a lot of color commentary.

The academic study of American sports has boomed during the past generation. At the same time, the writing of history has undergone profound change. The "new social history" and "history from the bottom up" of the 1970s and 1980s focused much attention on the daily lives of ordinary people. When they examined such lives, historians found not only family and work but recreation as well. At the same time, cultural historians began to examine the historical origins and experience of popular culture—the expressive outlets of people who did not compose symphonies, publish philosophical treatises, or design office buildings but who went to movies, read pulp fiction, and rooted for the home team. Finally, as historians of women and African

Americans excavated and reinterpreted the history of those groups, they unearthed much that had previously been overlooked in the sporting experience. The study of sports has benefited from all of these developments.

Certainly we have. In the years since we first published books in this field, Elliott Gorn's *The Manly Art* (1986) and Warren Goldstein's *Playing for Keeps* (1989), sports history has begun to break out of its ghetto, where practitioners talk only to one another and the rest of the historical profession looks down its nose. In this book, we have tried to push ourselves and the field a little harder in order to make connections between the history of sports and the larger story of American culture and society.

This short work is by no means a comprehensive survey of American sports history. Its purpose is to describe and interpret some central themes of that history. We have sought to show, first, how the study of sport cannot be divorced from other social and cultural developments; second, just how changes in, for example, the organization of production and consumption have affected the growth and experience of sports; and finally, how sports have served as a key arena for the formation and definition of gender and class identities.

As a result, rather than survey all of sports history over the past three hundred and fifty years, we have concentrated on certain central issues: battles between religious folk and nonbelievers over recreational practices; racial prejudice and integration in sports; the class origins of football, baseball, boxing, and basketball; the entry of women into sports; the relationship of sports to masculinity and femininity; the playground movement, educational institutions, and sports; television, money, drugs, and the culture of consumption.

Part I, "America Becomes a Sporting Nation," deals principally with the years before 1900, and Part II, "Sport and Its Discontents," centers on the twentieth century. While our structure is chronological, we have felt it important to roam backward and forward as necessary. Co-authorship tends to blur lines, and we both admit to liberal borrowings from each other, but Elliott Gorn bears primary responsibility for Part I, Warren Goldstein for Part II.

We would both like to acknowledge Gerry McCauley for locating a fine home for this book at Hill and Wang. There Arthur Wang provided the regular nudging, unfailing good cheer, confidence in his authors, and first-rate editorial sense for which he is justly renowned. Eric Foner's insightful and penetrating criticisms of earlier versions of this manuscript helped us focus, refine, and rethink our arguments, in the process making this a much better book. Ronald Story provided an exceptionally helpful critical reading of the entire manuscript as it was nearing completion, an effort for which we will remain long in his debt. Elaine Chubb both untangled our prose with good humor and kept us from making numerous errors of fact. Finally, Larry Malley has been a constant source of good advice, encouragement, and friendship.

We each have our own debts. Warren Goldstein thanks his colleagues in the American Studies Program at the State University of New York/College at Old Westbury: Laura Anker, Rosalyn Baxandall, Elizabeth Ewen, Barbara Joseph, Karl Grossman, Naomi Rosenthal, Elaine Scott, and Denton Watson. They have reason to be proud of what they have created: an intellectual and professional environment both open and stimulating to the practice of cultural history, one from which he has benefited enormously. Finally, he thanks his wife, Donna Schaper, for her unfailing attempts to make sure that a book about sports would risk playing a bit between its covers; and Isaac, Katie, and Jacob Goldstein, to whom he dedicates this book, for insisting—with compelling logic—that writing about sports is not at all the same thing as playing baseball in the backyard.

Elliott Gorn thanks Andrew Cayton at Miami University, who read the first three chapters and saved him from several missteps. Other colleagues at Miami University provided friendship and support over the years, among them Arthur Casciato, Jack Kirby, Allan Winkler, Sheldon Anderson, Mary Cayton, Michael O'Brien, Mary Frederickson, Carl Pletsch, and Peter Williams. A fellowship from the Stanford Humanities Center and a Miami University summer grant aided the completion of this work. Finally, he thanks his daughter, Jade, who continues to teach him the true spirit of play.

PART I

. . . .

America Becomes a Sporting Nation

1 / Colonists at Play

. . . .

"Virgin Land"

American children during the 1950s played with Hula Hoops, those plastic rings about three feet in diameter that circled around your hips if you gyrated just right. But sometimes children used Hula Hoops in a different way from that advertised by the toy manufacturer. One kid, for example, might roll a hoop down the street while others stood on the curb and tried to throw rocks through it.

Many American Indian tribes played a similar game. Edward Curtis, an early ethnographer of native American life, described in *The North American Indian* (1909) a hoop-and-pole game enjoyed by the Salish Indians of the Northwest Coast. A hoop six inches in diameter was rolled past players standing about forty feet away. The object of the game was to impale the hoop by sending a spear or arrow through it into the turf. Such contests, Curtis noted, were never held during salmon-spawning season, because "the invisible spirits of the salmon, passing

Indian youths in Florida, ca. 1566, shooting bows and arrows, throwing balls, running races *(Library of Congress)*

through the village on their way upstream, might be struck by a missile and become angered, not to return that way again."

Play may be universal, and a particular game might be popular among the most diverse people, but as these two examples suggest, context and meaning are everything. The Salish enjoyed the hoop-and-pole game as pure competition, and certainly playing it honed their hunting skills. But Curtis's remark about the spirits of the salmon suggests how different the Salish culture was from that of 1950s suburban American children who also hurled objects through rolling hoops.

English explorers and colonizers of North America did not find "virgin land." The millions of native people who occupied the continent enjoyed a variety of games and recreations. Some were unique to the New World, such as stickball (also known as lacrosse), an elaborate team game popular throughout the Eastern Woodlands of North America. There were also Indian versions of wrestling, football, and fighting with sticks (known as cudgeling in England). But even where their games resembled those of Europeans, disparate cultural contexts gave them different meanings.

Indian games accompanied fertility ceremonies, burial rites, healing practices, and efforts to control the weather. It was not just that games were part of religious practices; the sacred pervaded the Indians' existence. James Mooney reported in the *American Anthropologist* (1890) that Cherokees who played stickball must not engage in intercourse for a month before a game, nor could they eat rabbit for fear of becoming timid, nor frog lest their bones turn brittle. Before a game, Cherokees built a fire and danced through the night to the sounds of drums, rattles, and sacred chants. Shamans prepared athletes for matches with prayers, body paint, pipe smoking, and other ritual practices designed less to ensure victory than to enhance them spiritually. For gifted athletes playing stickball and other games, participation was not voluntary, because placating spirits, or warding off disease, or ensuring adequate rainfall were crucial tribal concerns. Games, then, were embedded in ritual; contests could be fun and exciting, but even as tribesmen enjoyed themselves, athletic events kept them connected to their sacred beliefs, which gave meaning to the world and their place in it.

No doubt the English who colonized North America and the Indians whose land they took exchanged ideas about play; many English country amusements, like Indian games, were filled with symbolism of fertility and the harvest. Moreover, their pastimes could be remarkably similar. Take away the netted sticks of lacrosse players and replace their little ball with an inflated bladder, and the game is similar to English football of that era. In both cases, two teams ranging in numbers from dozens to hundreds tried to get the ball past a goal on a field without sidelines, whose length might vary from yards to miles.

Nonetheless, Englishmen and Indians do not seem to have borrowed freely from each other. Certainly the colonists' Protestant faith abhorred "paganism." But more generally, the wilderness was so frightening that they felt most comfortable and secure maintaining their own cultural practices. Traditional pastimes that they brought from their home parishes allowed colonists to remain true to themselves as Englishmen, no easy task in a forbidding wilderness. What they held on to were not just particular games and sports but whole clusters of attitudes and practices in which leisure-time activities were rooted. Settlers did not just transport English pastimes to the New World; they also brought their *ideas* about the role of play—recreational ideologies we might call them—across the ocean.

English Sports

In addition to the English, ethnic peoples such as the Dutch in New York, Germans in Pennsylvania, Scotch-Irish scattered through the Appalachian valleys, and Africans in the South maintained ancestral games. But for over two hundred years, England's colonies remained, for the most part, outposts of English culture. Cockfighting, horse racing, and animal baiting; hunting, angling, and fowling; throwing quoits (similar to horseshoes), cudgeling, and rounders (an antecedent of baseball); contests in which we would recognize the outlines of modern wrestling, football, and cricket—indeed, a hundred games of chance and skill, played according to a thousand unwritten local rules, were brought to the colonies.

Sports and games were part of England's cherished realm of leisure. Renaissance writers evoked the pastoral tradition of classical authors and the biblical imagery of paradise before the Fall. In both cases, leisure formed a mythic ideal and a counterpoint to the necessity of daily labor. Work was associated with pain, toil, even servitude; play, with freedom and gentility—necessity and sin on one side, pleasure and ease on the other. Especially under Henry VIII and Elizabeth, the English people celebrated leisure, and their lore blossomed with references to the national love of play. The legend that Sir Francis Drake insisted on finishing a game of lawn bowls while his fleet waited ready in port to sail against the Spanish Armada only endeared him to his countrymen; Drake had the composure of a true gamesman.

The aristocracy set the pace for the rest of the country. Horsemanship became a central part of the courtly tradition, as did the revived medieval tournament, along with grand hunting parties, match games like tennis, and even wrestling bouts. Common folk, too, cherished play. Particular games became associated with various feast days of the ecclesiastical calendar. Informal contests, governed by local rules and provincial customs, gave excitement to special occasions. Rough football games played by masses of brawling men were mandatory on Shrove Tuesday; Easter games included feats of running, jumping, throwing, and wrestling; and Sabbath afternoons saw a variety of amusements, played in accordance with local traditions, fertility symbolism, and Church rituals.

Richard Carew's marvelous description of "hurling" contained in his *Survey of Cornwall* (1602) gives us a sense of the exuberance, bordering on riot, of such games:

> . . . Some two or more Gentlemen doe commonly make this match, appointing that on such a holyday, they will bring to such an indifferent place, two, three, or more parishes of the East or South quarter, to hurle against so many other, of the West or North. Their goales are either those Gentlemens houses, or some townes or villages, three or four miles asunder, of which either side maketh choice after the neernesse to their dwellings.

Local elites initiated the game, dozens or even hundreds of players opposed each other according to parish rivalries, square miles of countryside were the fields of play, and well-known landmarks the goals. "When they meet," Carew continued, "there is neyther comparing of numbers, nor matching of men: but a silver ball is cast up, and that company, which can catch, and cary it by force, or sleight, to their place assigned, gaineth the ball and victory." The style of play, however, resembled a brawl more than games as we know them:

Whosoever getteth seizure of this ball, findeth himself generally pursued by the adverse party; neither will they leave,
till . . . he be laid flat on Gods deare earth . . . The Hurlers
take their next way over hilles, dales, hedges, ditches; yea,
and thorow bushes, briers, mires, plashes and rivers whatsoever; so as you shall sometimes see 20, or 30 lie tugging
together in the water, scrambling and scratching for the
ball . . .

Such matches—antecedents of modern football that varied
widely according to local custom—were common in early modern
Britain. Any number of men could participate, the playing field
was the entire countryside for miles around, and teams were
formed out of communal identities such as parishes or townships.
The gentlemen who arranged the contests generally offered prizes
for the winners and a feast for all after the game. These local
nobility or gentry were patrons of the community whose largesse
secured the loyalty of their more lowly neighbors. In this way,
the games were cultural glue, binding men together with shared
identity despite the class divisions produced by England's intensely hierarchical and aristocratic social system. But it must
be remembered that such popular recreations did not erase social
distinctions; games often depended on the presence of rich and
poor, nobleman and commoner for their very existence.

The singular violence of these contests made them convenient
venues for settling old scores and perpetuating social tensions.
Hurling, Carew concluded, prepared men for war, putting courage in their hearts and strength in their bodies; but it also left
many with broken bones, bloody heads, and injuries that short-
ened their days. Above all, hurling was emblematic of a host of
brutal sports all of which helped define a male ideal. Parishes
might lose or individuals get bloodied, but all who played demonstrated their membership in the circle of masculinity. In a
patriarchal society, even the poorest man who proved his grit,
his valor, his ferocity, reinforced his dominance over women and
children.

Only a decade and a half after Carew described hurling

matches, James I—who reigned during the founding of the first permanent American colonies—issued his famous "Kings Majesties Declaration to His Subjects concerning lawfull Sports to bee used," better known as the *Book of Sports* (1618). The king's decree defended traditional sports and pastimes:

> Our pleasure likewise is, Our good people be not disturbed, letted, or discouraged from any lawful recreation, Such as dancing, either of men or women, Archery for men, leaping, vaulting, or any other such harmlesse, Recreation, nor from having of May Games, Whitsun Ales, and Morris-dances, and the setting up of Maypoles, and other sports . . .

The *Book of Sports* was a very controversial document. James promulgated it not merely to encourage his people to have a good time. Sabbath amusements had become an important issue to a large minority in English society, the Puritans, those Protestant reformers who believed that daily life must conform much more closely to the divine plan revealed in the Bible. This meant rooting out "Popish" accretions of custom and tradition that, according to the Puritans, had no basis in early Christianity. As early as 1583, Philip Stubbs's *Anatomie of Abuses*, a Puritan indictment of the "corruptions" of the Church of England, condemned all sorts of traditional recreations, from feast days to bearbaiting, from Christmas celebrations to cockfighting. The English Puritans were not against all amusements, but they believed that honest labor was a Godly activity, and that Sunday, the Lord's day, must be reserved for prayer and thoughtful introspection. Ministers refused to proclaim the king's decree from their pulpits. And in those parishes where the Puritans gained political ascendancy, they stopped all Sunday amusements, feast days, and raucous pastimes, all that they deemed sensual or self-indulgent, all activities that opened the floodgates to violence and passion, all that distracted men and women from diligent work and pious worship.

James I rebuked his Puritan opponents and cultivated those who resisted their rigid morality. He argued that Puritan fanaticism frightened people; rather than convert from Catholicism to the Church of England, they rejected the Protestant message and remained in the "Romish" fold. Moreover, the king stressed the old idea that sports helped prepare men for war, so that to hinder lawful recreations was to injure the national defense. Finally, James argued, if individuals were prevented from enjoying themselves after services on their only day off, they would turn from healthy recreation to such vices as drunkenness; worse, they would be susceptible to the seditious speeches of the idle and discontented.

Puritans and traditionalists often squared off over feast and holy days, lusty occasions marked by drinking, gambling, and rough play. The Church of England had retained the Catholic tradition of celebrations—holidays to honor miraculous events, the deaths of martyrs, the canonization of saints. In Somerset, for example, a "church-ale" was held annually to commemorate the founding of a parish church. The occasion resembled nothing so much as a Brueghel painting of a peasant holiday. Feasting, dancing, and athletic contests were the order of the day, and considerable local ale, sometimes brewed by the parson himself, was imbibed. Wandering minstrels provided music, and itinerant entertainers offered juggling, dancing, puppet plays, and other diversions.

Such events released normal inhibitions, momentarily replacing the routine of rural life with pleasure and abandon. Vast quantities of drink were consumed, out-of-wedlock pregnancies increased, brawls broke out, and blood sports such as bull- and bearbaitings were staged. Country people relished church-ales, wakes, feast days, and similar celebrations. The parson raised money for his parish, the local squire displayed his magnanimity and power, and the rural folk got a much needed break from the monotony of their lives. Needless to say, such events horrified the "precise people," as Puritans were called. Here were the pagan excesses of Rome sponsored by allegedly Protestant churches; here, in the name of Christianity, the eyes of common folk were diverted from God to a veritable orgy of debauchery.

The conflict between religious dissenters' belief in a well-ordered society, on the one hand, and the desires of Church and Crown to encourage more traditional free and easy ways, on the other, grew explosive when these ideological positions were fused with a struggle over power. Social rank did not determine where people stood on this conflict, but there were clear tendencies— aristocracy, gentry, and peasantry overrepresented in the traditionalist camp; urban professionals, shopkeepers, the middle class, and small landholders more on the side of religious reform. Popular recreations became a site for these conflicts, especially when Archbishop Laud of the Church of England had the *Book of Sports* reissued in 1633, forcing individuals to declare themselves openly for or against traditional amusements on feast days or the Sabbath.

The stakes continued to rise between dissenters and loyalists until civil war broke out. The Puritans consummated their revolution in 1649 by beheading King Charles I and establishing the Commonwealth under Oliver Cromwell. They imposed a rigid Sabbath and went further than ever before in uprooting the old feast day celebrations. Profane pastimes, Puritan Thomas Hall declared in *Funebria Florae, the Downfall of May-Games*, were an invitation to sinfulness:

> If I would debauch a people, and draw them from God and his worship to superstition and Idolatry, I would take this course; I would open this gap to them, they should have Floralia and Saturnalia, they should have feast upon feast (as 'tis in Popery), they should have wakes to prophane the Lord's day, they should have May-Games, and Christmas-revels, with dancing, drinking, whoring, potting, piping, gaming, till they were made dissolute, and fit to receive any superstition, and easily drawn to bee of any, or of no religion . . .

To the Puritans, small indiscretions led to larger and larger sins, so the laws were drawn tight around popular recreations. Sports, games, and athletic competitions did not die off, despite the onslaught, but they became much less prominent in English culture during the Puritan reign.

With the Restoration of the 1660s, the pendulum swung again toward more vigorous recreations. The rural character of English society changed slowly, and the old feast days and holiday revels still conformed to the seasonal cycles of work and relaxation. With renewed social power, aristocrats and gentlemen reasserted themselves, and they once again patronized traditional games and pastimes, while local parsons, farmers, and townsfolk, too, enjoyed the freedom and exuberance of the old ways. Rural laborers saw feasts and celebrations as something they had earned, a sort of informal compensation for loyal service. And males, especially young ones, renewed the bloody old sports— such as cockfights and bullbaitings—that helped define a particular style of masculinity.

Men of wealth were no doubt sincere in their belief in mutuality: great man and commoner needed each other, had mutual rights and obligations to each other. The privilege of rank bestowed the duty of benevolence. But the nobility and gentry also understood that failure to placate their social inferiors could lead to trouble, for popular pleasures helped accommodate workers to their lot. Declared one article published in 1736 in the *London Magazine*, " 'Tis well known that such Diversions are chiefly enjoy'd by the common People; who being fatigued by labouring continually for a sorry Living, find a Relaxation highly necessary for them." A little generosity by the elite bought the commoners' goodwill and secured their loyalty:

> For several Months before these Festivals come, they please themselves with the Expectation of approaching Joys. Then, think they, we shall not only rest from our mean Employments, but shall act the Part of Richer and more Creditable People; we shall appear with our best Clothes, and with the Help of our Savings not only live well, but divert ourselves with the merry Humours of Harlequin and Punchanello. These Imaginations brighten their Thoughts, dispel the

Clouds of Melancholy, and make them dispatch their Business with Pleasure and Alacrity.

The mere memories of a grand festival, the author concluded, lived long in people's imaginations, and buoyed them through their labors.

Some contemporary observers explicitly advocated popular recreations as a means of social control. Adam Smith argued in *The Wealth of Nations* that they helped check the power of "fanatical" religious sects, for exuberant pastimes dispelled the melancholy on which such groups fed. Gentleman-scholar John Brand went further: popular pastimes not only helped workers accept their lot but siphoned off discontent that otherwise might lead to political rebellion.

But even advocates of popular recreations must have pulled up short at the riotousness, the social leveling, the sheer menace inherent in some events. We can feel the powerful emotions these activities elicited in the description of a cockfight that the German traveler Zacharias Conrad von Uffenbach witnessed in London and described in his *Travels* (1710). As soon as the birds were brought in, the crowd began to shout and argue; commoners sat with gentlemen, but all acted "like madmen"; wagering rose to a crescendo as the trainers attached razor-like spurs to the birds' feet. The battles themselves were blood-soaked frenzies: ". . . It is amazing to see how they peck at each other, and especially how they hack with their spurs. Their combs bleed terribly and they often slit each other's crop and abdomen with the spurs. There is nothing more diverting than when one seems quite exhausted and there are great shouts of triumph and monstrous wagers; and then the cock that appeared to be quite done for suddenly recovers and masters the other." Momentarily, high and low found themselves on the same social level: "Those who put their money on the losing cock have to pay up immediately so that a hostler in his apron often wins several guineas from a Lord. If a man has made a bet and is unable to pay, for a punishment he is made to sit in a basket fastened to the ceiling, and is drawn up in it amidst peals of laughter." Such social mixing was only temporary, and strictly confined to special venues like the cockpit.

As Uffenbach's narrative of life in London suggests, it was not only the old rural amusements that revived after the Puritan reign; a burst of new activities exploded in the cities, too. By the eighteenth century, public events grew in size, frequency, and variety; new games arose; increasing wealth and population density created a growing consumer demand for entertainment; and sports began to stand alone as spectator events in their own right, not necessarily part of larger celebrations such as saints' days. Among the most prominent activities were horse racing on circular tracks; boxing matches, which began to attract both wealthy aristocrats and the urban working class; and old country pastimes like cockfighting, which now found a home in urban taverns.

This urban leisure culture was patronized by the old upper class but also by newly wealthy merchants. The London gentry created a fashionable social life of balls, soirees, and sports. Perhaps even more important to the transformation of popular recreations was the expanding importance of inns and taverns, and the relative decline of the church as the center of activities. Publicans not only tolerated sports, they promoted them—horse races, prizefights, bearbaiting, and the rest—in order to keep trade brisk. Here were the very beginnings of a critical shift, away from the paternalism of the countryside, with its ties of power between the local nobility, the parish clergy, and rural laborers, toward the modern version of recreation as part of commercialized consumer culture. Still, throughout the eighteenth century, gentry patronage, whether in the cities or in the countryside, remained indispensable. A champion boxer, for example, could not survive without a great man who financed his training and put up the stakes for his matches. Nor were sports purely moneymaking ventures—not until the nineteenth century would gate receipts become the essential condition for staging events.

Because many of these early sports were filled with aggression, competition, and violence, they sometimes threatened to unleash social disorder. Certainly class or even ethnic divisions at a given event were potentially dangerous in the context of heavy drinking and gambling. Yet the countervailing bonds of patriarchy usually kept social and personal divisiveness in check. In their very violence and competitiveness, sports united men with displays of masculine power. The swagger of a man who played in bloody football games, or even the strut of one who, with a large wager, identified himself with a particular fighting cock, were emblems of manhood that excluded women, children, and the elderly. In bloody sports, men momentarily rejected those who demanded that they act responsibly; more precisely, the displays of physical prowess writ small in sports were symbols of the same patriarchal power that enforced masculine prerogatives in society, politics, and the family.

As popular recreations gained prominence in English society, opposition also grew, so much so that late-eighteenth-century reformers threatened to hound the most raucous sports into extinction. Burgeoning cities were home to an entertainment-hungry working class but also to a newly powerful and self-conscious middle class, an early capitalist class of property owners who abhorred the license and abandon associated with popular recreations. Particularly prominent were individuals in manufacturing or in trades with large and specialized labor markets. Their quest for productivity demanded diligence, sober self-control, and hard work, hardly the characteristics of profane men at a prizefight. Effective labor discipline in this youthful capitalist economy meant that workers must internalize such traits as industriousness, thrift, and prudence, must shun the drinking and gambling and swearing of the racecourse and the cockpit.

Not only were the opponents of urban sporting traditions bourgeois in their social backgrounds; they were also, quite frequently, members of evangelical sects, dissenters who retained much of the style and moral outlook, if not the specific doctrines, of the Puritans. Such individuals led important reform movements, among them temperance and antislavery. But in their faith that humans could perfect their earthly behavior and choose salvation, they had little patience with the sloppy moral habits of others, much less with the idleness, the sensuality, the self-indulgence they saw in popular recreations. Moreover, a significant number of the religious reformers were women, who were offended by the masculine posturing and brutality associated with many old sports. The nexus of bourgeois and evangelical reformers often garnered the support of legislators and magistrates, adding political power to economic and moral force. English law and English courts increasingly reflected the new emphasis on sober self-control, regularity, and orderliness.

Prizefighting provides the clearest example of these tensions. The ring was esteemed the "national sport of England," and this golden age lasted roughly from the last quarter of the eighteenth century through the opening years of the nineteenth century. "I have known the time," George Borrow wrote in his autobiographical *Lavengro* (1851), "when a pugilistic encounter between two noted champions was almost considered as a national affair; when tens of thousands of individuals, high and low, meditated and brooded upon it, the first thing in the morning, and the last thing at night, until the great event was decided." Despite the fact that prizefighting was illegal, thousands of men—including aristocrats and ministers of state—witnessed the great matches involving champions like Richard Humphreys, Daniel Mendoza, Tom Crib (or Cribb), John Jackson, Jem Belcher, and John Gully. Working-class men, many of them quite poor, offered the muscle and grit, while the old gentry and nobility provided cash to stage matches, and protection from the law. But by the nineteenth century, the growing power of the middle class—of those whose wealth came more from manufacturing and commerce than from inheritance—brought the end of boxing's golden age. The bourgeoisie and the evangelicals made war on all that seemed wild and licentious, and police interference grew until it was all but impossible to stage fights.

The American colonies were heirs to England's bifurcated leisure heritage. On the one hand was the productive ethic of Calvinism, not opposed to all diversion but suspicious of excessive worldly joys. Those who envisioned godly communities in the New England wilderness found "human nature"—especially male human nature—inherently untrustworthy. Too much leisure time gave free rein to men's base instincts. Sober religious folk kept amusements hedged within useful and moderate bounds, bounds that threatened to constrict until they contained nothing at all. In a new land, these people felt, the old ideals of true Christianity and virtuous hard work might yet be realized. But others molded their fantasies of the New World on the age-old ideal of a leisured paradise. They envisioned an easy and bountiful life on fresh and fertile soil. Plenty, not poverty, repose, not toil, would be their lot. The English heritage of fairs, feast days, and sports became the palpable expression of their leisure ethic. Colonists carried both traditions to North America, and settlers would try to shape their lives to fulfill these old dreams.

The Virginia Ethic

A few years before the American Revolution, Philip Vickers Fithian—a New Jerseyan, a Princeton graduate, and a tutor for the aristocratic Carter family of Virginia—described in his journal two events that help us understand sports in the Southern colonies. One fall morning in 1773, he rode to the Richmond courthouse to watch a horse race. Fithian noted that the horses' owners had wagered heavily on the event, and that spectators made innumerable side bets just before the race began. "One of the Horses," he wrote in his journal, "belonged to Colonel John Taylor, and is called *Yorick*—The other to Dr. Flood, and is called *Gift*—The Assembly was remarkably numerous; beyond my expectation and exceeding polite in general." The horses raced five heats on a one-mile circular track, while observers recorded their times and distances. Colonel Taylor—a wealthy planter, and among the most successful horse breeders in Virginia—emerged victorious. The race, Fithian concluded, had been a gentlemanly affair, conducted before a well-behaved audience.

Less than a year later, in the summer of 1774, Fithian witnessed another event near Richmond. Two "fist battles"—rough-and-tumble fights, as they came to be called—were scheduled for a

Saturday afternoon. Such contests had little to do with stand-up boxing under the rules of the English prize ring, for here, Fithian observed, "every diabolical Stratagem for Mastery is allowed and practised, of Bruising, Kicking, Scratching, Pinching, Biting, Butting, Tripping, Throtling, Gouging, Cursing, Dismembring, Howling, &c." Fithian noted the "triffling and ridiculous" causes of these common battles: one man supplanted another as a lover; or he impugned another's social status with epithets like "lubber," "buckskin," or "Scottssman"; or one mislaid the other's hat, or knocked a peach from his hand, or offered a dram without first wiping the mouth of the bottle. Most shocking, "this spectacle, (so loathsome and horrible!) generally is attended with a crowd of People!" Or perhaps, Fithian speculated, the audience only looked human but was really the offspring of "the meaner kind of Devils with Prostitute Monkeys."

The events Fithian described thrived on Virginia soil. Rough-and-tumblers were lower-class white males, while the horse breeders were wealthy planters. Poor men sometimes tried to enhance their social standing by competing against their betters; rich men sponsored blacks and poor whites who raised pit bulls or bred fighting cocks; men of diverse backgrounds might mingle as spectators at any given event. Male Virginians shared a regional taste for sports, and sports, in turn, came to symbolize their shared power as men in a patriarchal system. But social distinctions always remained. In Virginia, and later in the other Southern colonies, great disparities of wealth and the racial chasm separating blacks from whites made individuals' social status a constant source of anxiety. Sports became one venue where these anxieties were played out.

All of England's North American colonies inherited the two-sided leisure tradition: Calvinist suspicion of worldly pleasures contrasted with a long heritage of sports and pastimes. But austerity grew stronger toward the North, while the love of leisure found fuller expression as one moved South. After all, the Church of England was established in Virginia, while antiestablishment Congregationalists dominated Massachusetts. Still, the settlers of colonial Virginia, much like their New England counterparts, arrived with ideals of re-creating English society as they knew and idealized it. They expressed the desire to spread English Protestantism in the New World, convert the "savage" Indians, and check the growth of the Catholic empire. Calvinist beliefs in original sin, predestination, and election manifested themselves at one time or another in all of the colonies. Yet Virginia always seemed a little more at ease with the joys of the flesh than Massachusetts, and as time went on, economic circumstances, demography, and the environment tipped Virginia culture ever more toward the camp of traditional recreations.

Shortly after the founding of Jamestown in 1607, as hundreds died of famine and disease, Captain John Smith complained that for many settlers, "4 hours each day was spent in worke, the rest in pastimes and merry exercise." Over the next century, colonial governments tried several times to outlaw gambling, as well as such sports as horse racing and cockfighting, but always with limited success. The tobacco boom that began in the 1620s reinforced the play impulse. With the burgeoning demand for tobacco in world markets, Virginia life in the first few decades took on the tone of a raucous mining camp. The colony was settled less by families than by unattached men: impoverished English bachelors indentured themselves to escape poverty; poor couples sent their boys into the wilderness to labor for years as virtual slaves; second-born sons of prominent families went to the New World to seek their fortunes. Some individuals made large amounts of money on tobacco, and many as quickly lost their earnings to those willing to gratify cravings for elegant clothes, strong drink, and high-stakes gambling. In this exploitative, often brutal social environment, many of the wild entertainments of Old England flourished.

Out of this uncertain social situation, key men—planters and traders, often from well-off and respectable families but lacking means of their own—managed to impose order. Greed merged with opportunity as they sought a way to exploit scarce labor. Before long, they imposed an unscrupulous system of indentured servitude that allowed a few to control the labor of many. Whether as tenants, bond servants, or apprentices, countless men found that their poverty and indebtedness jeopardized their freedom and bound them over to work for others. Here was the basis on which a handful of men accumulated fortunes and established themselves as a social elite. By the third generation of settlement, as the colony attained some economic and social stability, labor exploitation took a final turn. Though more or less tractable, white Englishmen could suddenly prove fiercely independent, as Bacon's Rebellion of 1676 revealed. More important, as mortality rates dropped, the possibility of permanent investment in labor —slavery—became feasible. No single conscious decision was responsible for Virginia planters choosing black slavery over white servitude. But slowly a variety of economic, demographic, and psychological factors lifted the yoke from Virginia's poor whites and placed the burden on African blacks.

If this transformation did not level white Virginia society, it created opportunities for some small farmers to prosper modestly. By the beginning of the eighteenth century, the labor force was clearly demarcated by color. A wide social chasm still separated wealthy from middling and poor whites, but the presence of an underclass of black slaves helped obscure those differences, giving all free white Virginians a sense of heightened status and a democratic political style, despite prevalent patterns of deference and privilege. As Edmund S. Morgan argues persuasively, revolutionary-era Virginians led the fight for American liberty with pen and sword because men such as Jefferson, Madison, and Washington lived in a society that had "solved" the problem plaguing republicanism for decades. Permanent black slavery provided both a stable system for controlling the poor and an economic base elevating large numbers of whites to the status of free and independent yeomen.

All of these circumstances opened an important place for popular recreations in Virginia society. Far from causing work to overwhelm leisure, the early boom economy with its lack of settled domestic life encouraged men to follow bouts of hard moneymaking with interludes of abandon, especially under the influence of copious drink. Moreover, the sheer dismal brutality of early Virginia—disease, servitude, and exploitation truly made most people's lives solitary, poor, nasty, brutish, and short—created a callous ethos quite compatible with the bloody sports of old. Finally, the rhythms of plantation life itself, of sowing, tending, and harvesting, produced alternating periods of work and idleness rather than regular sustained labor. The crucial point here is not how hard people worked—tobacco planters, indentured servants, and slaves toiled very hard indeed—but how they valued work. England's leisure ethic more than its work ethic became a compelling cultural ideal for Virginians.

The Virginia elite (and eventually the elites of other plantation-based colonies) took as its model the English rural gentry. Wealthy Virginians thought of themselves as English gentlemen. They read the English press, followed English fashions, played English sports, all as part of a class style. Wealth was less a sign of God's grace or the by-product of an upright life than an affirmation of status. For English gentlemen—and although Virginia planters might be colonials, they *were* English gentlemen—ostentatious display of leisure was a way to identify themselves as members of a distinct ruling class, regardless of the poverty or ruthless competitiveness of their ancestors.

Before the end of the seventeenth century, one last factor encouraged a distinct Southern ethic of leisure. To put it baldly, black chattel slavery made it difficult for whites to venerate work, easy for them to idealize play. How could whites value hard work unequivocally once labor was associated with degraded, servile blacks? How pretend that work was ennobling, character-forming, even sanctified in a society whose hardest workers were stigmatized as dangerous, half-civilized heathen, capable of nothing but brutish tasks? The logic was impeccable: if enslaved blacks *had* to work, play was proof of freedom and of elevated social status. Labor was a burden of blackness; leisure, the prerogative of whiteness.

For all of these reasons, sporting displays became a major preoccupation among Virginians. Games and amusements were important to all classes, but the gentry had the time, motivation, and means (horses, after all, were owned by only a small portion of the population) for great displays of consumption and conviviality. By the eighteenth century, about two or three hundred tidewater families comprised Virginia's aristocracy. Bound by kinship ties, they shared a gracious life in which leisure lay at the heart of their class identity.

Young colonial aristocrats often went to be educated in England, where they observed the gentry code firsthand. For example, on his return to Virginia, William Byrd II participated in the whole panoply of English sporting customs on his enormous family estate at Westover. He played billiards, laid out a bowling green, joined others in cricket, ninepins, and skittles. Wealthy Virginians like Byrd seized every opportunity for merrymaking, especially dancing, partying, and gambling over a sociable bottle. Like their English brethren, they laid out circular tracks for horse racing, enjoyed fox hunting, bred fighting cocks, and learned such combat sports as wrestling, fencing, and cudgeling. Religion and law buttressed these practices more than assailed them. Ministers of the Anglican Church, whose congregations often depended on the patronage of local gentry, offered little resistance to the ethic of leisure, while county courts recognized gambling debts as legally binding.

Although Virginia society was obsessed with social rank, status was not fixed by hereditary titles and fortunes, as in a true aristocracy. Because a man's exact social position might be a little unclear, even subject to change, displaying the emblems of high status became one way to achieve it. Since conspicuous consumption of play could be a bench mark of rank, the quest for status through sports often became intense. For example, James Bullocke, a tailor, defeated Mathew Slader, a "gentleman," in a 1674 horse race on which each man staked two thousand pounds of tobacco. The county court informed Bullocke that it was "contrary to Law for a Laborer to make a race being a sport for Gentlemen," and fined him one hundred pounds of tobacco for his indiscretion. Indeed, so incredulous was the court that a common tailor presumed to beat a member of the gentry that Slader was confined to the stocks for an hour, the court judging his loss to be "an apparent cheate." To give another example, Virginia governor Francis Nicholson organized competitions for the annual St. George's Day celebration in 1691, offering prizes in shooting, wrestling, backswords, and horse and foot racing; but the governor made it clear that these events were open only to society's "better sort." Sports were a prerogative of patriarchy, but not all patriarchs were equal.

Such elite sports replicated in microcosm the reality of gentry society: intense individual assertiveness within overall solidarity. The "merry-dispos'd gentlemen" of Hanover County who celebrated St. Andrew's Day in the 1730s with quarter-horse races enacted a private ritual that vented their competitiveness, even as it helped define their shared elite status. The *Virginia Gazette* reported that spectators were allowed to watch the sports of their betters, provided they comported themselves "with Decency and Sobriety, the Subscribers being resolv'd to discountenance all Immorality with the utmost Rigour." While observers were expected to be well behaved, sport as a vehicle for displays of prowess, wealth, and status encouraged men to compete with reckless abandon, to drink, gamble, and assert themselves as if their very social position, even their masculinity, depended on it. Here was an enduring tension: time and again, public officials inveighed against the drinking, swearing, and especially gambling that accompanied horse races; time and again, men wagered amounts that at once risked their fortunes, secured their honor, and made them heroic in the eyes of their peers.

As the eighteenth century progressed, Enlightenment ideals and revolutionary ideologies spurred new notions of political equality, yet sports remained highly stratified. Poor and middling whites continued to stage their own quarter-horse matches; blacks and whites attended the gentry's races; but it was the great planters who systematically imported English Thoroughbreds into America, built English-style circular tracks designed for the new horses' endurance, and made the sport into a grand affair that reflected their wealth and power. After mid-century, new jockey clubs opened not just in Virginia but throughout the coastal South. They sponsored the building of fenced tracks and charged admission, less to turn a profit than to control who attended the races. Moreover, a corps of skilled breeders, jockeys, trainers, and stablemen developed. At the great races, participants started wearing colorful and distinctive apparel, and clubs began to measure and record formal handicap weights and racing times. Indeed, towns like Fredericksburg and Williamsburg turned such races into annual week-long events. Under the gentry's leadership, horse racing became the most popular, best-organized, and most important American sport from the colonial era well into the nineteenth century.

Other sports followed the same pattern: the gentry gave humbler folk a leisure model to emulate, rich and poor came together to share a common male culture, yet boundaries of status never fully dissolved. Cockfighting offers a good example. Yankee traveler Elkanah Watson described in his *Men and Times of the Revolution* a cockmain—a series of fights—in Southampton County, Virginia:

> The roads as we approached the scene were alive with carriages, horses, and pedestrians, black and white, hastening to the point of attraction. Several houses formed a spacious square, in the center of which was arranged a large cockpit; surrounded by many genteel people, promiscuously mingled with the vulgar and debased. Exceedingly beautiful cocks were produced, armed with long, sharp, steel-pointed gaffs, which were firmly attached to their natural spurs. The moment the birds were dropped, bets ran high. The little heroes appeared trained to the business, and not the least disconcerted by the crowd or shouting. They stepped about with great apparent pride and dignity; advancing nearer and nearer, they flew upon each other . . . the cruel and fatal gaffs being driven in to their bodies, and, at times directly through their heads. Frequently one, or both, were struck dead at the first blow, but they often fought after being repeatedly pierced, as long as they were able to crawl, and in the agonies of death would often make abortive efforts to raise their heads and strike their antagonists.

Whichever side won the most matches took the main prize. Spectators might travel great distances for these events, especially when they were held on Easter, Whitsuntide, or other holidays. Occasionally women attended, attracted, it was said, by dances given at night after the cockfights.

Despite Watson's description of promiscuous mingling, the upper and lower classes usually kept to separate spheres. Some taverns catered to the "dregs of the people," as one clergyman complained in 1751, "where not only time and money are vainly and unprofitably squandered away, but (what is worse) where . . . cards, dice, horse-racing, and cock-fighting, together with vices and enormities of every other kind" were practiced without end. Certain events, too, became associated with the lower social orders. Fithian's "fist battles" were pretty much confined to poor white backwoodsmen by the late eighteenth century; gentlemen had by then adopted the ways of formal dueling.

Brutal eye-gouging matches were said by members of the elite to be emblematic of lower-class depravity. In his *Travels in America* (1806), Englishman Thomas Ashe described a fight he witnessed in Wheeling, Virginia. The trouble started with an impromptu horse race; two-thirds of the town quit work to attend. One race led to another, close heats resulted in arguments, words gave way to blows, and soon the belligerents narrowed to two men, one a Virginian, the other a Kentuckian. Ashe described their combat. After some cautious sparring, the Virginian lunged at his opponent, as the crowd roared:

> The shock received by the Kentuckyan, and the want of breath, brought him instantly to the ground. The Virginian never lost his hold; like those bats of the South who never quit the subject on which they fasten till they taste blood, he kept his knees in his enemy's body; fixing his claws in his hair, and his thumbs on his eyes, gave them an instantaneous start from their sockets. The sufferer roared aloud, but uttered no complaint.

Before it was over, the Kentuckian bit off the Virginian's nose, and in return, the Virginian ripped the Kentuckian's lower lip below his chin. The crowd cheered the victorious Virginian, the Kentuckian returned to town to have his face repaired, and new rounds of drinking, gambling, and racing resumed. Back in Wheeling, a Quaker whom Ashe had befriended explained that such events occurred every week, and that rough-and-tumble fights left countless men with mutilated faces.

Virginians' love of popular recreations extended all the way down the social structure to black slaves, who were occasionally allowed to enjoy their ancestral pastimes along with newly adopted English ones. Fithian observed in his *Journal* in 1775 that Easter Monday was a general holiday: "Negroes now are all disbanded till Wednesday morning & are at Cock Fights through the County." A week later he noticed before breakfast "a ring of Negroes at the Stable, fighting Cocks." In their free time, slaves held their own athletic competitions—racing, leaping, wrestling—and a few blacks were encouraged by their masters to enter the prize ring against other slaves, or to train fighting cocks, or to handle and ride racehorses. Rather than eliminate sports and recreations, the rigors of slavery made play especially precious for those who controlled so little of their own time.

Unlike blacks, however, poor and middling whites had an additional incentive for embracing the play ethic of the elite. Simply put, the poor could emulate the rich, sometimes even compete against them, and thereby bask in reflected glory. By promoting leisure activities among its inferiors, the gentry encouraged this identification of interests across the social chasm. "Public Times," for example, were the spring and fall court and assembly sessions, during which great and humble alike thronged county seats. Mid-eighteenth-century Williamsburg swelled to three times its normal population during these events. Festivities of all kinds coincided with Public Times, including horse races, plays, dancing, fiddling, and singing; prizes were offered for acrobatics, cudgeling, wrestling, horse racing, even greased-pig chasing.

In important respects, Public Times resembled the wakes and feast days of early-modern Europe in which both peasants and townsmen momentarily reversed the repressive roles of daily life. While poor and middling folk probably considered themselves entitled by their labors to these special events, the powerful men who sponsored Public Times took them as a chance to display their magnanimity and reaffirm ties to the community. In the end, such revels emphasized the social stratification beneath communal solidarity, because the distinction between patron and patronized—between those who paid the bill for food, drink, and prizes, or who let others use their racecourses or hunt on their lands, and those who accepted their largess—always remained clear. Thus, a cockfight in which "genteel people . . . promiscuously mingled with the vulgar and debased" helped legitimate gentry rule, even as it seemed to promote social leveling. Horse races could operate in similar fashion, such as the one observed late in the eighteenth century by the English actor John Bernard and described in his *Retrospections of America*: "a motley multitude of negroes, Dutchmen, Yankee peddlers, and backwoodsmen, among whom, with long whips in their hands to clear the ground, moved the proprietors and betters, riding and leading their horses . . ." All shared in the event, but the barriers of wealth and power remained high.

Thus, sports in Virginia—and by the eighteenth century, in all of the Southern colonies—were deeply rooted in the social order. Popular recreations were one way that men located themselves in the status hierarchy, kept score, and tried to advance a bit in the standings. For gentlemen, slaves, and all in between, cockfights, horse races, and even fox hunts had become regional passions. These sports and others inherited from England facilitated fierce competition between individuals and social groups. But sports also united men with their own cultural style. Both rich and poor shared traditional pastimes as an affirmation of their "Englishness," as tests of strength, agility, and skill, as rituals marking seasonal change, and as celebrations of traditional rites of passage. Simply put, popular recreations were pleasurable by the cultural standards men knew, by their shared customs and habits. Even while reinforcing social distinctions and defining class boundaries, then, sports were a regional passion.

Perhaps most important, Southern sports were rituals of manhood. Despite great variations of class and even race, certain common themes brought sportsmen together, the most obvious being gender. Sports were for men; playing sports was a masculine prerogative in a male-centered social structure. Games allowed men to compete with each other and try to establish dominance through superior strength or skill. Even horse races were often violent affairs in which gentlemen risked their necks but made sure that their opponents incurred equal risk. To participate, of course, demonstrated virility, but simply being a spectator—cheering lustily, wagering wildly, losing defiantly— proved one's manhood, one's worthiness to be accepted by peers.

Sports were about honor, and each event tested a man's claim to be part of the masculine world. More precisely, a Thoroughbred race defined who was admitted to the gentleman's sphere, while an eye-gouging battle tested the mettle of lower-class white males and thereby defined their circle of honor. Extravagant risks, unflinching bloodiness, competition bordering on madness— these were at the core of sporting life. Sports helped define the terms of admission to male groups, valorized particular traits of masculine virility, and thereby devalued all that was womanly and feminine. Honor meant more than mere pride. It was an intensely communal concept that depended on display to the outside world and the affirmation of one's status equals. A man who wagered recklessly, rode with abandon, or fought without fear demonstrated that he was worthy of honor.

Honor was part of a larger hierarchical and patriarchal social system. A member of the gentry brought no credit to himself by defeating a poor man in a horse race; on the contrary, he degraded himself by stooping to that level. Honor could be conferred only by social equals in the tightly knit world of personal relationships. Winning or losing mattered less than the public willingness to risk all. Reconsider Fithian's "fist battles" in this light: young men fought when they felt insulted, and they vindicated themselves by their public willingness to engage in combat that proved their mettle among equals. And even those outside the circles of honor learned the lessons of domination, for the white male's unflinching bloodiness—at gouging matches, at horse races, at cockfights—intimidated social inferiors, and kept women and slaves in line.

The Southern colonies' devotion to sports was not without its opponents. A Calvinist strain sometimes made war against free and easy ways, and in the eighteenth century, religious opposition to popular recreations grew as Baptists and Methodists—adherents of sects that appealed to middling folk—challenged the Anglican hegemony. The intermittent waves of religious revivals brought renewed commitment by many individuals, North and South, to a more austere and godly life. During the era of the American Revolution, mass conversions swept thousands of Southern poor folk into the fold. Their restrained cultural style was a rebuke to the old ways, and if the planter elite was not totally reformed, the new cultural austerity sometimes made them a bit more cautious and forced those who loved grand displays onto less public grounds.

Nevertheless, the Southern colonies had been most hospitable to English traditional popular recreations. The historian C. Vann Woodward points out that early observers such as John Smith, Robert Beverly, and William Byrd, as well as many modern-day commentators, have noted a distinct "Southern ethic" in American history. Upholders of the ethic described leisure and good fellowship as its central tenets, while those who decried it saw laziness punctuated by violence as its chief result. All agreed, however, that the Southern ethic valued free time and rejected labor as the all-consuming goal of life. This ethos appeared early in Jamestown and continued through the colonial era, into the new nation. When Southerners esteemed commerce or enterprise, it was less because piling up wealth contained religious or moral value than because making money facilitated the good life. They rejected the Puritans' worldly asceticism and the Yankees' stereotypical miserliness in favor of attitudes associated with "pre-capitalist" societies.

While gentlemen-planters were not part of a hereditary aristocracy, they took their cue from great landed Englishmen, and it was these elites who set the tone for Virginian, and later Southern, society. Conspicuous consumption was a hallmark of the region because outward displays of luxury and fine living were sources of power, marking a man's elevated status. Honor, chivalry, paternal obligations, noblesse oblige, personal rather

than formal relationships, ancestral pride and close family ties
—these elements of a traditional worldview held on more tenaciously in the South than in the North. Fox hunts, week-long
horse races, even bloody cockfights and eye-gouging matches
were not mere episodes; they were expressions of a way of life.

We must take care not to interpret the Southern ethic as
aberrant or unique. Non-regular working rhythms, conspicuous
display, and love of finery, games, and sports had deep roots in
human cultures. The compulsions to work steadily and regularly,
to make leisure a subordinate value accepted only for its ability
to increase one's capacity for labor, and to divide work and play
into compartmentalized realms were the novel ideas. It was not
that Southern colonists failed to work hard; it was that they did
not place labor at the center of the moral universe. For that odd
notion, we must look elsewhere.

The New England Way

Just after the founding of the Plymouth Plantation in 1620, a
notorious rakehell named Thomas Morton led a small band of
settlers to Merry Mount at the edge of the godly community
and defied Pilgrim authority. The governor of the colony, William Bradford, declared Morton the "Lord of Misrule"—a reference to the wild celebrations of carnival, practiced throughout
Catholic Europe—and accused him of founding a school of athe-
ism. Bradford described the renegades' revels in his *History of
Plymouth Plantation*:

> They also set up a maypole, drinking and dancing about it
> many days together, inviting the Indian women for their
> consorts, dancing and frisking together like so many fairies,
> or furies, rather; and worse practices. As if they had anew
> revived and celebrated the feasts of the Roman goddess Flora,
> or the beastly practices of the mad Bacchanalians.

Morton also composed rhymes and posted them on the maypole, rhymes that were not only lascivious but, in Bradford's eyes, slanderous to the colony's leaders. The governor moved against Morton. Colonial officials cut down the maypole and disbanded the revelers. They arrested Morton for selling arms to the Indians and shipped him back to England in irons.

The case of Thomas Morton highlights the troubled status of play in the Northern colonies. From the outset, Puritan restraint and the English leisure heritage eyed each other with suspicion. Governor Bradford, heir to the dissenting religious tradition yet also a practical man charged with making sure that the colony survived, sought a godly compromise. For example, he believed that the Bible did not sanctify Christmas, that the holiday was merely one more Catholic corruption of pure Christianity. But in 1621, some new settlers told him that it was against their consciences to work on the day of Christ's birth, and the governor decided not to press the matter. When he and his followers returned from their Christmas Day labors, however, they found the newcomers "in the street at play, openly; some pitching the bar, and some at stool-ball, and such like sports." What most piqued the governor was not that these people played but that they did so openly while others worked: "If they made the keeping of it matter of devotion, let them keep their houses; but there should be no gaming or revelling in the streets." Human beings, the Pilgrims knew, would sin, but it was important that the public realm be kept pure, and that the diligent not be tempted from their labor.

While Governor Bradford's actions reveal to us the distaste of the devout for popular recreations, the settlers who danced around the maypole or played village games on Christmas Day demonstrate that not everyone accepted the leaders' policies. Like their Virginia counterparts, Puritan magistrates in Massachusetts and other New England colonies sought to curb excess when they legislated against such games as shuffleboard, quoits, and lawn bowling. These colonial leaders were more successful than their southerly counterparts at reining in traditional recreations, because more New Englanders believed in the temperate life. Nonetheless, the very existence of laws regulating popular recreations indicates that pastimes enjoyed enough support to make the pious uncomfortable. Many, perhaps most, colonists resisted Puritan strictures and tried to re-create the traditions of the English countryside. Here was a social division that would endure for decades.

The tension between sober self-control and joyful play could become a personal struggle, and Puritan leader John Winthrop provides a striking example. Believing himself too enamored of worldly pleasures, Winthrop, soon to be governor of the Massachusetts Bay Colony, constantly scrutinized his life. He contemplated giving up hunting, noting that the practice was overly strenuous, expensive, and dangerous. But the decisive reason why Winthrop decided to lay down his musket was most telling: he was a poor marksman. It surely would have been sinful if Winthrop so abandoned himself to hunting that he neglected his workaday duties or his obligations as a church member. But equally serious, his efforts at recreation cost more in effort than they repaid in pleasure. For Winthrop, hunting failed the Puritans' test of any recreation: play that refreshed a man for work was worthy; play that wasted time and left him enervated was not. Using this standard, Winthrop found more appropriate recreations for himself: "I examined my heart, and findinge it needfull to recreate my minde with some outward recreation, I yielded unto it, and by a moderate exercise herein was much refreshed." Humans needed "worldly delights" lest they become melancholy; moderation was the right path for all earthly practices, and scrutinizing one's conscience helped one find the middle way. Drink was from God, Puritans believed, but drunkenness from the devil; sex was one of the delights of marriage, adultery one of the most heinous sins.

It should be no surprise, then, that Puritans favored activities that accomplished useful ends: house-raisings, corn-husking parties, ordinations, commencements, and spinning and quilting bees. They also rejuvenated their spirits with such "innocent" activities as singing, ball games, hunting and fishing, backgammon, even cardplaying and dancing in the privacy of one's home.

Meanwhile, their children amused themselves with imported marbles and dolls and played tag, leapfrog, deer and hounds, and other traditional English games. Neither prudish, nor sedentary, nor fanatical, Puritan men, like their English ancestors, celebrated such special occasions as annual election days and militia musters with traditional contests in shooting, wrestling, and running, as well as combat sports like cudgeling and sword fighting. However, when these very same activities became part of "Romish" celebrations such as saints' days or Christmas, or when they led to excessive drinking, then a line had been crossed. Even gambling had its place: Puritans held lotteries to raise money for worthy causes. But excessive wagering was anathema because the successful gambler acquired wealth without labor, the unsuccessful one jeopardized his family's future, and both pridefully tempted fate.

Throughout the seventeenth century, the devout continued their path of studied moderation, expanding by degrees the realm of play as prosperity grew, and as the Restoration brought a more open and secular cultural tone to English life. Increase Mather declared in "An Arrow Against Profane and Promiscuous Dancing" (1684): "The Prince of Philosophers has observed truly, that Dancing and Leaping, is a natural expression of joy: So that there is no more Sin in it, than in laughter, or any outward expression of inward Rejoycing." Mather's son Cotton continued on the century-old path of moderation, though he, too, condemned as wicked Sabbath play, as well as all rough sports like cockfighting. Thomas Gouge's *Young Man's Guide through the Wilderness of This World to the Heavenly Canaan* (1672) expressed the matter metaphorically. Games, he told young men, "should be as Sauces to your Meat, to sharpen your appetite onto the duties of your Calling, and not to glut yourselves with them." Benjamin Coleman shifted the metaphor in his *Government and Improvement of Mirth* (1707), but the same message remained: "It spoils the *bow* to keep it always bent, and the *viol* if always strain'd. Mirth . . . lifts up the hands that hang down in weariness, and strengthens the feeble knees that cou'd stand no longer to work." Keeping with the spirit of moderation, the law often was honored more in the breach than the observance. Thus, by the middle of the seventeenth century, football was illegal in Boston, but games were countenanced so long as they became neither too bloody nor too raucous.

Puritans' ideas about the proper role of leisure were deeply influenced by their attitudes toward work, and both grew out of their religious worldview. After the fall from Eden, they believed, all of humankind was tainted with sin. Yet in His mercy, God saved a small number from eternal damnation. These people, for reasons known only to their Creator, were elected for salvation before time began; He had predetermined everyone's eternal fate, and these few He chose not to damn. Since the Almighty made His irrevocable decision before the universe began, a person's earthly efforts had no impact on his or her spiritual condition. Although it was impossible to know for sure if one was saved or damned, through constant self-scrutiny an individual might discover evidence of the Lord's grace. Leading an upright life according to God's Commandments, along with strenuous introspection for signs of salvation, could provide hints that one's soul was not irredeemably corrupt.

For Puritans and like-minded folk, proper religious conduct meant far more than simply observing ritual forms. Work—all work—was a calling. Laboring hard and well in one's worldly occupation was a religious obligation, and the daily routine of life was thereby infused with godly significance. The diligent farmer or tradesman did the Lord's bidding as surely as the minister. Labor pleased God, and it followed that success in one's earthly endeavors might just be a sign of inner grace. But even while individuals strove to succeed in this world, they must never overvalue the material fruits of success. Signs of salvation, not the good life, were what one sought in pursuing one's calling.

Here was what the sociologist Max Weber called the Protestant work ethic. Perhaps the most important ramification of this way of thinking was its shifting of labor discipline from external compulsion to internal control. Laboring in the wilderness had metaphorical as well as literal meaning, for the Puritans believed they must plow, hoe, and harrow the human spirit, struggle with their sinful selves, and build a moral life bit by bit. Self-discipline was a daily sign of the Lord's grace, of the heavenly reward that awaited the end of one's labors. In theory, if not always in practice, worldly asceticism—striving for temporal success while placing little value on the fruits of one's labor—kept Puritan minds from dwelling too long on material things. Good Christians focused their thoughts on work itself, on the sacredness of labor; they did not overvalue the earthly comforts gotten by their diligence.

Whatever inclinations toward individualism the Protestant ethic contained, they were balanced by other cultural values brought from England. A self-consciously communal people, New Englanders strove to re-create the village and family life of the English countryside. An emphasis on unity, order, and hierarchy gave them a sense of closely shared experience. Their patterns of communal rural settlement were replicated throughout the region. While they may not have always lived up to their own standards, work was inseparably part of Puritan social ideology, a transcendent value, for through work people not only searched for signs of personal salvation but also built a godly commonwealth, an American Israel, a city on a hill.

Given the Puritan mission, suspicions of all that seemed boisterous, sensual, or passionate were easily aroused. Tensions developed between the leaders and New England's lower classes, especially the unchurched majority who sought the traditional pastimes of the English countryside. From the beginning, however, village parsons looked the other way during an occasional bearbaiting, and taverns offered games of chance despite the laws against gambling. While there may have been questions over the precise boundaries separating proper from improper recreations, there is no reason to think that common folk in the New England colonies chafed under draconian Puritan rule, that they longed to burst out in an orgy of wild amusements. We know, for example, that while there was very little heavy gambling among Massachusetts' social, political, and religious leaders during the seventeenth century, the amount of gambling among servants and the poor was apparently not very large either. A rough consensus seemed to make moderation a regional style.

However, as sports became more prominent in Britain, as new

migrants familiar with them came into the colonies, and as population density increased, games and recreations grew more common and more elaborate in New England. Stray references give
evidence of young men playing football (soccer) in the streets,
and newspaper advertisements reveal that at least some colonists
had a sophisticated knowledge of horse racing. "This is to give
notice," declared the *Boston Gazette* in 1725, "to all gentlemen
and others that there is to be Thirty Pounds in Money run for
. . . by Six Horses, Mares or Geldings, Two miles . . . to carry
9 stone Weight, the Standard to be 14 hands high . . . the 3 first
Horses to run a second Heat . . ." New modes of play also arose,
especially at the first glimmerings of a consumer society early
in the eighteenth century. Merchants sold toys and card tables,
dancing instructors began to give lessons, and tavern and cof-
feehouse owners occasionally sponsored games. Thus, the owner
of Boston's British Coffee House advertised in 1714 that a bowling green now adjoined his establishment, where "all Gentlemen,
Merchants, and others, that have a mind to Recreate themselves,
shall be accommodated."

Throughout the early generations, then, New Englanders
found many occasions for leisure and sports. A few flouted the
law or defied religious authorities, following in the footsteps of
Thomas Morton of Merry Mount. Neither religion nor harsh
frontier conditions precluded traditional pleasures, as some sports
historians have assumed. Most New Englanders were never as
restrained as the oligarchy would like or as freewheeling as other
colonists; a blend of law, faith, and custom hedged their recreations within moderate bounds. But if New Englanders enjoyed
their popular recreations, what failed to emerge throughout the
seventeenth century and well into the eighteenth was an ethos
of leisure that conferred powerful social rewards, a full-blown
cultural challenge to the Puritan work ethic. In the mid-eigh-
teenth century, John Adams acknowledged the exuberance of
tavern life, even as he condemned it: "Here, the time, the money,
the health, and the modesty, of most that are young and many
old, are wasted; here diseases, vicious habits, bastards, and legislators, are frequently begotten." Popular recreations never be-

came a way of life as they did for the Southern gentry. Nor did Northern colonists tend to make raucous sports a hallmark of male values, of patriarchy. In a word, New Englanders were much less likely than Virginians to assume that humans worked in order to play; rather, play renewed men for work.

The Middle Colonies

Pennsylvania and New York developed somewhat different patterns of play. English colonists here found themselves among German, French, and Dutch people who had their own ways. Nevertheless, the broad outlines of traditional recreations—rural pastimes, church-related celebrations, peasant traditions, old folk games—confronting the sober and precise ways of religious dissenters was played out again. However, by the middle of the eighteenth century, the booming cities of the middle colonies, especially New York and Philadelphia, became the centers of new commercial recreations. Here we find the earliest glimmers of what American sports were to become in the nineteenth and twentieth centuries: urban, commercialized, audience-seeking spectacles.

But in the beginning, the middle colonies most resembled New England. William Penn, founder of the Quaker settlement, declared in *No Cross, No Crown* (1669) that men must not "eat, drink, play, game and sport away their irrevocable precious time, which should be dedicated to the Lord, as a necessary introduction to a blessed eternity." The Quakers' plain dress and unadorned speech, their devotion to labor and worldly asceticism, led them away from frivolity, and they did their utmost to curb the excesses they perceived in the colony's non-Quaker population. The Quakers, or Friends, grew more rigid as they confronted newcomers who rejected their ways. Elders lashed out at the spread of wasteful living, especially among German immigrants. By 1700, the battle lines were drawn. Still in control of the Philadelphia town council, Quakers outlawed the theater, blood sports, and games of chance. Other citizens challenged the

Friends and found sympathy from the colonial government. The Philadelphia Quakers responded with statutes that banned not only traditional games but also "any other kind of game whatsoever now invented or hereafter to be invented." Such extremism attests at once to the Friends' piety and to the determination of their opponents to enjoy popular recreations.

Growing numbers gave the upper hand to the non-Quakers, and as the century progressed, Philadelphia acquired a reputation for "immorality" and "wickedness." Not only did English and German rural folk keep pouring in with their traditional recreations but, equally important, opposition to the Quakers was led by a growing and powerful landed proprietary gentry that now prospered in Pennsylvania. By the second half of the eighteenth century, these men rivaled the Quaker elite in affluence; indeed, the gentry became one of the most exclusive and prestigious groups in British North America. Bound together by kinship and political interest, sharing common professions such as the law, possessing vast amounts of land, they came to dominate the executive and judicial branches of the provincial government and the town government of Philadelphia.

Not only did the proprietary gentry challenge Quaker political power, it held a cultural vision quite alien to that of the godly commonwealth. This is clearly revealed in the social ties binding gentlemen, ties that paralleled their political and economic connections. Most were members, along with other prominent Philadelphians, of the Mount Regal Fishing Club, the Dancing Assembly, the Hunting Club, the Society of the Sons of St. Tammany, or the Philadelphia Jockey Club. Men of the gentry also made particular taverns and coffeehouses their gathering places, where they shared congenial drams, games, and songs. In the midst of William Penn's holy experiment, then, a wealthy elite defined its social identity in part through its leisure pursuits, and formed an interlocking directorate of play. And the gentry's prestige helped legitimate the growth of popular recreations in general, much to the Quakers' displeasure.

New York, too, faced the tension between religious restraint and more free and easy ways. The original Dutch settlers, especially landed aristocrats and small planters in the Hudson Valley, eagerly played their ancestral games such as golf, lawn bowling, skittles, and gander pulling (in which men on horseback tried to pull the greased head off a live gander, tied by its feet to a tree limb). The Dutch used ice skates and sleighs for play as well as work, and they introduced Easter eggs and Santa Claus to American holiday celebrations. However, when New Netherland became New York in 1664, Dutch Calvinists and colonial Puritans made common cause and tried to impose new restraints. While the new austerity had some influence, traditional pastimes continued in the countryside.

Like Philadelphia, moreover, New York City witnessed the rise of a wealthy gentry class around the beginning of the eighteenth century. Prosperous merchants and officials of the British colonial government began patronizing theaters, coffeehouses, and social clubs, took up coaching, and held semiannual horse races at Hempstead, Long Island. Opposition arose quickly. Townsfolk pushed their council to pass legislation curbing some of the gentry's activities. Yet New York piety was never as strong as that of Boston or even Philadelphia, and men with newly acquired wealth and the inclination to enjoy it would not be denied. A merry life of balls, dancing, and fine fashions as well as sports—racing, cockfighting, and animal baiting—acquired a following among new merchant princes, colonial officials, and many common folk. Anglican minister John Sharpe, for example, noted in his diary that he attended several cockfights between 1710 and 1717. Sponsors of such events even tried to attract women to the cockpit by promising a ball after the matches. Moreover, the New York gentry started one of the nation's pioneer jockey clubs; in 1736, they built America's first enclosed circular track and charged admission, less to make money than to keep out undesirables.

So by the eighteenth century, a leisure ethic was beginning to take hold in the cities. This new culture of leisure found palpable expression in taverns such as New York's London Coffee House, Philadelphia's Turk's Head, and Boston's Bunch of Grapes. Public houses eased the longings of English immigrants and colonial officials for the life they left behind. Throughout the century, gentlemen gathered to drink and gossip, to swap news and opinions, to debate and tell stories. The most respectable establishments often boasted the largest public room in town, where ordination balls, great dinners on saints' days, celebrations of royal birthdays, and patriotic rallies were held. Formal and country dances took place in the publicans' rooms, while picnic, cookout, and fishing parties gathered there, then returned in the evening for refreshment. People came to collect their mail, to see plays, to sing, and to observe such special events as balloon ascensions. And they came both to play and to watch sports.

Indeed, from the early eighteenth century well into the nineteenth, publicans, especially those in Northern cities, were the nation's most important sports promoters. They set up pits for cockfights, kept bears and bulls for baiting, and later helped raise the stakes for boxing matches. They organized contests in running, leaping, and quoits, arranged billiard and ninepins matches, provided fowls for shooting contests, and offered prizes to the winners of the events they sponsored. They facilitated games of chance in their rooms, held the wagers of men who bet on the events, and sometimes even promoted horse races on their own adjoining tracks. Increasing trade was one motive for their efforts, and in this sense, publicans stood at the wellspring of commercialized leisure. The local tavern—from the most elegant gentleman's inn to the meanest tradesman's saloon—was not just a business but a community center that helped bring individuals together in a shared culture. The growing wealth and security of the cities offered new means to enjoy leisure, and taverns provided access to play and sports. Publicans helped men participate in a larger variety of activities more freely and openly than ever before.

So the fate of the old English country amusements varied widely in the colonies. In general, the religious and social outlook of Puritans, Quakers, and Dutch Calvinists created laws and a cultural tone that restricted the scope of popular recreations. While no region in America fully replicated England's parish system or ecclesiastical calendar, Virginia and the other Southern colonies came closest to reenacting the traditions of the English countryside. Rural colonists in New England and the middle colonies continued some of the old pastimes, but in a piecemeal way, and they were more likely to stage their popular recreations on practical occasions—training days or militia musters—rather than on ancient holidays that rural folk claimed for their own— Plow Monday or Shrove Tuesday. Still, throughout the colonies, during various public occasions as well as informal gatherings, old folk games and pastimes continued as expressions of local rivalries and daily village life.

Even more important for the future, the growing influence of cities and towns as centers of trade fostered the very beginnings of a consumer culture. By the middle of the eighteenth century, prosperous merchants, along with English colonial officials and military officers, sought to emulate the life of urban English gentlemen. The elites of Boston, New York, Philadelphia, Baltimore, and Charleston not only were powerful in their own circles but shared a cultural style that brought them together in a wide range of social activities from dinner parties and balls to sports. These activities, often sponsored by exclusive clubs, allowed members of the new urban gentry to transcend their provincialism and view themselves as men sharing a way of life.

Captain Francis Goelet's description of his 1746 business trip to Boston illustrates the point. Shortly after arriving, this New Yorker found himself at a turtle dinner, complete with toasts and songs, for forty gentlemen:

> Exceeding Merry until 3 a Clock in the morning [Goelet reported], from whence Went upon the Rake, Going past the Commons in our way Home, Surprised a Compy Country Young Men and Women with a Violin, at a Tavern Dancing and making Mery . . . We took Possession of the Room, hav'g the Fidler and the Young Man with us with the Keg of Sugar'd Dram, we were very merry, from thence went to Mr. Jacob Wendell's where we were obliged to drink Punch and Wine and abt 5 in the morning made our Exit and to Bed.

Goelet managed to place himself in the company of like-minded men even though he was far from home, and lavish entertainment was the common ground on which they met.

Sports became part of this bonding for the late-colonial elite. By the eve of the Revolution, several wealthy men, Northern and Southern, ran their horses in a circuit of races from Leedstown, Virginia, through Annapolis, Philadelphia, New Jersey, and New York. Similarly, cockfighting became the passion of many men of the gentry, so that, for example, fortunes and reputations from several colonies were staked at the Germantown, Pennsylvania, cockmain staged in 1770 by James De Lancey of New York and Timothy Matlack of Philadelphia.

All of this added up to more than a series of recreations. A new class had arisen, urban in outlook and wealthy with profits from trade. The cultural style of that group owed much to the London gentry, for which symbols of status had grown increasingly important, and to the Southern gentlemen of the Chesapeake, who amassed fortunes earlier than other North Americans. While the new class did not entirely adopt the Southern cult of honor, rough masculine sports became increasingly important to the group's view of itself, for here were models of patriarchal power. Driving in elegant chaises, spending extravagantly for suppers, going to the spas—these were the marks of economic success. But betting heavily on horse races, or raising fighting cocks, or besting someone in a shooting match marked a value system that rewarded male aggressiveness.

Sports and the New Nation

By the eve of the Revolution, then, wealthy gentry men—Northern and Southern, rural and urban, mercantile and agricultural —had helped foster sporting traditions on American soil. There had always been voices of caution, even resentment. But when prosperity failed to last, and the British government in America became identified as the oppressor, anything that smacked of aristocracy drew criticism. As the Revolution approached during the 1770s, the association of sports with frivolity and decadence left them open to attack, for the ideal of chaste republican virtue did not sit well with the spirit of play. In the hothouse of revolutionary politics, attitudes changed quickly. "Balls, concerts, assemblies—all of us mad in the pursuit of pleasure . . . not a pause . . . prudence kicked out of doors," Gouverneur Morris wrote to Ann Allen Penn from New York in 1774.

Yet later that same year, as the crisis with Britain deepened, delegates to the First Continental Congress urged the colonists to "discountenance and discourage every species of extravagance and dissipation, especially all horse-racing, and all kinds of gaming, cock fighting, exhibitions of shows, plays, and other expensive diversions and amusements." By the eve of battle, the colonies seemed transformed. As one Philadelphian put it, "The troublous times have come . . . Everything bears a warlike aspect. We hear no more of races, of cockfighting . . . bullbaiting or bearbaiting; these men have something else to think of, they discuss the war views, they prepare for war." The same ambivalence toward leisure that characterized early colonial life burst forth again in the midst of the revolutionary crisis.

When the war came, it brought men together in unprecedented numbers, and the seriousness of the undertaking made recreations problematic. This was no time for frivolity, yet men must find escape from the danger of war and the boredom of camp. General George Washington tried to deal with the situation. In 1777, he urged his officers to promote exercise and vigorous amusements among their troops: "Improve all the leisure time your brigades may have from other duties in maneuvering and teaching the men the use of their legs, which is of infinitely more importance than learning the manual exercise . . . Games of Exercise for amusement may not only be permitted, but encouraged." As a landed Virginia gentleman, Washington loved fox hunting and horse racing. But as an heir to Protestant suspicions of play, as a believer in republican self-restraint, and as the leader of a revolutionary struggle, he insisted that recreations be useful. Sports had their place, but games of chance failed to "improve" leisure time. Washington forbade soldiers to play with cards or dice, and ordered his subordinates to employ their spare time "training and disciplining their men."

With Washington's blessing or not, the soldiers of the Continental Army participated in a variety of pastimes. By throwing together thousands of individuals from disparate communities, the Revolution helped spread local variations of traditional play. Soldiers momentarily escaped the hardships of camp and battlefield with folk games, and they even raced horses, gambled, and fought cocks, all explicitly forbidden by the Continental Congress. Indeed, the French general Rochambeau, unaccustomed to Calvinistic strictures against idleness and wasted time, established an officers' club in his camp where he and his subordinates played at the gaming tables together, much to the improvement of morale, according to one Continental captain.

So, at the very beginnings of American nationhood, play and leisure, sports and popular recreations occupied contested ground. The gentry's love of display offended evangelical suspicion of all things sensual; the working people's raucous escapes from daily tedium opposed the middle-class ideal of self-control; the urban elites' love of conspicuous consumption denied republican insistence on self-restraint in the name of communal welfare. All of these trends and countertrends would grow increasingly important as the new nation developed.

But it must be added that stasis as much as change characterized the era. Perhaps the single largest generalization about American sports at the end of the colonial period would be that the majority of people were middling rural folk, and that their recreations were mostly customary, local, participatory, loosely organized, and patterned after English country amusements. Sports were part of a larger pattern of folk recreation, in which such activities as quilting bees, cornhuskings, and barn raisings continued to merge work with play, to make hard labor more palatable with the spice of dancing, singing, feasting, storytelling, and competitive games. Rough muscular sports—wrestling, shooting, tug-of-war, and maul-throwing—as well as such work-based competitions as plowing matches, logrolling, and tree cutting emphasized useful skills. On the frontier, physical prowess was always in demand, and brutal fighting underscored the premium that the environment placed on ferocity, while hunting and fishing merged pleasure with utility so that the distinction between work and play disappeared altogether.

Americans did not "learn to play," as one historian of sports has put it; migrants from England and Europe arrived with their own popular recreations. The ways that colonials played, however, bore little resemblance to our twentieth-century practices. No one in the colonies ever claimed that athletics built character, or made men out of boys, or inculcated the ethic of fair play. There was no sporting goods industry, and the only athletic stadiums were a few crude racing tracks. Sports used readily available implements, and most often occurred spontaneously whenever people got together—swimming in a pond or skating on it in the winter, bowling on the town green or at the crossroads tavern, playing rounders in the street or football in a pasture. The distinction between players and spectators was always tenuous, and the categories of amateur and professional did not even exist.

Labor and play blended into each other much more freely than we are accustomed to today, because leisure time and work time were not so rigidly segmented. Moreover, sports were not played according to standardized official rules; they were part of local culture, passed on by example or word of mouth, with rules varying from one place to another. Races, fistfights, and other activities were not arranged by professional promoters but grew out of direct challenges, most often between individuals who knew each other, so sports at once provided entertainment and resolved personal disputes. Missing from early sports, then, were whole layers of communications and transportation, of professionalism, regulatory bodies, records, and statistics, all of which we take for granted, and which influence even the informal games of children today.

As late as 1820, three in four American families lived on farms. Equally important, rural folk grew all that they possibly could for home consumption, along with modest amounts of staple crops to trade or sell. While not totally self-sufficient, most

Americans until after the colonial era produced mainly for home consumption or local barter and were only tenuously tied into marketplace transactions. In New England, Pennsylvania, and even in the South, farmers and their families fed themselves with what they produced, and raised a small surplus to trade in the local village economy. Long past the colonial era, America remained above all a loose-knit nation of isolated farms, tiny villages, rutted roads, and primitive markets.

Folk sports and pastimes were embedded in this society and helped shape it. Home production, cottage industry, local and community markets, barter mixed with limited currency and specie, close kin dependencies—all kept popular recreations hedged within narrow geographical limits. Family, neighborhood, and town gatherings offered the opportunity for traditional activities, so the ball games and running races, the wrestling matches and leaping competitions, the quoits, bowling, sleighing, football, town ball, cudgeling, archery, and other games and sports continued to act as powerful expressions of local ties. Competitive games symbolically merged individual assertiveness and group unity. Community- and kin-based relationships, more than marketplace or contractual ones, were at the heart of early sports in America.

Finally, sports such as horse racing, cockfighting, and football helped define manhood. Powerful men displayed their status by building tracks or sponsoring events, while humbler ones gained a sense of their own masculinity as participants or spectators in games. And despite differences in social rank, sports united men in a shared patriarchal culture. Details varied from locale to locale, but early sports encouraged men to display their competitiveness and their physical abilities. Sports valued skill, cunning, power, and ferocity; they encouraged men to think in terms of winning and losing, of dominating or being dominated. Sports thereby helped construct a particular vision of masculinity, one that emphasized aggression and physicality. The ethos of early sports, especially the bloodiest ones, assumed a hierarchy of physical prowess, and they thereby became models of domination, emblems of patriarchal rule.

2 / "Saints and Their Bodies": Sport Through 1860

• • • • • • • • • • • • • • • • • • •

The Adams Family

Charles Francis Adams discouraged his sons from wasting time on play. "Sports and games he held in horror," Charles Junior lamented in his *Autobiography* (1916). "His theory was that the proper thing for every young man was to get to work as soon as he could scrabble through college, begin to make a living, marry, and become, as he would express it, 'a useful member of society.' " Like his grandfather John and father, John Quincy, Charles Senior was nothing if not a useful member of society. He served in both houses of the Massachusetts legislature and in the American Congress, published reform newspapers, ran for Vice President on the Free-Soil ticket, distinguished himself as Lincoln's minister to England, and edited his progenitors' personal papers.

Yet even Charles Senior's ancestors leavened work with play. President John Adams enjoyed sailing, kite flying, wrestling, and shooting. In winter he skated, in summer he swam, and in between he pitched quoits. His son John Quincy Adams took time from Presidential duties to attend horse races and swim in the Potomac. Quincy Adams even caused a small scandal when he purchased a billiard table for the White House. But by the middle of the nineteenth century, Charles Senior had laid aside his ancestors' example and taught his sons that there was too much work to be done to squander time on play.

Charles Junior exaggerated the dearth of active recreations during his antebellum youth. His younger brother recollected in *The Education of Henry Adams* (1906) that well-born Boston boys were more familiar with barrooms and billiard halls than their parents knew. Most lads found time for skating, swimming, and sleighing, as well as hockey, town ball, and football. Yet with the exception of an annual violent snowball fight on Boston Common pitting Latin-school boys against young toughs from the slums, the Adams brothers felt their childhood games lacked passion. Recreations were incidental to life, and parents gave little encouragement to play. "In my boyhood," Charles Junior lamented, "nothing whatever was done to amuse children. They might amuse themselves or go unamused, that was their affair!"

Looking back from his early-twentieth-century perspective, Charles Junior believed that English boarding school as described in Thomas Hughes's novel *Tom Brown's School Days* (1857) would have repaired the damage done by his sheltered upbringing: "I ought to have been sent away from home and rubbed into shape among other boys; I should have been made to undergo a severe all-around discipline; I should have been forced to participate in all sorts of athletic games; I ought to have been rounded into shape as much like other boys as school life could round me."

Being "rounded into shape" by a "severe all-around discipline" hardly describes the ethos of traditional recreations; eighteenth-century planters, rural folk, or merchant princes did not seek self-discipline at cockfights. Yet the sports world Adams longed for was just being born in America on the eve of the Civil War. If young Adams faulted his father for not encouraging games and sports, the elder Adams acted in accordance with powerful cultural imperatives of his day. Boarding academies created in the image of Thomas Arnold's Rugby School in England, where athletics served the Victorian ideal of character building, were still years away for well-to-do youths who grew up in the antebellum era, and most children of working families would wait the better part of a century for high-school athletics and the urban playground movement. Organized sports as we know them—amateur and professional, for youths or adults—hardly existed.

But change was on the way. Powerful forces were reshaping America, and play would not slip by unaltered. New ideas about sports and leisure arose alongside the older attitudes toward popular recreations. By the time of the Civil War, a few sports, ancestors of today's games, were being played with regularity. At the same time, new arguments were advanced supporting sports and recreations, and these arguments came from the sorts of people who had previously frowned on them.

Victorian Culture and the Attack on Traditional Sports

As might be expected, the revolutionary zeal against traditional amusements abated most quickly in the South. Horse racing boomed during the 1790s, as new Thoroughbred stock was imported. Despite wartime suppression of raucous pastimes, New York and Philadelphia quickly followed the South's lead. Cockmains were fought, bear- and bullbaiting returned, and horse racing commenced anew. Yet these events were conducted surreptitiously, and not without much hand-wringing. The *Philadelphia Gazette* of 1802, for example, condemned the "great mischiefs and vices" at the track, while the *Daily Advertiser* in 1805 spoke of the "intoxication, riot, lewdness" that attended the Germantown races.

Criticism also came from another quarter in the Quaker City. In June 1802, the grand jury received a petition against Hart's Racecourse, located on the Hunting Park Estate:

This English dissipation of horse-racing may be agreeable to a few idle landed gentlemen, who bestow more care in training their horses than educating their children, and it may be amusing to British mercantile agents, and a few landed characters in Philadelphia; but it is in the greatest degree injurious to the mechanical and manufacturing interest, and will tend to our ruin if the nuisance is not removed by your patriotic exertions.

The petition was signed by fifteen hundred mechanics and twelve hundred manufacturers.

During this era, "manufacturers" and "mechanics" usually referred to individual craftsmen working in their homes or shops, often with the aid of their families and one or two apprentices. Printers, cobblers, cabinetmakers, tailors, coopers, iron molders, silversmiths, goldbeaters, clockmakers, cordwainers, and other artisans made goods by hand and vended them in local markets. The ancient system whereby an apprentice might hope to rise to master mechanic still operated. But there were growing signs of breakdown in the mutual rights and obligations between masters, journeymen, and apprentices. As personal attachments between craftsmen and the workers who lived in their households cracked under the weight of expanding markets, as filial duties and loyalties slowly became translated into monetary values, the rift widened between shop owners and employees.

Perhaps when the petitioners referred to the racecourse ruining them, they meant that their journeymen and apprentices were spending too much time at the track, drinking and gambling, rather than working. What is especially clear from the petition is the distinction between producers of goods and those who lived off the labor of others. The references to "English dissipation" and "British mercantile agents" played on America's durable Anglophobia, here expressed in paradoxical stereotypes of Englishmen as effete and rapacious, effeminate and tyrannical. For decades, aristocratic patronage of horse racing, blood sports, and similar amusements served as an argument against them in a democratic land. Lacking England's debased poor and idle rich, some argued, America could avoid the curse of depraved amusements.

But the early nineteenth century witnessed a growing antipathy between landed and mercantile wealth, on the one hand, and manufacturing interests on the other, grounded in the former's desire for free trade and the latter's need for protection against foreign competition. Places like Hart's Racecourse became symbols of this social division. The "idle landed gentlemen" and merchants who patronized the track set an example of privilege, wasted time, and lack of concern for the future. Small independent producers—craftsmen and manufacturers in increasingly competitive markets—could not abide such extravagance. Horse racing offended the sensibilities and needs of those who lived by the virtues of production.

No doubt the majority of Philadelphia artisans did not view Hart's track as ruinous. Probably the petitioners were worried that their young charges—apprentices and journeymen—were becoming too independent, too defiant, too wasteful of time doing things like betting on horse races. Yet the craftsmen's petition was also a sign that many Americans were willing to abandon the leisure tradition associated with artisan culture. Hart's Racecourse foreshadowed broader conflicts in American life, and these grew out of crucial transformations of nineteenth-century society.

This early Philadelphia example points to an important theme of the antebellum era: the relationship between work and play in an economy that was increasingly geared toward production for national and even international markets. Manufacturing was something that men could control, especially as the process of production was reorganized in the early nineteenth century. Slaves could coax only so much cotton out of an acre of land; but tinker with the methods of spinning or weaving cotton, simplify the process so that low-paid unskilled workers could do the work, use water power and machines where possible, and the ability to increase production seemed endless. The pressure to produce came not only from the possibility of making more money but also from the fear of falling behind. When markets became glutted and prices fell, then production must increase just to stay even; owners worked harder to avoid bankruptcy and workers labored longer to keep starvation at bay.

New industries, labor specialization, and expanding markets in the blossoming American economy imposed a degree of steadiness and self-control previously unknown in artisan life. Textile mills, for example, required not simply hard work but discipline and concentration. The tediousness of labor, its unrelenting regularity, was most difficult for workers. And it was in precisely those sectors of the economy where the division of labor grew ever finer that a burgeoning Evangelical Protestant movement made significant headway. Religious revivals provided both owners and laborers with a useful cluster of values, including sobriety, steady habits, self-improvement, productivity, and the careful husbanding of time and money. This emphasis on Protestant self-control helped adjust men to new work relationships, held out the promise of virtuous prosperity, and, above all, seemed to give the alien industrial order transcendent meaning firmly grounded in age-old religious traditions.

The changes came slowly, haltingly, over decades. Production processes were rationalized at different times, depending on market demand, capitalists' initiative, and the technologies available. Equally important, workers responded in a variety of ways. Some became entrepreneurs who used the new organization of production to advance themselves; some resisted the debasement of artisan skills, loss of control over their working lives, and falling standards of living through union organizing; some accepted what they had to in the work world, but held on to their free time as their own and reasserted as best they could the old popular recreations.

This last group resisted most strongly the tide of change. Traditionalist journeymen clung tenaciously to their street life, centered in saloons, volunteer fire companies, gambling houses, circuses, and minstrel shows, all raucous places despised by reformers. While preachers gathered the faithful, the unregenerate—increasing numbers of whom were Irish immigrants—chose burgeoning urban street culture over the pious and productive ethic. These unreconstructed workers, however, were cut off from the new centers of wealth, social power, and religious legitimation. The shift from face-to-face relationships between master and man under the artisan system to purely monetary ones demanded a powerful sense of delayed gratification in those who would succeed. If the cities felt these changes most acutely, the countryside, too, was transformed by the twin forces of the marketplace and evangelism. The free and easy habits of old and the new demands for moral rigidity were irreconcilable, requiring people to stand up and be counted in the great cultural battle.

Despite the rising chorus against popular recreations, the sports of old survived and sometimes even thrived in the first decades of the nineteenth century. Their most important supporters were the landed gentry, merchants, apprentices, and journeymen of the old artisan trades, immigrant workers, and a growing urban underworld of drifters, hangers-on, town toughs, and criminals. Horse racing, rowing matches, cockfighting, and animal baiting were the major spectator events, North and South. While such activities were already of long standing in America, the growing scale of some of these events marked a real departure. Interest expanded, the numbers of contests increased, and organizational sophistication deepened. A few events became truly national in scope.

Horse racing led the way, reaching its most spectacular development in the two decades before the panic and depression of the late 1830s. New tracks and jockey clubs arose with each passing decade; 56 Thoroughbred meetings in 1830 became 130 in 1839, and the number of tracks nearly doubled in the same period. By 1836, Thoroughbred sales and transactions amounted to more than half a million dollars. To facilitate fair wagering, track organizations and new sporting journals—especially John Stuart Skinner's *American Turf Register and Sporting Magazine* (1829) and William T. Porter's *Spirit of the Times* (1831)— standardized handicap weights, planned yearly schedules, arranged the settlement of bets, fixed rules of entry, timed heats precisely, and attempted to establish a national jockey club. Increasingly, local clubs charged admission, less to make a profit than to defray expenses and control clientele. Sometimes, to ensure a respectable crowd, track officials discouraged the presence of professional gamblers, pickpockets, or prostitutes, while they encouraged "ladies" to attend. William T. Porter summed up the importance of the upper echelons of the gentry to the track's development when he declared: "We are addressing ourselves to gentlemen of standing, wealth and intelligence—the very Corinthian columns of the community."

Horse races became America's first nationwide sports spectacles when a few meets pitting Northern horses against Southern ones galvanized national attention. In 1823, three years after the Missouri Compromise patched up the dispute over the expansion of slavery, the Northern champion Eclipse raced against the South's Sir Henry for twenty thousand dollars on Long Island's Union Course. "For several days before the race," *Niles' Weekly Register* reported, "the stages and steamboats arriving at New York were burthened with anxious passengers—many of whom, no doubt, had travelled 500 miles to witness the important contest of speed! It was estimated that not less than 20,000 strangers were in the city of New York—all the hotels, inns, taverns and boarding houses were jammed with people from the bottom to the top, and on the day of the race, the city was as deserted." William Blane, an English traveler in America, believed that the race stirred more interest than a Presidential election: "In all the papers and in every man's mouth were the questions, 'are you for the North or the South? The free or the slave states?'" Estimates ranged as high as seventy thousand spectators at the race, and Northern jubilation over Eclipse's victory radiated throughout the region. Mail carriers in upstate New York witnessed Eclipse's colors flying, inscribed with the words "Eclipse forever—Old Virginia a little tired." While a handful of other big races stirred fan interest, none surpassed the 1842 match between the Northern champion Fashion and the South's Boston. Forty senators were said to have attended, and grandstand seats cost ten dollars each. Overcrowding and problems transporting people to and from the track resulted in a minor riot in which fences were torn down and ticket booths smashed.

By the 1820s, boat races, too, attracted thousands of spectators. When, in 1824, a crew from the British frigate *Hussar* challenged the Whitehall Aquatic Club to a rowing match for one thousand

The 1845 race between the victorious Southern favorite Peytona and the Northern horse Fashion on the Union Course, Long Island. Lithograph by N. Currier *(Library of Congress)*

dollars a side, upward of fifty thousand New Yorkers stood from the North River down to Castle Garden at the Battery and cheered the American victory. Observing such races was a democratic pastime, but participation was not. Young gentlemen dominated boating through the Knickerbocker Club of New York, the Savannah Boat Club, and similar associations in Boston, Philadelphia, Baltimore, and Charleston. Four-to-six-man crews raced for as much as twenty thousand dollars, and individual bettors occasionally risked tens of thousands of dollars on three to five miles of rowing. As with horse racing, intercity and interregional rivalries elicited intense interest, and victorious crews were feasted and toasted long into the night by their admiring friends.

Sporting events of this magnitude, however, were rare. While spectator sports grew in popularity through the first decades of the nineteenth century, their appeal generally remained local, their scheduling irregular, and their organization primitive. Because blood sports were illegal, they remain shadowy to us, but certainly cockfighting and bull- and bearbaiting occurred fairly regularly in New York, Philadelphia, Baltimore, and even Boston. English traveler Isaac Holmes estimated in 1820 that two or three cockmains were held in New York City every week, and he visited one breeder who kept seventy birds. Whereas Southerners openly advertised matches in newspapers, Northerners generally had to rely on handbills and word of mouth to spread the news of upcoming contests. Still, the sport had great underground popularity throughout the antebellum era.

Most of what we know of bull- and bearbaiting in this era comes from their opponents. An 1801 letter to the *New York Spectator* complained that fifteen hundred to two thousand spectators in the Bowery joyfully watched several dogs attack an incapacitated bull. Another citizen bore witness against an 1824 bait held in Baltimore:

> The bull was a fine, well-bred creature; seven or eight dogs were turned loose on him at once. They soon tore his ears off, and shockingly lacerated his head which made the poor thing bellow hideously and run about in every direction to the length of his chain, maddened with pain. In ten minutes he had killed one dog and lamed others; when I turned away in disgust.

Seats at these events ranged from twenty-five cents to a dollar. Despite the fact that this represented as much as a day's pay—urban laborers and canal workers did well to earn $4.50 a week in this era—witnesses claimed that the grandstands were usually full. Still, these contests grew less popular after about 1820, perhaps because it was harder to hide a bull than fighting birds, or maybe because cockfighting had a more elite clientele, and therefore received greater protection from the law.

Nonetheless, new blood sports, imported from England and readily conducted in backstreet taverns, came into their own as the century progressed. Rat baiting appeared in New York City around 1830 and achieved sudden favor with gamblers, saloon owners, and the urban underclass. In the "classic," one hundred rats were placed in a pit eight feet long, and a carefully trained fox terrier waded in to kill as many of them as possible in a given period of time. The best dogs could dispose of all one hundred in about twenty minutes. In the "handicap," a timekeeper determined how long a dog took to kill its weight in rats.

A fight between a bull and a bear in New Orleans. From the *London Illustrated News*, April 23, 1853 *(Library of Congress)*

For variety, men wearing great boots occasionally teamed up with the terriers in timed rat-killing competitions. Like other blood sports, ratting had a certain sophistication—dogs had special trainers and handlers, referees resolved disputes, timekeepers kept watchful eyes on the clock, and old men and boys were hired to catch live rats. Matches were held in saloons, livery stables, and private pits, and spectators paid from a quarter to a dollar and half to witness a handicap, as much as five dollars for a classic. Kit Burns's Sportsman's Hall in New York could accommodate two hundred and fifty spectators for these events, and even Boston had its own pit in the North End.

So the most highly developed American spectator sports in the early decades of the nineteenth century remained English recreations promoted on a local, sometimes regional, occasionally national level. Often these were raw affairs, replete with gambling, drinking, and swearing. Such sports implicitly offered an unreconstructed conception of masculinity; the men who attended them witnessed elemental competition that rewarded aggressiveness, violence, and domination above all else. In sports like these one found not just brutality but a grim vision that depicted the world of men as relentlessly callous. There was honor for winners and losers, to be sure, but above all there was respect for grit and prowess, contempt for weakness or frailty. Here, in other words, was little to comfort those who valued sober self-control, tender feelings, and romantic faith in progress.

The sensibility expressed in such sports could not have stood in sharper contrast to the new bourgeois culture that was coming to the fore in England and America. Rising businessmen and new converts to Evangelical Christianity were the shock troops of Victorianism. They placed no barriers between moral and economic virtues. Like their Puritan ancestors, most nineteenth-century Protestants would not have argued that wealth was a sure sign of moral worth, but they did believe in a natural connection between prosperity and morality. The millennial hopes expressed by Evangelical preachers, the belief in progress, in eternal life, in individual and spiritual perfectibility, were as real to the saints as the profits that accrued from temperance, thriftiness, and hard work. Slowly, haltingly, countless communities underwent social and economic transformation, and the result was not merely a series of altered localities but a new dominant culture. No single date marks the change, yet certainly before mid-century national markets, mass print media, telegraphy, voluntary associations, and, above all, a powerful consensus of values united most white, Northern, Protestant, middle-class Americans.

The values Victorians cherished and the institutions they built cannot be understood apart from their cultural style. "Duty" and "virtue," words that have an archaic ring to our ears, were key Victorian concepts, underscoring the era's sense of moral urgency and ethical certitude. Victorian didacticism grew out of the belief that moral principles were objective, and social values universal. This absolutism deepened the self-righteousness of

Victorian writing and broadened its scope to include prescriptive pieces on everything from etiquette to exercise, and from singing to sex. The goal of the didactic style was to convince people so deeply that they internalized a sense of social obligation and developed self-reliance. A change of behavior must come from a change of heart.

Victorian culture, it should be clear, was on a collision course with the old free and easy recreations. Whereas the Puritans had tolerated drinking and lottery playing in moderation, nineteenth-century Evangelicals condemned those practices as utterly sinful. Similarly, eighteenth-century Methodists customarily offered itinerant ministers a social dram, but for many Americans during the antebellum era, that was unthinkable. Protestants always eyed the joys of the flesh with suspicion, but the new Evangelicals insisted on an unprecedented level of asceticism from their converts. At one time or another, they condemned virtually every recreation, not only gambling, horse racing, and cockfighting but also boating, fishing, and storytelling; not just drinking, prizefighting, and bearbaiting but also chess, checkers, and croquet.

In a much-reprinted article entitled "The Billiard Table" (1828), James Hall aptly captured people's fears:

In the centre stood the billiard table, whose allurements had enticed so many on this evening to forsake the quiet and virtuous comforts of social life, and to brave the biting blast, and the not less "pitiless peltings" of parental or conjugal admonition. Its polished mahogany frame, and neatly brushed cover of green cloth, its silken pockets, and particolored ivory balls, presented a striking contrast to the rude negligence to the rest of the furniture; while a large canopy suspended over the table, and intended to collect and refract the rays of a number of well trimmed lamps, which hung within its circumference, shed an intense brilliancy over that little spot, and threw a corresponding gloom upon the surrounding scene. Indeed, if that gay altar of dissipation had been withdrawn, the temple of pleasure would have pre-

sented rather the desolate appearance of the house of mourn-
ing . . . The stained and dirty floor was strewed with
fragments of segars, playbills, and nut shells; the walls
blackened with smoke seemed to have witnessed the orgies
of many a midnight revel.

Hall worked his metaphors carefully. Here the billiard table,
brightly illuminated, elegant, dangerously alluring; but framing
it, engulfing it, a mean and dingy room, cut off from the warmth
of conjugal life. Floors filthy with cigar butts and peanut shells,
walls blackened with smoke—this was a world bereft of female
influence, befouled by undomesticated men. Not only was the
pool hall a depraved substitute for the family, it was a mock
church; the table was a "gay altar of dissipation" for worshippers
in a house of death.

Billiards' reputation for attracting dissolute men made it an
easy target, but the list of unacceptable activities grew as the
grounds of attack shifted. Idleness gradually overshadowed other
sins—gambling, drinking, swearing, Sabbath breaking—opening
the way for a very broad attack. Declared *The New Englander*,
a Congregationalist magazine, in 1851:

Let our readers, one and all, remember that we were sent
into the world, not for sport and amusement, but for labor;
not to enjoy and please ourselves, but to serve and glorify
God, and be useful to our fellow men. That is the great
object and end of life. In pursuing this end, God has indeed
permitted us all needful diversion and recreation . . . But
the great end of life after all is work . . . The Christian
fathers have a tradition that John Baptist, when a boy—
being requested by some other boys to join them in play—
replied, "I came into this world not for sport." Whether
the Baptist ever said this, we are unable to decide. But
whether he did or not, it is a remarkable saying. It is a true
saying—however cutting may be the reproof which it carries
to not a few of our fellow men. It is a saying which we may

all with propriety adopt. "We came into this world not for sport." We were sent here for a higher and nobler object.

Such lessons were repeated constantly.

In an article called "Christianity and Popular Amusements" (*Century Magazine*, 1885), young Washington Gladden recalled that as he grew up in Oswego, New York, he desperately wished to become a member of his family's church. But the sermons he heard each week taught him that this would entail "giving up all my boyish sports—ball playing, coasting, fishing." In a similar vein, William Alcott advised the youthful readers of his very popular *Young Man's Guide* (1836) that "every man who enjoys the privilege of civilized society, owes it to that society to earn as much as he can, or in other words, to improve every minute of his time. He who loses an hour or a minute, is the price of that hour debtor to the community. Moreover, it is a debt which he can never repay."

Not just the waste of time but the flagrant rejection of productive values irked reformers. When the Thoroughbred Eclipse defeated Sir Henry in 1823, *Niles' Weekly Register* berated the thousands who came to the Union Course to wager on their favorite: "Few have gained much by it—but many have lost what should have went to the payment of their just debts . . . The money expended or lost, and time wasted . . . is not far short in its value of half the cost of cutting the Erie Canal." Men must choose between payment of just debts and the sporting life, between internal improvements and wastefulness. A serious cultural clash inhered here. On the most superficial level, wild sports threatened to disturb public peace and safety. More important, those who wasted their time and gambled their money rejected productivity and genteel decorum as ultimate values. Failing to bend to the new work discipline, engaging in protracted bouts of play, such individuals not only threatened the social stability on which profits depended but called into question the very legitimacy of Victorian culture.

While the Northeast was the center of Victorianism, the West and South felt the effects of the new ways. Wild sports often flourished on the frontier, particularly in all-male environments like the California mining camps. But such activities were soon suppressed as farmers, businessmen, and workers elbowed aside miners, hunters, and trappers. In the South, not only the great planters but also poor whites and slaves continued their old sports, though they, too, faced growing opposition from the revivalists. Declared the editor of Georgia's *Christian Index* in 1840:

> . . . We think the injunction of the Apostle quite sufficient—Abstain from all appearance of evil. Now can it be a compliance with this requisition to be seen playing ball, marbles, bacgammon or any such thing? Surely no. The parties may say indeed, 'We don't bet anything, we intend no harm, it is only pastime'. Very well, and the card player and horse-racer may say the same—But how would it look for Baptists or Methodists to be seen playing cards and running horses?

Circuit riders and country preachers did their part to drive out gander pullings, gouging matches, and bearbaitings and to persuade the godly to shun the sinners.

The righteous were partially successful. Young Andrew Jackson, for example, had a reputation as one of the wildest hell raisers in Tennessee. " 'Hurrah, my Dominica! Ten dollars on my Dominica,' " Jackson bellowed during an 1805 cockfight in Nashville. " 'Hurrah, my Bernadotte! Twenty dollars on my Bernadotte! Who'll take me up? Well done, my Bernadotte, my Bernadotte forever.' " Jackson's early political career benefited from his frontier image of grit and virility, yet as President in the 1830s, he trod lightly. Jackson avoided cockfights and stopped training Thoroughbreds.

Blood sports came in for the harshest criticism, for here, in addition to the usual gambling, drinking, and swearing, were unabashed displays of violence. Reformers charged that cockfighting and animal baiting deadened men's feelings, leaving them incapable of benevolence. How could a society that made each man responsible for his own behavior and custodian of his own fate tolerate sports that undermined self-control? By mid-century, cruelty to animals grew to be as important as the debasement of humankind to those who would outlaw blood sports. This new emphasis was part of a growing trend away from viewing the animal kingdom as existing purely for people's use, toward the romantic ideal of humans and animals sharing tender feelings and sympathies, an anthropomorphism encouraged by the increasing separation of urban individuals from wildlife and livestock. New York in 1828, Massachusetts in 1834, and a total of twenty states by 1866 outlawed blood sports.

Whether reformers loved animals more or sportsmen less, their attack grew out of central assumptions of the age. Faith in human perfectibility underlay many of the era's social causes, including antislavery, temperance, feminism, peace movements, and prison reform. Scenes of cruelty and injustice assaulted Victorian belief in an ever-brightening future. Cockfights were not just in poor taste; to those who beheld gleaming visions of a godly community and well-ordered society, such spectacles revealed a side of human behavior totally at odds with virtue. Attending these wild activities, men broke away from the refining influence of women to revel in the rough fellowship of their peers. Around the cockpit, as drink and blood and wagers flowed, men forgot the future and lived for the sheer hedonistic pleasure of the moment. Symptomatic of the loose habits of artisan, gentry, and immigrant cultures, blood sports were but the worst offenders of Victorian feelings. They revealed all of the sins of popular recreations writ large.

And those sins were not just committed against piety and productivity; they were equally sins against bourgeois ideals of manhood. Victorian culture upheld new conceptions of male and female roles. The heightened division of labor was also a gender division: men inhabited the public sphere where they earned their salaries; women stayed home and received no compensation. Guardians of the hearth, women were made into the moral and spiritual centers of family life. Delicate creatures, wives and mothers raised pious families, smoothed men's rough edges,

Free black American Tom Molineaux fought for the championship of England twice, in 1810 and 1811. He lost both battles to Tom Crib. Engraved
by George and Robert Isaac Cruikshank *(William Schutte Collection)*

brought them to morality, to tender feelings, to God. Men, in
turn, expected to go out into the world, then return to the joys
of domestic life. For Victorians, the high virtue of manliness did
not mean primal aggression or virility. On the contrary, true
manliness was a matter of responsible behavior and self-control.
Manliness inhered in good character, steady habits, and forth-
right business practices. Attending a bullbait was not a manly
act; working for legislation against blood sports was.

The Beginnings of Modern American Sports

In December of 1810, an American boxer stood in a prize ring
thirty miles north of London to fight for the championship of
England. Tom Molineaux was a black man, a former slave, it
was said. The British seemed as concerned about Molineaux's
nationality as his color, for it would have been a disgrace to allow

a foreigner to reign as champion in the "national sport of England." Molineaux fought spectacularly, but finally lost in the thirty-ninth round to Tom Crib, one of the great fighters of all time. Pierce Egan, a renowned chronicler of the English sporting scene, declared that Molineaux "proved himself as courageous a man as ever an adversary contended with . . . The Black astonished everyone, not only by his extraordinary power of hitting, and his gigantic strength, but also by his acquaintance with the science, which was far greater than any had given him credit for." Molineaux and Crib fought a second time less than a year later, with much the same result. These were great fights; thousands of Englishmen attended, including countless aristocrats who patronized boxers with their fortunes, took lessons from them in the manly art of self-defense, and spent much of their time slumming in the dives and back alleys of London where the culture of the ring thrived.

In America, however, scarcely anyone knew Molineaux's name. Certainly his color made a difference. But equally important was the strangeness of the sport of boxing to Americans. Except for occasional battles on the New York wharves, usually involving English seamen, prizefighting was virtually unknown in the United States, so most Americans simply were indifferent to the fate of two men—any two men—who chose to brutalize each other for pay. The practice must have seemed bizarrely English to Americans.

Almost exactly fifty years later, on the eve of the Civil War, another American sailed for England in search of the championship. This time, there was an explosion of interest in the fate of Irish-American John C. Heenan as he prepared to fight the English champion, Tom Sayers. Declared *The New York Times* of the upcoming battle, "With the mass of the people it is just now the great topic of speculation . . . throwing completely into shade all political themes and everything else which can afford to wait." Not that boxing had grown respectable. The editor of *Frank Leslie's Illustrated Newspaper* sermonized that pugilists were the heroes of saloons, gambling parlors, and brothels, and that prizefighting was the last subject that should find its way into a family newspaper. Yet, fearing the loss of a golden opportunity, *Leslie's* sent reporters and artists to London and flooded the newsstands with tens of thousands of papers. The ring represented all of the libidinal outpourings that were anathema to the Victorian middle class: drunkenness, gambling, cursing, open displays of near nudity and violence. The sport remained illegal and widely condemned. Paradoxically, prize-fighting had become one of America's most popular spectator sports by the 1850s.

The outpouring of public interest in boxing during the Sayers-Heenan bout was a dramatic sign of growing interest in sports. Countless local, incremental changes made such occasional great events possible. In Pittsburgh, for example, we glimpse the ebb and flow of sporting life. The disorderly frontier town at Fort Pitt had been a roughneck's haven around the beginning of the nineteenth century. But after citizens organized the city of Pittsburgh, religion persuaded some and the law forced others to change their ways. For decades, public vigilance imposed an unwelcome circumspection on sporting men. However, by the middle of the nineteenth century, Pittsburghers once again attended illegal horse races, cockmains, and dogfights. Like many other burgeoning American cities, Pittsburgh was a boom town, and it attracted a large, heterogeneous population, eager for action.

But respectable pastimes also took their place alongside taboo events. An 1840 editorial in the *Daily Pittsburgher* declared that city dwellers failed to take enough exercise: "Throughout all nature, want of motion indicates weakness, corruption, inanimation and death." The paper cited an "illustrious physician's" belief that men must exercise to become fully developed in mind and body. In the same year, Mr. S. Barrett, "Professor of Gymnastic Exercise," opened his Pittsburgh Gymnasium, where, for ten dollars a year, adults could learn cavalry and sword exercises in addition to gymnastics. To secure an impeccable clientele, Barrett admitted physicians and clergymen free of charge. For the next generation, a variety of new sports such as rowing, cricket, and pedestrianism (running races) thrived in Pittsburgh.

Many American communities replicated Pittsburgh's experience, for the Victorian assault on sports and recreations never succeeded completely. Not only did the influx of immigrants into the growing cities revitalize old practices and introduce others, but changing social, cultural, and economic patterns spawned a new sporting impulse. If the Victorians adapted modern means of communication to their purposes, steam-powered printing, telegraphy, and the penny press were equally useful in disseminating sporting news. While the advent of the daily sports page came only a full generation after the Civil War, the antebellum period witnessed America's earliest sports reporting. The first sporting magazine made its appearance in the second decade of the century, three new magazines in each of the next three decades, four in the 1850s, and nine in the 1860s. Most of these were aimed at a wealthy audience. For example, five dollars purchased an annual subscription to such quality monthlies as the *Knickerbocker Magazine* or the *Southern Literary Messenger* during the 1830s, but the elegant *New York Sporting Magazine* was doubly expensive. In its pages, gentlemen learned the latest on the track, the chase, and even the baiting pits, while colored engravings brought images of champion Thoroughbreds into tastefully furnished parlors.

Spirit of the Times editor William T. Porter in 1835 made his elite appeal explicit: "Our course will be among the refinements, the luxuries, and the enjoyments of society." Two years later, he added that his magazine was "designed to promote the views and interests of but an infinitesimal division of those classes of society composing the great mass . . ." Porter patterned his publication after the aristocratic English magazine *Bell's Life in London*. For ten dollars a year the *Spirit of the Times* offered gentlemen not only sporting news but also frontier sketches, backwoods humor, and news of the theatrical world. At the height of its popularity, forty thousand subscribers took the journal, and for countless men who read and discussed its pages in local taverns, the *Spirit of the Times* helped define an ideal of upper-class life modeled after that of the English gentry.

Serving the other end of the social spectrum was the penny press, dailies that sold literally for a penny. Beginning in the

1830s, rising literacy rates and the revolution in printing technology broadened potential readership to include the growing urban working class. But papers like the *Sun* and the *Transcript* in New York, the *Philadelphia Public Ledger*, the *Baltimore Sun*, and the *Boston Daily Times* were not merely inexpensive versions of more elite dailies. They eschewed gentility to report sports, crime, gossip, and scandals. They developed sophisticated news-gathering techniques, they exposed fraud in high places, and they thumbed their noses at Victorian proprieties with salacious writing, disreputable advertising, and sensationalism.

James Gordon Bennett and his *New York Herald* exemplified all of these characteristics in exaggerated ways. Bennett encouraged the public taste for news of crime and vice. He attacked churches, reformers, revivals, all who considered themselves part of polite society. He sometimes found himself in fistfights with those he offended. At his most innovative, Bennett pioneered the use of railroads, telegraphs, and special reporters to cover the news. He responded to Victorian sentimentality with blunt realism and mocked his critics' prudery with scandalous abandon. At his worst, Bennett was cynical, misanthropic, exploitative; his populist appeal often seemed like little more than a means to expand the *Herald*'s circulation. Most important for our purposes, he made sporting news available to New York City's working class. Sports coverage was irregular, but if a major horse race, prizefight, or running race was about to happen, Bennett bent the *Herald*'s full efforts toward reporting it.

Other institutional changes aided the cause of sporting culture. By the 1850s, telegraph lines formed an information network that transmitted Presidential proclamations as well as baseball game results; railroads brought raw materials and finished goods to market, but also carried Thoroughbreds to racetracks; the same steamboats that transported the godly to revivals brought toughs and gamblers to prizefights. The manufacturing and marketing of sporting goods such as cricket bats, bows and arrows, billiard tables, and hunting and fishing gear also began around mid-century.

The expansion of American cities further spurred the growth

of sports. Between 1840 and 1860, America urbanized at a rate never attained before or since. During Andrew Jackson's Presidency, only two American cities held more than one hundred thousand people; by 1860, eight reached that population. Even the sheer physical size of urban areas grew dramatically from roughly a one-mile average radius in the late eighteenth century to almost five miles by the mid-nineteenth century. Immigration, of course, accounted for much of this expansion. In the thirty years between 1815 and 1845, 850,000 immigrants came to America, but in the next eight years, 1.25 million more poured in, largely because of the Irish potato famine. By 1860, about one half of the residents of New York, Chicago, and St. Louis had been born abroad. No longer isolated islands in a rural sea, cities grew ever more vital as the centers of national and international markets.

Urban growth meant new social problems, and popular literature at once moralized and titillated readers with stories of crime, prostitution, gambling, and other sins of the metropolis. The cities' growing importance as manufacturing and trade centers gave them economic clout and enhanced their social and cultural influence over the rest of the country. Even as schoolbooks, dime novels, and popular lithographs exalted rural virtue, even while countless writers condemned the sinful dissipation, moral depravity, and class inequities of the growing population centers, even as men longed for a romanticized life on the land, all testified to the heightened influence of urban mores, to the economic and cultural pull of new city ways.

Although most Americans still lived in the countryside during the antebellum era, it was in the growing cities that sports developed most rapidly. Here displaced journeymen, migrants from the countryside, and new immigrants found themselves thrown together as propertyless employees. Urban growth in this era closely paralleled the expansion of specialized wage labor, and these in turn were both cause and effect of the increasing importance of mass-marketed goods in daily life. The cramped environment of expanding cities, the long working hours and remoteness from the countryside, and, above all, the new emphasis on time thrift and regular working rhythms militated against the easy familiar flow of the old rural pastimes.

While these trends far from destroyed the older popular recreations, they did create a new set of restrictions and possibilities. Commercialization expanded the variety of popular pastimes, but commercial activities were also less tightly woven into the fabric of communal life than were age-old folkways. Increasingly, recreation was transformed into entertainment, cultural goods purchased with earnings. Minstrel shows, melodramas, popular "museums" like P. T. Barnum's in New York City, circuses, pleasure gardens, and sporting events all became cultural commodities. Put another way, the growing division of labor in the cities was paralleled by heightened specialization of function between performers and audiences, between creators and consumers of culture. Entertainment itself was being transformed into a commodity for sale in the marketplace.

In sports, these trends were just getting under way in the decades before the Civil War. Boxing came into its own during this era with a series of spectacular fights, the price of admission being included in steamboat and railroad fares to the bouts. In terms of the attention given to individual events, prizefighting was the most noteworthy sport of the era. Long-distance footracing, called pedestrianism, also enjoyed great popularity. Although tens of thousands of fans attended Jacksonian-era horse races, and hundreds of thousands read about them in the papers, the track did not fare particularly well during the middle decades of the century. But harness racing, especially in the cities, became the single most popular sport of the era. Also, by the eve of the Civil War, baseball had outgrown its beginnings as a children's game and developed a structure of clubs; a few teams even began charging spectators and paying players.

Men from various social strata participated in sports, but the most controversial group was known as "the fancy" or the sporting fraternity. Comprised mainly of working-class males, members of the sporting fraternity either were unmarried or spent most of their time apart from their families, and hung out in plebian commercial districts—for example, New York's Bowery.

An occasional wealthy rakehell joined their revels, and some of their sports were supported by machine politicians or such wealthy benefactors as the steamboat heir John Cox Stevens. But most of the fancy were workers in traditional trades (such as butchering), unskilled and day laborers, members of the urban underworld, and immigrants, particularly the Irish. Above all, this bachelor subculture defined itself against the genteel canons of the day; in volunteer firehouses, saloons, gambling parlors, theaters, militia company headquarters, and brothels, men gathered to carouse.

Boxing, cockfighting, and billiards found a home in plebian neighborhoods; tavern keepers staged dogfights, ratting contests, and running meets. Frederick Van Wyck, the son of a socially prominent family that mixed with Vanderbilts, Morgans, and Roosevelts at the Union League Club, loved to go slumming in the dives of lower Manhattan. Van Wyck described a night at Tommy Norris's Livery Stable in his *Recollections of an Old New Yorker*: "When you start with a dog fight as a curtain raiser, continue with a cock fight, then rat baiting, next a prize fight, then a battle of billy goats, and then a boxing match between two ladies, with nothing but trunks on—after that I think you have a night's entertainment that has enough spice—not to say tabasco sauce—to fill the most rapacious needs."

Prizefighting under the bare-knuckle rules was the favored sport of the urban underground. Boxers were ethnic and neighborhood heroes, leaders of tough street gangs that provided muscle on election days for various political factions. Champions like James "Yankee" Sullivan, Tom Hyer, and John Morrissey won their fame in brutal matches held surreptitiously in defiance of the law. The 1858 championship bout between Morrissey and John C. Heenan, the "Benicia Boy," will serve as an example. Both men had reputations as street fighters, though young Heenan had never fought in a ring under bare-knuckle rules. After signing articles of agreement to put up five thousand dollars each, then training for several weeks, the fighters took the train from New York City to Buffalo, accompanied by hundreds, perhaps thousands, of sporting men, some from as far away as New

Frank Leslie's Illustrated Newspaper (October 30, 1858) condemned the prizefight between John C. Heenan and John Morrissey in 1858, but gave the event ample coverage *(William Schutte Collection)*

Orleans. From Buffalo, boats were chartered to Long Point, Canada. Although both men were of immigrant parentage, Morrissey was depicted in the press as the menacing Irish tough (he had been brought to America from Tipperary as a babe), while Heenan, no choirboy himself, was given a more respectable, more American image, perhaps because he had been born in the States.

The fight turned out to be a good one. Despite predictions of gang violence, order prevailed. Heenan was seriously weakened by an abscess on his leg, but he dominated the fight for ten rounds. The first one lasted over four minutes (under the rules, a round ended when a man was either punched or thrown down, and a fight lasted until either man could no longer continue), and Heenan pummeled Morrissey at will. But bare-knuckle boxing made "bottom"—endurance—a great virtue, and by the eleventh round, Heenan was so exhausted he could no longer throw punches, while the bloodied Morrissey seemed to be gaining strength. Finally, Heenan collapsed insensible. When he came to, fans paraded both men around the ground in a carriage, toasted their health, paid or collected their debts, then steamed back to Buffalo, where they arrived, rockets firing, horns blowing, crowds cheering on the docks, at 2:30 a.m. Some papers estimated that a quarter of a million dollars in wagers changed hands in New York City. With its days-long festivities, the Morrissey-Heenan fight was a high point of the bachelor subculture during the bare-knuckle era.

Others saw it differently. Horace Greeley's *New York Tribune*, a bastion of propriety and social reform, declared of the fight scene: "Probably no human eye will ever look upon so much rowdyism, villainy and scoundrelism, and boiled-down vicious-ness, concentrated upon so small a space . . . Scoundrels of every imaginable genus, every variety of every species, were there assembled; the characteristic rascalities of each were developed and displayed in their devilish perfection." *Frank Leslie's Illustrated Newspaper*, which gave extensive coverage to the bout, editorialized: "A worse set of scapegallowses . . . could scarcely be collected; low, filthy, brutal, bludgeon bearing scoundrels—the very class of men who have built up the Tammany Hall party in New York . . ." But while condemnations of the ring were loud, prizefighting had a solid base of support, and even the respectable press felt compelled to cover the fight.

Within the bachelor subculture, young working-class men spent large amounts of time in each other's company. Many of them joined urban gangs, which, when they were not fighting each other over points of honor raised by turf disputes or ethnic rivalries, were working for machine politicians as ballot-box stuffers or election-day enforcers. These men created a world of rough masculine camaraderie, drinking, whoring, fighting, ca-rousing, or just hanging out with the boys. The bachelor sub-culture emphatically rejected the middle-class Victorian version of proper male behavior, and the bloody, elemental combat to be found in the prize ring gave deepest expression to their sensibility.

Indeed, the bachelor subculture developed its own masculine aesthetic that reveled in male beauty, as this description from the *Spirit of the Times* of the 1842 prizefight between Chris Lilly and Thomas McCoy attests: "If Lilly's appearance was fine, McCoy's was beautiful. His skin had a warmer glow than the former's; his form was more elegantly proportioned, and his air and style more graceful and manlike. His swelling breast curved out like a cuirass: his shoulders were deep, with a bold curved blade, and the muscular development of the arm large and finely brought out . . ." The homoeroticism of this passage (and there were many like it) was unmistakable. Men in the bachelor subculture could be objects of beauty to one another because their emotional lives were so closely tied together, because they chose to spend their lives much more with men than with women.

Besides the old sports of the fancy, long-distance footracing also gained tremendous popularity in antebellum America. The ubiquitous John Cox Stevens initiated the commercialization of racing in 1835 with an offer of one thousand dollars to any man who could run ten miles in under an hour. He advertised the challenge in national and local newspapers and had several articles printed on the history of pedestrianism. With all of this publicity, a crowd estimated at twenty to thirty thousand people showed up at the Union Course in Long Island to watch a field of runners take up Stevens's challenge. During the next twenty-five years, crowds of up to fifty thousand spectators saw men race one another for as much as $4,000. Most purses ranged from a few dollars to a few hundred, so in an era when $250 represented what many workers earned in a year, running could provide a substantial supplement to the incomes of farmers, artisans, and laborers. Indeed, runners such as John Gildersleeve and William Howett made handsome livings traveling from race to race, even promoting themselves with public challenges.

Virtually every state witnessed pedestrian races during the 1840s and '50s, but, as was typical, this sport was most highly developed in New York City. For a mere dime, members of the urban working class might enjoy an afternoon's amusement. Mingling with the fans at Long Island's Union Course and other venues were pickpockets, hustlers, prostitutes, and professional gamblers. Sometimes overcrowded stadiums, nationalistic pride, flowing grog, and spiraling wagers raised emotions to a fever pitch. Maintaining order posed a real problem in an era that had not yet developed crowd control techniques. On October 14, 1844, for example, intense promotion lured thousands more spectators than Hoboken's Beacon Course could accommodate, and fans stood on every bit of space that afforded a view of the track. Fights broke out, drunks staged a mock race, and it took an hour for mounted police and "mob managers" armed with long clubs to clear the track so that the race might begin. Despite such problems, these were festive occasions, replete with song and laughter, drink and good cheer. The spectacle of the crowd, the holiday spirit in the stands, the runners' colorful uniforms, the intense drama of the competition—all filled these races with excitement.

Harness racing was, by some measures, the most successful sport in the years before the Civil War. Once leadership in Thoroughbred racing passed out of the hands of Southerners, Northern horsemen tried to take control, but a depressed breeding market, a lack of strong jockey clubs to regulate the sport, and an absence of promoters who could put together good matches kept the track in the doldrums. While the aristocratic Thoroughbreds experienced hard times until after the Civil War, the trotters flourished. By the 1850s, more spectators watched harness racing than any other sport, and there were about seventy tracks nationwide, seven in the New York metropolitan area alone. The city's greatest harness-racing venue, however, was Third Avenue; trotters raced up and down the road, and at taverns along the way, men gathered to discuss the sport and arrange new contests.

In contrast with the sport of kings, harness racing fostered a mythology of wholesome equality; unhitched from its cart, the tradesman's horse of legend wins the day at the track. "Wherever the trotting horse goes," declared Oliver Wendell Holmes in the *Atlantic Monthly* in 1857, "he carries in his train brisk omnibuses, lively bakers' carts, and therefore hot rolls, the jolly butcher's wagon, the cheerful gig, the wholesome afternoon drive with wife and child—all the forms of moral excellence . . ." The myth of democratic participation was an enduring one, despite the fact that good trotters were owned almost exclusively by prosperous businessmen, and the cost of fine horses increased steadily from the 1850s through the 1870s. Indeed, the leading New York trotting men were steamship magnate Cornelius Vanderbilt and newspaper owner Robert Bonner, whose legendary rivalry testified to the exclusivity of harness racing.

Bonner, a devout Presbyterian, refused to enter races, believing that they promoted gambling. Yet competitiveness arose between the two men as they drove their teams along the avenues of New York. Vanderbilt publicly challenged any team of horses to beat his, and put up a $10,000 winner-take-all stake. Bonner would not compromise his principles, but on May 13, 1862, he brought his team to the edge of the Fashion Course on Long Island. At the end of the day's races, which Vanderbilt won, Bonner asked that his horses be clocked around the mile track. His team came in three seconds faster than Vanderbilt's best time. Having just "defeated" his rival by a substantial margin, Bonner declared that while he opposed gambling, he would make a gift of $10,000 to anyone who could beat his time.

With the rise of boxing, pedestrianism, and harness racing, America witnessed more large-scale spectator sports than ever before. But despite the events that drew thousands of fans and hundreds of newspaper stories, contests with mass appeal remained relatively uncommon. Professionalism in sports was still unusual, profits secondary, organizations informal, and scheduling irregular. In short, if athletic contests as commodities grew more common during the antebellum era, sports continued to be occasional events, not the regularly scheduled, lucrative, well-managed spectacles of today. Far more important than professionalization and commercialization in organizing mid-century sports was the voluntary association of individuals based on class, ethnic, or occupational background. In sport, as in religion, politics, or business, voluntary associations were the glue holding diverse Americans together.

In booming new cities where strangers were thrown together in an impersonal marketplace, sports clubs offered to humanize relationships. The young Germans, for example, who migrated to America after the abortive revolution of 1848 brought their turnvereins with them. The first turnverein was started in Germany in 1811 by Friedrich Ludwig Jahn, and these societies blended nationalism, anticlericalism, and utopian socialism. Universal education and a systematic program of gymnastics, according to the members (or turners, as they became known), prepared men for political and social democracy. Although they faced hostility from American nativists and from large communities of "church" Germans already settled in this country, these "forty-eighters" found in the turner movement an alternative to American individualist ideology, and a place of refuge where they could spend time with like-minded people. Turnvereins appeared wherever forty-eighters migrated, and became havens of German culture, scholarship, and gymnastic training.

During the 1850s, Scottish immigrants began replicating their ancient track and field games in America. Caledonian clubs sought to perpetuate the manners, customs, music, literature, dress, and sports of the Scottish homeland. They helped satisfy Scots' need for an ethnic community centered on traditional folkways. By the late nineteenth century, the Caledonian Games' racing, hurdling, jumping, pole vaulting, shot-putting, and hammer throwing formed the basis for modern track and field, but as early as mid-century, upward of twenty thousand New Yorkers turned out to witness the Scots' annual competitions. English immigrants found a home away from home in the game of cricket. By 1860, more than one hundred American cities were home to about five hundred cricket clubs, and something like ten thousand men and boys—mostly British, but Americans, too—actively participated in the game before the Civil War. Sports, then, allowed immigrant groups to forget momentarily the alien American environment and re-create an idealized vision of their homelands.

Not only ethnic groups but social classes as well founded sports clubs. At the upper end of the social spectrum, men of wealth and power organized a handful of elite sporting institutions. These were part of a larger club movement arising among wealthy individuals during the antebellum era. Metropolitan, University, and Union Clubs, for example, at once symbolized and buttressed class prerogatives. Such organizations reinforced distinctive class styles of dress, speech, and values, while creating networks of personal and business connections, free from interference by men of lower status. During the 1840s and '50s, cricket, racquet, yacht, and rowing clubs began to take their place alongside other exclusive men's organizations. John Cox Stevens, for example, founded the New York Yacht Club in 1844, which attracted some of the city's leading men. When Stevens's yacht *America* defeated eighteen British rivals in the first America's Cup race (1851), other cities quickly organized their own yacht clubs, which sponsored a variety of social activities including races, balls, and cruises. Boat clubs, crew teams, and regattas sprang up at prestigious Ivy League colleges; and in 1852, Harvard and Yale oarsmen competed in the nation's first—albeit informal—intercollegiate athletic contest. The embryonic alliance between sport and business is especially clear in this example, because the Boston, Concord and Montreal Railroad sponsored the regatta and paid all expenses as part of a business promotion.

The most important sport associated with the club movement was baseball. Children's games known as rounders, town ball, one old cat, stoolball, and baseball had been played at least since the eighteenth century in England and America, and all involved hitting a ball with a stick. But only around the middle of the nineteenth century did the "New York game"—the baseball configuration we recognize today, with its diamond-shaped infield and nine players on each side—emerge as the dominant form. An organization initiated in 1845 in New York City by a bank clerk named Alexander Cartwright and known as the Knickerbocker Base Ball Club was the first team that survived more than a year or two. (Alas, Abner Doubleday did not invent the game in Cooperstown, New York.)

By the late 1850s, dozens of clubs had been formed. These were fraternal organizations, devoted to good fellowship, to feasting and sociability, as well as to the game. Members tended to be urban artisans, clerks, and proprietors of small shops, all part of respectable local cultures. Clubs played each other on an ad hoc basis. A few games attracted a thousand or more spectators; but much more often, members of a given club practiced and played against each other, usually two or three times a week. While men recognized standards of good play, the fraternal rituals of the clubs overshadowed winning and losing. Like other local urban institutions—volunteer fire companies, Masonic orders, party ward organizations, workers' benevolent associations—baseball clubs allowed men from similar social and economic backgrounds to meet and fraternize. Each baseball club had a constitution, bylaws, and officers; members paid dues and held meetings. Distinctive uniforms soon caught on, as did club names—the Mohawks, the Mutuals (for the volunteer fire company), the Eckfords (for the shipbuilding firm). So while the game as it was played by 1860 would be recognizable to a modern-day fan—two teams of nine players each, nine innings, hitter, pitcher, runs scored and outs made in familiar ways (though walks were nonexistent and strikeouts rare)—baseball was not yet played by trained professionals, as it would be by the 1870s.

Baseball may well have been the most important sport of the antebellum era. Although some Victorian critics condemned the game for the usual offenses, it was much less raucous than the old sports of the bachelor subculture. Players were proud of their status as members of the respectable working class, as skilled artisans, or as men who had advanced to white-collar status and petty proprietorships. The game was pervaded by the language of work and craft, no surprise since many of the clubs drew their members from particular trades such as shipbuilding, butchering, and printing, trades in which workers had managed to retain considerable pride, skill, and control. Moreover, many players went out of their way to defend baseball's reputation. Not only did the game attract far fewer gang members, Irish immigrants, and unskilled laborers than prizefighting but players advocated the sport for its wholesome exercise, manliness, and cooperation. Club members deliberately fashioned a game ethic that would not overstep Victorian fears of unregulated passions or loss of self-control, and in this way they deliberately tried to make baseball acceptable to mainstream Americans.

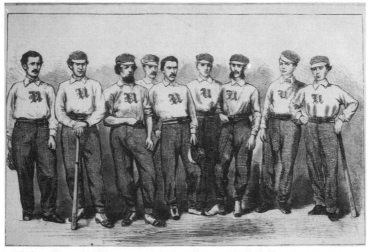

Until the triumph of the great Cincinnati Red Stockings of 1869 (made up mostly of transplanted northeasterners), the best baseball in the country was played in the New York metropolitan area. The Unions of Morrisania (The Bronx), New York, were perennial contenders and occasional champions during the 1860s *(National Baseball Library and Archive)*

The concern of many clubs in these early years to prevent the sport from becoming a vulgar commercial amusement was a reaction against the plebian culture of the streets loathed by high Victorians. Although baseball grew up in the same cities as minstrel shows, melodramas, brothels, saloons, dance halls, and gambling parlors, the sport was not, like boxing and cockfighting, so closely associated with the bachelor subculture. The proliferating New York baseball clubs of the 1850s were rarely tainted with the political factionalism, ethnic violence, and bloody machismo of the Bowery. Whereas boxing, with its overtones of male honor, turf wars, and drunken brawling, stood in direct violation of all that Victorians cherished, baseball was much more accepting of bourgeois proprieties. It was significant that while boxers and members of the sporting fraternity spent much of their time in the volunteer firehouses, the more respectable baseball clubs spread throughout New York just as the volunteer companies were giving way to professionals in the late 1850s.

Even before the Civil War, however, there was tension in baseball. A few particularly successful clubs began paying players and charging admission. By the 1870s, baseball had become professionalized, as fans, players, and sportswriters sought the highest possible quality of play. During the antebellum era, however, many players and fans argued that the game was a healthy alternative to the seamy world of urban amusements. And at the same moment, a handful of successful, well-respected Americans were beginning to articulate a defense of sports and recreations in the name of key Victorian ideals.

Muscular Christians and Brawny Brahmins

The rise to prominence of new sports in the antebellum era evoked mixed reactions. While certain activities, such as cockfighting, remained forever beyond the pale of Victorian respectability, others slowly gained support. America's national pride was deflated by foreign travelers—especially Englishmen—who commented on the poor physical condition of Americans. "A Boston boy is a picture of prematurity," British consul Thomas C. Grattan observed in 1859:

> It can be said that every man is born middle-aged in every city in the Union. The principal business seems to be to grow old as fast as possible. He enters college at fourteen and graduates at seventeen into the business world. The interval between their leaving school and commencing their business careers offers no occupation to give either gracefulness or strength to body or mind. Athletic games and bolder field sports being unknown . . . all that is left is chewing, smoking and drinking . . . Young men made of such materials as I describe are not young men at all . . . They have no breadth either of shoulders, information or ambition. Their physical powers are subdued and their mental capability cribbed into narrow limits.

James Silk Buckingham, Frances Trollope, Charles Dickens, Harriet Martineau, and Sir Charles Lyell were among the foreign visitors who rendered similar judgments. For a frontier-smashing, progress-worshipping young nation, the charge that Americans lacked manly vigor rankled. The very idea that working too hard gave rise to immoral habits seemed especially ironic, given Victorian faith in the virtues of work.

Still, some Americans agreed with the critics. An 1856 article in *Harper's Magazine* described American boys as "an apathetic-brained, a pale pasty-faced, narrow-chested, spindle-shanked, dwarfed race—mere walking manikins to advertise the last-cut of the fashionable tailor." When Tom Hyer fought Yankee Sullivan in 1849, N. Parker Willis pondered the ongoing rivalry between Britain and the United States. "America," he declared, "could doubtless afford at some cost of order and staid propriety to purchase an enthusiasm for physical culture and masculine vigor and beauty." But Oliver Wendell Holmes put the matter most bluntly in the *Atlantic Monthly* (1858): "I am satisfied that such a set of black-coated, stiff-jointed, soft-muscled, paste-complexioned youth as we can boast in our Atlantic cities never before sprang from the loins of Anglo-Saxon lineage . . ."

Sports and exercise received a boost from the era's interest in health reform. Temperance, vegetarianism, and sexual hygiene were central concerns for some reformers, while others advocated fresh air, regular bathing, and exercise as the keys to health. Several intellectual trends that had developed since the late eighteenth century helped support the new ideas. By emphasizing humankind's freedom to choose salvation, Evangelicals placed change and transcendence at the heart of faith. Moreover, the Enlightenment spirit of improvement found new direction in the romantic cult of the perfectible individual. And medical science now tended to assume a connection between ideation and the material world, so that physical health was linked with mental, moral, and spiritual improvement. Mind and body, in other words, became ever more tightly linked. Enlightenment, republican, and romantic intellectual trends all drew sustenance from the ancient Greeks, including their belief in the importance of physical development. Meanwhile, medical authorities and educators paid increasing attention to European trends in hygiene.

The "discovery" of health and exercise bolstered central Victorian assumptions. "How much sin does he accumulate," Dr. Edward Reynolds asked his audience at Andover Theological Seminary in 1831, "who, having enlisted as a soldier or leader in the cause of Christ, renders himself, by neglect, wholly or in part unfit for duty." Indeed, the very title of Dr. John Jeffries's essay "Physical Culture, the Result of Moral Obligation" demonstrates how concern for health blended with the Victorian style. Innumerable medical tracts on physiology, hygiene, and physical education appeared in the middle third of the century, all animated by the underlying assumption that self-reliance, morality, and spiritual development depended on good health.

The Victorians' spirit of improvement, their faith in an ever-brighter future, caused them to place great emphasis on the proper schooling of children. Mental cultivation was education's first priority, but the editor of Philadelphia's *Ariel* in 1831 believed that physical exercise complemented children's intellectual development: "They should be taught systematically to exercise themselves, and firmness, energy, muscularity, health, strength and activity will take the place of imbecility and weakness both of mind and body." It was far better to guide children toward moral and productive recreations than leave these matters to chance: "By setting proper bounds to late sleeping in the morning, reading novels and silly tales, visiting theatres and a thousand other methods of idling away time, in which youth consume a large portion of their most valuable years, we shall have ample time for improving the corporeal faculties."

Horace Mann, the great nineteenth-century educator, agreed that mental and spiritual growth depended on physical fitness, and that sedentary habits could cause one's body to deteriorate until it was an unfit dwelling place for the soul. Leaders of American colleges expressed similar sentiments. Francis Wayland, president of Brown University, argued that not only did lack of exercise impair mental faculties but "the want of it produces also a feebleness of will, which is as fatal to moral attainment as it is to intellectual progress." Mark Hopkins of Williams College viewed exercise as a wholesome alternative to students' excessive drinking, eating, and smoking. And Mary Lyon, founder of Mount Holyoke College, declared in 1832 that "those who enjoy bodily idleness enjoy sin. Exercise is part of the very constitution of man." Duty, hard work, and godliness—the marrow of Victorianism—became linked to rational physical education.

Exercise was upheld in the name of two other Victorian values, domesticity and rural virtue. Catharine Beecher, the most influential spokesperson for the cult of domesticity—which defined women as nurturing and emotionally supportive, as the moral bulwark of the home—advocated physical training in her *Course of Calisthenics for Young Ladies* (1832). By the 1840s, Lydia Huntley Sigourney was advising women on proper diet, clothing, and exercise, arguing that mothers were accountable to God for helping their families maintain sound minds and bodies. Victorians also viewed country life as a source of American goodness. John Stuart Skinner, editor of the nation's first sporting journal, *The American Turf Register and Sporting Magazine* (1829), advocated field sports, along with swimming, skating, and gymnastics, as alternatives to urban taverns, oyster houses, and other pernicious "haunts of dissipation." Skinner condemned blood sports and generally abstained from covering them, but field and stream, he believed, would revivify city dwellers. Wholesome, moral alternatives to urban depravity, natural sports refreshed citizens for the main business of life.

All of this can be seen as the first glimmerings of an emergent sports ideology. Not only were activities themselves changing, old ones dying and new ones arising, but sports were beginning to be viewed as a moral force, especially those sports that could lay claim to such virtues as self-discipline or bodily development or rural innocence. All of the various health concerns of the antebellum era, including sanitation improvements, vegetarianism, temperance, even new massage and bathing techniques, reflected the twin Victorian ideals of social progress and self-control. Taking charge of one's own physical condition became a prerequisite for a virtuous, self-reliant, spiritually elevated life.

Moral improvement, self-mastery, and godliness were all invoked in the name of sports. More than anything else, it was the characteristic Victorian tone—earnest, self-righteous, didactic, millennial—which reveals that health, recreation, and even sports were beginning their assimilation to bourgeois morality.

By mid-century, an avant-garde of moral leaders—clergymen, intellectuals, journalists, and reformers—took up the cause begun as early as the 1830s by physicians and educators. Middle-class, well educated, mostly Unitarian, the New England transcendentalists believed that spirituality infused the entire material world. They assumed that humankind was perfectible, and that individuals controlled their own destinies. To this they added a rejection of the excessive materialism they saw in American society, and an immediate sense of the sacred oneness of God, nature, and humankind. Above all, the transcendentalists were concerned with the divine spark that inhered in each human being. And since the body was the resting place of the soul, people were obliged to maintain it as a worthy sanctuary.

Ralph Waldo Emerson, father of the movement, advocated the full development of all human abilities in *Conduct of Life* (1860). Nature sought "symmetry between the physical and intellectual powers . . . power of mind with physical health." So physical education must accompany moral and intellectual development: "Archery, cricket, gun and fishing-rod, horse and boat are all educators, liberalizers, and so are . . . swimming, skating, climbing, fencing, riding, lessons in the art of power . . ." An admirer of active and powerful men, Emerson believed that physical vigor was at once a metaphor and a prerequisite for good intellectual work. "Out upon these scholars . . . with their pale, sickly etiolated indoor thoughts! Give me the out-of-door thoughts of sound men, thoughts all fresh and blooming."

Similarly, Henry David Thoreau declared that "the body existed for the highest development of the soul," and he advocated activities that immersed people in nature—walking, running, swimming, sailing, and rowing. Believing that education's main goal was to allow a child's innately good nature to come forth, Bronson Alcott introduced play and physical activities into his experimental schools, maintaining that in the playroom children learned how to associate harmoniously with others. Margaret Fuller felt so strongly about the need for rigorous exercise, she argued that the United States should follow the lead of European nations and make physical training of children a state function. Perhaps Walt Whitman best captured the spirit of optimism shared by the rest. In *Leaves of Grass*, he celebrated the divinity of the body:

> *If anything is sacred the human body is sacred,*
> *And the glory and sweet of a man is the token of*
>   *manhood untainted,*
> *And in man or woman a clean, strong, firm-fibred*
>   *body, is more beautiful than the most beautiful face.*

Protestant suspicion of the flesh remained too strong for most Americans to take so rosy a view; powerful Victorian assumptions still gave short leash to bodily pleasures. Nonetheless, some influential voices had joined the sports-and-fitness chorus.

Some of the new converts had lent their names to one or more of the era's great humanitarian crusades, such as antislavery, temperance, prison reform, and women's suffrage. All shared the age's heady spirit of improvement and romantic faith in human perfectibility. Although it never developed the organizational structure of other reform movements, the impulse toward sports and recreations comprised a kind of loose-knit reform crusade of its own. The critical point here is that the same ideological constellation of the Protestant and bourgeois ethic that had led to an attack on sports, especially boisterous working-class and gentry sports, now increasingly came to the defense of reformed recreations. The spirit of improvement, hard work, and self-control could all be reinforced through the right sorts of sports and recreations, undermined by the wrong ones.

Ralph Fletcher's *A Few Notes on Cruelty to Animals* (1846) made the choice clear. Fletcher argued that humans had no right to abuse helpless creatures for sport or profit. On the other hand, gymnastic exercises greatly improved both individual and na-

Rational exercise at Dr. Hammersley's gymnasium in Boston *(Library of Congress)*

tional character. The conclusion was obvious: this "powerful and interesting amusement" offered a moral and manly substitute for debasing blood sports. Frederick W. Sawyer agreed, and he argued in his influential *Plea for Amusements* (1847) that recreations were far more important than people realized: "The moral, social, and religious advancement of the people of this country, for the next half-century, depends more upon the principles that are adopted with regard to amusements generally, and how those principles are carried out, than to a great many other things of apparently greater moment." Sawyer argued that mats, ropes, and weights were instruments of national perfection; indeed, he declared new gymnasiums "would contribute more towards raising us up a healthy, brave, manly, and handsome race of men and women than all of the 'doctors' arts and opiates' this side of the moon."

By the 1850s, many wondered aloud if American youth had the vigor, the will, the energy to replicate their elders' success. Writer Bayard Taylor—in his 1855 lecture "The Animal Man"—had only contempt for America's "simpering sons of rich fathers," those "tallow-faced, narrow-chested, knock-kneed, spindle-shanked" lads who compared so unfavorably to Europe's robust youths. Had foppishness replaced the pioneer spirit, private corruption overrun American democracy, materialism poisoned social progress? Indeed, was prosperity smothering masculine energy? Energetic sports offered a promise of renewal. The *Cincinnati Star of the West* in 1856 captured the optimistic spirit of the new fitness advocates:

> While we concede to the fullest extent the sinfulness of neglecting the spiritual and intellectual faculties of our nature, we cannot see that it is any less a sin to neglect the physical. God made man to develop all his faculties to the highest possible degree—to stand erect with broad shoulders and expanding lungs, a picture of physical and moral perfection.

By the 1850s, the alliance of religion, morality, and sport acquired a label. "Muscular Christianity" first manifested itself in English public schools and universities. The Reverend Charles Kingsley's *Alton Locke* (1850) gave early expression to the cult of heroic English gentlemen, tempered by manly sports, educated to a fine practical intellect, and consecrated with devotion to Church and country. Such men, it was said, made their nation invincible; they colonized the world, ruled England, and built the nation's industrial might. Even more than Kingsley's work, Thomas Hughes's novel *Tom Brown's School Days* (1857) enjoyed instant popularity on both sides of the Atlantic. This romantic portrayal of life at Rugby School under headmaster Thomas Arnold idealized the sense of honor, fair play, and character development that English lads were said to imbibe with their strenuous games.

Privileged young men who attended America's colleges after mid-century started emulating Tom Brown's muscular ways. During the 1850s, students at Amherst, Brown, Harvard, Williams, and Yale led the way in initiating intercollegiate games. Amherst and Williams became the first colleges to play each other in baseball, in June 1859 (Amherst won 73–32—they played under "Boston" rules); football in its myriad variations remained part of freshman hazing in these years; and, beginning with an 1852 regatta between Harvard and Yale, crew became the earliest and most popular intercollegiate sport before the Gilded Age. "Will a kind fortune ever bring the day," asked the student editor of *Harvard Magazine* in 1858, "when the first scholar of his class can also claim the high honor of being the stoutest oarsman of the college?" Like their English counterparts, some Americans attributed moral benefits to collegiate sport. "If he attain a seat in a university boat," one writer asked, "must he rigidly practice austere virtues; and drill himself into such self-denials as tell on the moral character not less than on the muscular system?"

A handful of clergymen—mostly from liberal denominations such as the Unitarians, Universalists, and Episcopalians, but increasingly from the more conservative ones—articulated an American version of muscular Christianity. The Reverend Edward Everett, a Unitarian, believed that his countrymen overworked themselves, and he advocated sports to strengthen mind and body while putting men in communion with nature. His nephew Edward Everett Hale deplored the hypocrisy that sanctioned gardening on the pretense of usefulness, but condemned ballplaying, rowing, and skating because they lacked clear utilitarian value. Indeed, the boundary between Christian recreation and un-Christian amusement grew increasingly difficult to draw in these years.

The unresolved tensions over moral and immoral recreations were especially clear in the writings of the Reverend Henry Ward Beecher. Beecher was concerned that Americans develop internalized moral character. In good Victorian fashion, he urged his parishioners to cultivate the virtues of self-discipline and self-control, exhorted them to avoid the moral dangers of idleness and self-indulgence, and warned them against horse races, minstrel shows, and the theater. Yet Beecher was no milquetoast. He loved fast horses and even acknowledged his fascination with speed and power: "Fastness is a virtue . . . I drive fast on principle. I do it for the sake of being at one with nature . . . If I were engineer of a sixty-mile-an-hour express train, I should covet twenty miles an hour more." Beecher declared riding, swimming and boating, baseball, cricket, and gymnastics to be therapeutic. He urged Christian associations to help organize such sports in order to "give to the young men of our cities the means of physical vigor and health, separated from temptations to vice." He insisted on the benefits of steady exercise: "Don't be tempted to give up a wholesome airbath, a good walk, or a skate or ride every day as it will pay you back . . . by freshness, elasticity, and clearness of mind."

America's two most influential muscular Christians, Thomas Wentworth Higginson and Oliver Wendell Holmes, spoke out even more forcefully for sports. Their forum was the new *Atlantic Monthly*, whose contributors in the 1850s included Ralph Waldo Emerson and Henry David Thoreau, as well as Nathaniel Hawthorne, John Greenleaf Whittier, Harriet Beecher Stowe, and Henry Wadsworth Longfellow. A graduate of Harvard Divinity School in 1847, the Reverend Higginson threw his astonishing energies into a series of reform causes, including antislavery, temperance, and women's suffrage. But a love of outdoor sports turned his attention toward the subject of leisure.

In his most important essay on physical culture, "Saints and Their Bodies" (1858), Higginson lamented that not since ancient Greece had religious people possessed strong bodies. The assumption that godliness presupposed physical weakness had cloistered clergymen from "the strong life of the age." Higginson condemned parents who pushed their most puny, joyless, sedentary sons toward the ministry. While robust boys developed themselves in "manly" sports, budding clerics sermonized congregations of their sisters. When a crisis arose, the future Civil War colonel declared, "these precocious little sentimentalists wither away like blanched potato-plants in the cellar; and then comes some vigorous youth from his outdoor work or play, and grasps the rudder of the age, as he grasped the oar, the bat, or the plough handle." Only with health and strength could men confront great social issues: "Guarantee us against physical degeneracy, and we can risk all other perils—financial crisis, Slavery, Romanism, Mormonism, Border Ruffianism, and New York assassins . . ." Strong men built strong nations, but the shop and the countinghouse left little room for heroic action. Security made Americans soft, prosperity left them weak, fashion rendered them effeminate. While girls needed exercise as well as boys, it was sons who suffered most by motherly overprotection: "As the urchin is undoubtedly physically safer for having learned to turn a somerset, and fire a gun, perilous though these feats appear to mothers,—so his soul is made healthier, larger, freer, stronger, by hours and days of manly exercise and copious draughts of open air, at whatever risk of idle habits and bad companions."

Oliver Wendell Holmes, the *Atlantic*'s "Autocrat of the Breakfast Table," occasionally dedicated his monthly column to fitness and recreation. Besides being the best-known physician of his day, Holmes was a distinguished lecturer, essayist, and poet. Like many before him, he discussed the moral qualities of sports, arguing for participation in all of those that upheld Victorian values, denigrating those that did not. His prose merged idyllic descriptions of nature with aggressive athletic images: "I dare not publicly name the rare joys, the infinite delights which intoxicate me on some sweet June morning, when the river and bay are smooth as a sheet of beryl-green silk and I run along, ripping it up with my knife-edged shell of a boat, the rent closing after me like those wounds of angels which Milton tells of . . ." Most striking, Holmes framed his discussion of sports around the need to gain control over life. He declared as he approached his fiftieth birthday that so long as he could row fifteen miles at a stretch or one mile in less than eight minutes, "then I feel as if I had old Time's head in chancery [in a headlock], and could give it to him at my leisure."

Sports gave a man power over his body the same way an engineer had power over a piece of machinery. Riding a horse added the pleasure of governing another's will, physically extending one's self from the animal's ears to its hooves. "Now in this extension of my volition and my physical frame into another animal," Holmes added, "my tyrannical instincts and my desire for heroic strength are at once gratified." But if sheer power was so important to Holmes, he lamented not only Americans' bodily degeneration but also the fact that polite society still discouraged physical excellence: "As for any great athletic feat performed by a gentleman in these latitudes, society would drop a man who should run round the Common in five minutes." Manly sports, Holmes concluded, would counter America's "white-blooded degeneracy," would give men a renewed sense of power.

We should not attribute too much influence to such sports converts as Beecher, Higginson, and Holmes. Baseball games and harness races, boxing matches and pedestrian contests generated keen interest with or without the approbation of those who wrote for the *Atlantic*. Still, the intellectual avant-garde was important because it articulated an ideology of sports, a cluster of ideas that in future decades would help justify the coming explosion of games and athletics for society's dominant groups.

It is one thing to describe the new sporting attitudes that were just emerging among the intellectual elite, quite another to explain them. Advances in medical knowledge on the importance of exercise, the need to solve new public health problems associated with rapid urbanization, acceptance of the Enlightenment assumption of the unity of mind and body, a lack of recreations for the industrialized masses—all contributed to the new sporting impulse. But there were other factors, just below the surface. Ministers, reformers, educators, and journalists spoke from the assumptions and needs of their class. The new sporting ideal rejected the old love of display, conspicuous consumption, and bloodlust. It valued strenuosity over joy, self-testing over personal expressiveness, duty over impulse. Sport was slowly being assimilated to the Victorian spirit of self-improvement; wholesome recreations built character.

But what made the mid-nineteenth century fertile soil for the seedling sport ideology? Aside from other factors we have considered, the new advocates of sport addressed their own social crisis. Emerson's concern with power, Beecher's love of speed, Higginson's fears of effeminacy, Holmes's "tyrannical instincts" and his cravings for "heroic strength"—all of their images dwelt on masculinity, assertiveness, control over their environment.

Yet these very same men also discussed in detail their fears of cloying materialism, luxurious living, and foppishness. In Victorian America, goods were a sign of social success, and household creature comforts the outward manifestation that women were fulfilling their role of domesticating men. But the new sports advocates decried the bourgeois prosperity that made men soft. While extolling women for uplifting men, they worried over the "feminization" of their culture. Even "Mother Nature" became a problematic image, for she alternately nurtured and smothered men. Sports offered a symbolic way out; they asserted masculine aggressiveness to counter feminine softness.

We must not homogenize the diverse thoughts of such men as Emerson, Beecher, Higginson, and Holmes. Higginson, for example, was militantly abolitionist, leading mobs against fugitive slave hunters and supporting the violent actions of John Brown. Holmes, on the contrary, decried precisely those acts because they threatened social stability. But as George Fredrickson has argued, regardless of their differences, such men formed a distinct social class. Sharing a heritage of leadership based on old family ties, education, and often wealth, they took it as their common role to be intellectual leaders, cultural arbiters, and moral stewards. Respectable Americans looked to them and they to each other for social guidance. Yet, by mid-century, the old elite of clergy, intellectuals, and patricians found itself confronted with external and internal conflict. Democratic politics and new concentrations of economic and social power challenged the cultural legitimacy of the "Brahmin caste," as Holmes called men of his background. As the sectional crisis threatened social anarchy, such men felt their marginalization keenly. They worried that the life of the mind might lead to nothing but hapless self-cultivation; they feared their own impulse to turn inward as the world fell apart.

The Brahmins' interest in "manly" sports in the antebellum years was a sign of these tensions. Intoxication with power, assertions of virility, triumph over adversity spoke symbolic volumes to a group in crisis. The social tensions felt by Victorians often manifested themselves through sexual roles. In the bourgeois ideal, women must domesticate and civilize men, but some feared that this would blunt male assertiveness in the world of action. Good Victorians should stifle their sexual desires, yet the culture demanded that men and women maintain rigid gender identities. The same society that produced new consumer goods associated consumption with femininity and self-denial with "manliness." In other words, the highest Victorian values—productivity, independence, discipline, order, control, self-reliance—were the guiding lights of a particular class and gender, of bourgeois males. As commercial success, love of luxury, and "soft" living threatened manliness, as stifling thought smothered heroic action, a few cultural leaders groped for a source of salvation, and masculine sports offered hope. As the *Spirit of the Times* put it in 1857, arguing for school sports, "The object of education is to make men out of boys. Real live men, not bookworms, not smart fellows, but manly fellows."

Sports, in other words, became a vehicle for new conceptions of masculinity. In the competitive world of business and commerce, men occupied the public sphere, where energy and aggressiveness were rewarded. The bloodlust of the old ways was rejected. Those traditional sports characterized by orgies of violence remained anathema to bourgeois Victorians and were banished to the urban underworld. But revised masculinity, with its self-control and competitiveness, found articulation in such new manly sports as baseball and rowing. The language of sports advocates was telling. It was filled with visions of impotence and virility—fears, on the one hand, that American men might become "precocious little sentimentalists" or "simpering sons of rich fathers"; hopes, on the other hand, of new men grasping "the rudder of the age," of them standing "erect with broad shoulders and expanding lungs." Men who prided themselves on their rectitude might reject the bloody passions of the bachelor subculture while finding much to admire in the controlled aggressiveness of a baseball game. But women—so often characterized by bourgeois Victorians as the nurturing and delicate keepers of the home, the spiritual guardians of the private sphere—by definition should be outside the realm of such competitive and aggressive activities. Sports, then, had begun to delimit middle-class American ideals of masculinity and femininity.

Thus, what seems a simple phenomenon—the rise of organized sports during the antebellum era—was very complex, revealing all the schisms of class, gender, and ethnicity endemic to American life. Gentry sports and country amusements persisted in many areas, while disreputable older practices such as boxing and animal fighting were revitalized as part of urban, working-class, commercial culture. Important modernizing trends occurred as well; the beginnings of professionalization, admission charges, new promotion techniques, record keeping, and college and club organization had their start in sports such as baseball, pedestrianism, rowing, yachting, and harness racing. While voluntary association and the spirit of sociability remained the most important impetus for play, the profit motive had just begun to emerge. Even the disreputable, all-male world of billiards now found prosperity, and limited acceptance. On the eve of the Civil War, the largest New York City parlors each took in more than $10,000 annually, thousands of men earned money by teaching the game or hustling other players, and spectators paid as much as five dollars—roughly a week's pay for a laborer—to watch professionals compete in championship matches.

Sports developed not only out of the structural changes of economic growth, urbanization, and technological developments but also from the clash of ideologies, of visions of American life. Unreconstructed Victorians attacked the old leisure traditions because they promoted idleness and ungodly behavior. This point of view found its strongest support in Evangelical religion and the new middle-class work environment, but also attracted large numbers of women, and upwardly mobile segments of the working class. Those whose behavior was to be reformed had their own implicit visions of the good society, visions derived from traditional working-class, artisan, and gentry life.

But a new sports ideology reworked the old ideals to encompass the controlled expansion of moral recreations. In an era of urban overcrowding and strict labor discipline, well-regulated leisure activities could blunt worker rebelliousness. Whether or not average free time and disposable income increased during the antebellum era (an issue historians still debate), the new emphasis at the workplace on regularity and specialization of function set labor off from life as never before, and thereby created blocks of time that either God or the Devil might fill. Proper sports, reformers argued, refreshed workers' spirits, improved their productivity, and alleviated class tensions while strengthening the bonds of friendship and family. Balls and bats offered a wholesome alternative to brothels and bars. A few bold souls even dared to suggest that Sunday sports contributed to physical and moral health.

Equally important, mid-century America heard the first arguments that sports built character. The values articulated by the muscular Christians clustered around the concept of manliness defined purely in bourgeois terms. Gymnastics made men bold, truthful, and chaste; cricket engendered fortitude, endurance, and self-control; baseball promoted discipline, self-denial, and courage. Rugged masculine virtues, it was said, inhaled on the playing field with God's open air, countered the emasculation of luxurious living, the ennui of commercial transactions, and the impotence of cloistered intellection.

Should this effort to promote reformed sports be seen as social control, a middle-class attempt to manipulate the working class? Put so baldly, the idea seems absurd. How, after all, can men be forced to "play"? Besides, working-class people were quite able to refract the cultural mandate of others through their own experiences, to refashion sports to fit their own needs. Baseball as played by laboring men was never as genteel as middle-class players would have liked. Nor is there any reason to doubt that reformers sincerely perceived a need among the hardworking urban masses for expanded recreational opportunities. Besides, reformers sought to impose sports on themselves as much as on anyone else. The bourgeois authors of child guidance literature, for example, who advocated sports for health and morality, wrote for the youths of their own class more than anyone else.

The crucial fact is that reformed sports and recreations offered cultural solutions to a variety of social problems. All of this was only half-conscious, not yet fully articulated, but the trend was clear. Wholesome sports and recreations refreshed and uplifted the working class, replaced vicious amusements with moral ones, and inculcated new forms of discipline. Membership in sporting clubs and organizations offered group solidarity in anonymous cities, served as a clear sign of one's social status, and helped make new ideas such as competition and teamwork second nature. Sports held out symbolic regeneration to the genteel Brahmin caste, a sense of stewardship to social reformers, purposeful and wholesome leisure for the morally upright, ethnic unity for immigrant communities, and new outlets for relaxation, skill, and group solidarity to the working class. And for all of these groups, sports were being incorporated into new conceptions of masculinity. An alternative to the raucous old pre-modern recreations, reformed sports offered all these possibilities in a way that many Victorians—more precisely, middle-class Victorian males— could accept. Slowly, then, the ideas of men like Charles Francis Adams, Jr., muscled aside those of their fathers.

3 / "Vigorous, Manly, Out-of-Door Sports": The Gilded Age

. . . .

". . . Healthful and Invigorating Sports . . ."

"There is a certain tendency," Theodore Roosevelt worried aloud in an 1890 essay entitled "Professionalism in Sports," "to underestimate or overlook the need of the virile, masterful qualities of the heart and mind . . . There is no better way of counteracting this tendency than by encouraging bodily exercise and especially the sports which develop such qualities as courage, resolution and endurance." Before the Civil War, a handful of influential doctors, educators, reformers, and clergymen advocated sports and recreations. During the next generation, these occasional voices merged into a chorus. At the same time, the organizational structure of sports expanded enormously, facilitated by the same social and cultural changes that transformed Gilded Age America into a mature urban-industrial nation.

The Civil War introduced thousands of men to new sporting ideas and practices. The war engendered an ethos of sacrifice, of dedication to the heroic cause. But by temporarily suspending the norms of daily life, the war also encouraged the spread of leisure-time activities. The erratic demands of the camp and field replaced the regular rhythms of civilian life. The soldiers' routine of marching, drilling, or doing nothing might suddenly be shattered by violent action. All wars throw vast numbers of men together, upset domestic life, and suspend the old roles of producer, provider, and laborer; and combat rewards the violent aggressiveness that must be sublimated in normal times. America's Civil War was no exception. Initially, army recruiting destroyed sports organizations, amateur baseball clubs, for example. But as the conflict progressed, men organized themselves into company teams and regimental leagues. By the time of Lee's surrender at Appomattox, more Americans participated in organized sports than ever before. Baseball, football, shooting matches, pedestrian races, boxing, gymnastics—all had their place in camp and field. Those whom the war did not kill, or maim, or debilitate went home with a new appreciation of sports.

Equally important, during the next several decades America was thoroughly transformed by social forces that the war helped unleash. The conflict expanded markets, made enormous new demands on America's productive capacity, forced unprecedented government intervention in the economy, and spurred completion of the nation's transportation and communications network. War initiated new concentrations of corporate wealth and bureaucratic power, and it deepened the division between those who owned the nation's means of production and those who labored for wages. As American capitalism matured, ideological images of stern competition—of winning the race of life, survival of the fittest, harsh self-testing—grew increasingly prominent. The war not only transformed American society; it provided a well of memory, a master metaphor for the belief that conflict between individuals, classes, and nations lay at the heart of human existence.

It was in this context that sports as we know them took shape. By the end of the century, athletics were enlisted in the cause of the new social alignments and ideologies. Of course, the Victorian struggle against immoral recreations did not end with the

Cockfighting was one of the most popular spectator sports before the end of the nineteenth century. "Sunday in New Orleans," from *Every Saturday*, July 15, 1871 *(Library of Congress)*

Civil War. The attack on blood sports, for example, never succeeded completely, but reformers coerced and cajoled changes by redoubling their efforts. Tireless social activists like Henry Bergh, who founded the American Society for the Prevention of Cruelty to Animals, educated Americans through books and speeches, persuaded them with letters to newspapers, and coerced them by means of lawsuits and the police. Bergh called for "healthful and invigorating sports" to replace the bloody old activities. There was an important shift of language here. The singular "sport" —connoting rowdiness, defiance of social restraint, lower-class barbarism, all implied when a rakehell was called a "sport," or his ilk the "sporting fraternity"—was now replaced with the more inclusive "sports," meaning rational, wholesome, and purposeful athletic activities.

Despite such assaults, men watched pit bulls and fighting cocks tear each other apart at sporting houses like Harry Hill's in New York and the Spanish Cockpit in New Orleans. Blood sports still found powerful defenders, so police hesitated to break up events where influential citizens might be present: "Kid-gloved gentlemen," the New Orleans *Picayune* noted of a mid-1870s dogfight,

". . . jostled against squalid negroes, and spoiled the immaculate sheen of their boots with incrustations of sawdust . . ." Under headlines like "An Ass That Should Have His Ears Cropped," and "More Nonsense," sports writers condemned "busybodies" like Bergh for interfering with the amusements of the masses.

By the late nineteenth century, reformers themselves sometimes seemed more archaic than the sports they condemned, because standards of morality had changed profoundly. Clergymen and educators still agreed that saloons, brothels, and gambling dens were off limits. The "Continental Sunday" practiced by so many Catholic immigrants—Sabbath mornings for church, afternoons for ball games, beer gardens, the theater, and other pleasures—deeply disturbed Protestant advocates of an undefiled Lord's Day. But laborers, who generally worked a six-day week under the new industrial discipline, insisted that Sunday be reserved for recreation, and they were frequently supported by Catholic clergymen, and by politicians who winked at the old blue laws.

Condemnations of such sports as baseball continued: grown men idled away their time in children's games, boys neglected their chores, youths dreamed of becoming athletes rather than businessmen. The Reverend J. T. Crane in *Popular Amusements* (1869) called ballplayers shiftless and overpaid, condemned their drinking and feasting habits, and declared that baseball encouraged fighting and gambling. As the historian Ronald Story observes, tales abounded of fathers tracking down their adolescent sons and whipping them out of games, of mothers throwing boiling water at team organizers. But the tens of thousands of young men who played baseball in the Gilded Age, and the hundreds of organizations that sponsored amateur and semi-professional teams, attested to the growing acceptance of the game.

On one front, however, sports remained highly suspect. Women found more numerous athletic outlets than ever before, but the late nineteenth century also witnessed renewed warnings that athletic women trod on dangerous ground. As sports became increasingly implicated in middle-class definitions of masculinity, some critics condemned them as a threat to femininity. Female sports raised the fear of women getting beyond men's control; athletic women symbolized the physical competence that domestic ideology, with its emphasis on chasteness and delicacy, was at pains to deny. When a roller-skating craze swept the country in the 1870s and 1880s, for example, critics condemned the sport for causing men to squander their earnings, neglect their work, even steal to support their habit. But women were in far greater danger. They were vulnerable to seduction by skating teachers, or in their weakness they might elope with other skaters, and either situation, it was said, could lead to broken homes or even suicide. Similarly, an article by J. R. Headington in the *American Christian Review* in 1878 argued that croquet was the downfall of otherwise virtuous women, and traced their descent into the abyss:

 1. A social party.
 2. Social and play party.
 3. Croquet party.
 4. Picnic and croquet party.
 5. Picnic, croquet and dance.
 6. Absence from church.
 7. Imprudent or immoral conduct.
 8. Exclusion from the church.
 9. A runaway-match.
10. Poverty and discontent.
11. Shame and disgrace.
12. Ruin.

Nonetheless, such apocalyptic condemnations of sports and recreations grew increasingly rare. Many clergymen now accepted the liberal ideas that men such as Higginson had espoused a generation before. At times, sheer pleasure even became an end in itself. The Reverend Washington Gladden told young people in *Amusements: Their Uses and Abuses* (1866) that "sport, glee, fun, not the dismal, repressed, shame-faced variety, but the real hilarious, exuberant sort," was their lawful inheritance; and that there was, by divine appointment, "a time to laugh as truly as a time to pray." Liberal clergymen argued that sports spread the Gospel and encouraged good character. Church leaders recognized that recreation programs drew new members and forged tighter bonds within their congregations.

The rise of muscular Christianity in the second half of the nineteenth century was part of the growing concern of American churches with man's life in the world, with the alleviation of problems in the here and now, with the "social gospel." When the American Christian Committee examined thirty-five cities in 1867 to uncover the main obstacles confronting urban missions, debased amusements were identified as a crucial problem. Why not offer wholesome alternatives that would bring Americans to Christ? Such thinking was the seedbed of the Young Men's Christian Association. Founded first in England in 1844, and reaching North America in 1851, the "Y" gave youths—especially recent migrants from the countryside—a refuge against the temptations of the metropolis. Here Christian fellowship, intellectual stimulation, and wholesome physical exercise supplanted the loneliness of boardinghouses and the evils of commercial amusements. The Y became the institutional embodiment of a rejuvenated, muscular, middle-class ethos. By 1869, San Francisco, Washington, D.C., and New York City all had YMCA gymnasiums. Within twenty-five years, there were 261 Y gyms scattered across America. An interdenominational lay organization, the association's encouragement of sports—baseball, football, rowing, calisthenics, swimming, bowling, weightlifting—earned praise from America's best-known clergymen. The elevation of man's physical state to equality with his mental and religious condition attained symbolic expression when the Y adopted the inverted triangle as its emblem in 1895, signifying the three components of fully developed man: mind, body, and spirit.

The underlying assumption of the YMCA program was that supervised athletics under Christian auspices promoted religious and moral goals. Sports countered the licentiousness of commercial amusements, while engendering self-control, leadership, discipline, and tough-mindedness, all highly desirable masculine traits in a competitive capitalist society. The New England Society for the Suppression of Vice could close every dive, Boston reformers argued, but without moral alternatives, they would reopen instantly, ensnaring new victims and reenslaving old ones. On one level, the reformers' embrace of wholesome amusements testified to the resiliency of urban working-class cultures: plenty of people still needed reforming. Workers and members of ethnic groups participated in "wholesome" sports and athletics, but they also continued to patronize beer gardens, dance halls, gambling parlors, and saloons; the unwashed masses still strayed from the path of righteousness. In important respects, urban amusements were now more class-segregated than ever.

The pattern was similar with youth and playground sports, advocated by urban and municipal reformers late in the nineteenth and early in the twentieth century. Wholesome athletics certainly were part of a social control movement designed to channel people, especially working-class and immigrant youths, into safe activities. By the end of the century, many reformers believed that sports could be a socially stabilizing force that would help Americanize foreigners, pacify angry workers, clear the streets of delinquents, and stem the tide of radicalism. Sports could deflect tensions away from an oppressive social structure and channel energy into safe activities that taught the modern industrial values of hard work, cooperation, and self-discipline, and thereby help secure social order.

But this was only part of the story. Youth sports and the playground movement usually had support not only from elitist reformers but also from city folk themselves responding to their specific local environments. In Boston, for example, grass-roots community organizations and ward politicians were much more instrumental in developing urban playgrounds than were elite organizations. Reformers eventually seized the playground movement as a useful method of teaching discipline and citizenship, but the original impetus came from local people solving community problems in their own way. And early in the twentieth century, sports came to Boston high schools when students themselves grew tired of the monotonous gymnastics and military drills that were part of the old curriculum. Only after students organized their own athletics did administrators take up the cause of physical education, citing recruiting and eligibility scandals, the value of professionally taught sport for building character, and the special skills of trained coaches as their reasons for intervening. Social control, then, if it can be said to have worked at all, was a complex, dialectical, tentative process.

The public parks movement that swept the cities late in the nineteenth century provides another fine example. As an antidote to the moral anarchy, vice, and corruption in urban life, many city planners developed landscaped tracts, such as New York City's Central Park, for the public's leisure. Clear brooks, lush trees, and blue skies, reformers believed, were moral agents, improving the temperament of workers, elevating their thoughts, and uplifting their manners. Public parks brought a bit of the countryside to the urban landscape and raised the people's vision from poverty, dirt, and disorder to scenes of rural virtue and natural harmony. Parks could mollify class antagonisms, for here rich and poor came together in harmonious communion with nature. Unfortunately, rather than passively soaking up virtue, the urban multitudes brought beer, bats, and balls, ignored the KEEP OFF THE GRASS signs, and had a rollicking good time. Some people just refused to be reformed.

Sport and Society

So it is unclear whether reformers' efforts to discourage certain recreations and encourage others had much effect. Suffice it to say that moral guardians failed to eradicate wild old pastimes, and new sports flourished with or without the blessings of reformers. Between the Civil War and the turn of the century, baseball was the acknowledged national game, boxing exploded in popularity, football became a college mania, and basketball took firm root in urban athletic clubs. Croquet, polo, tennis, golf, and bicycling swept over the upper class—including women—in successive waves of popularity, while laborers participated in countless local amateur and semiprofessional teams.

Americans took part in more and more leisure activities because social conditions were ripe for it. Not only free time but also average disposable income increased for many workers, especially those in the booming white-collar service sector. In a sense, the old work ethic was a victim of its own success. As the specialized economy produced increasing amounts of goods and slowly solved the age-old problem of scarcity, as the workplace became ever more separate from home, family, and community, as the hours of labor grew sharply marked off from non-work time, an opening was created for the modern concept of leisure. Some businessmen and editors might argue that those who worked fewer than twelve hours a day were dangerous idlers, but a slow shift toward more free time—by the 1890s, the American Federation of Labor renewed organized labor's call for the eight-hour day—was clearly under way.

This is not to deny that for many workers "leisure time" was a cruel euphemism for chronic unemployment. The Gilded Age was an era of severe business depressions, and some reformers, fearful of labor unrest, believed that play offered a safety valve for the anger of a militant working class. Still, the nation's exploding productive capacity was changing Americans' perception of recreation. The dawning age of potential abundance necessitated the stimulation of new wants and desires. Despite the maldistribution of income that left many Americans impoverished, the nation's economy now expanded into new markets and produced new goods and services, many of them oriented toward leisure. The nascent ethos of play, of having fun, of "letting go," made a virtue of necessity.

Slowly, unevenly, consciousness and material conditions changed together. Factory clocks and rationalized schedules set a compelling beat, forcing a radical division between work time and leisure time. Production had forever shifted away from making objects for oneself and one's community to making goods

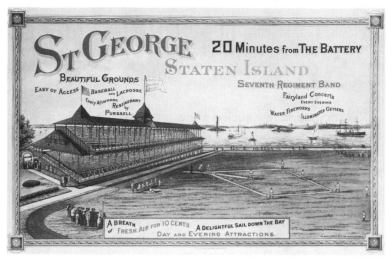

By the late nineteenth century, excursions out of the crowded cities became popular. In this 1886 lithograph, sports were part of a package that included music, fireworks, and a boat ride to Staten Island from New York City *(Library of Congress)*

for unseen others in return for cash. Now leisure, like work, revolved around the abstract concept of monetary exchange. Although Americans continued to create their own entertainment, the emergent national culture idealized the purchase of mass-produced commodities as a great human privilege and goal. Homegrown recreations competed for attention with mass entertainment, and the latter increasingly dominated and structured the former. To purchase leisure—to be a spectator at a great event, for example, or buy a bicycle or a baseball mitt—was to participate in an ever more important part of American culture: the consumption of goods produced by others.

As increasing productivity eroded the age-old assumption that material scarcity and therefore pain were the fate of humankind, the austere Victorian demand for absolute self-control crumbled as well. This is not to argue that all the values that made up the Victorian ideal of "character" instantly became obsolete. On the contrary, new business and government bureaucracies as well as huge factories and offices demanded tight self-regulation. But now many Americans labored in impersonal corporate and bureaucratic environments, where they sought not autonomy but success within the organization. Earning a living in a large business could be a deeply alienating experience, but the work world offered little choice, so in the realm of play and leisure people sought alternatives.

The transformation took decades, and most Americans were unaware of the contradictions between the old ethos and the new. Self-gratification vied with future-orientation as conflicting behavioral styles. For better or worse, however, buying things, especially non-necessities and leisure goods, gradually became a prime source of identity and status. By the turn of the century, the economist Simon Nelson Patten asserted that consumption more than production formed the basis of America's new economy of abundance. Moralists might complain, but economic necessity demanded that the joyous "self-expression" of spending replace the painful self-denial of saving.

As the old productive ethic loosened its grip, sports became an important part of the new consumerism. Baseball club owners sold an afternoon's leisure for fifty cents; publishers of major dailies such as Charles A. Dana, William Randolph Hearst, and Joseph Pulitzer increased circulation by creating regular sports sections with their own editors and staffs; and writers such as Gilbert Patten coined money with boys' books like the Frank Merriwell stories, which idealized college athletics. Slowly, imperfectly, but inexorably, the new consumer ethic transformed leisure from local expressions of group life into commodities for sale in national markets.

Cities were the cradle of modern American sports not only because overcrowding militated against many rural amusements but also because here the idea that life was a flow of commodities to be bought and sold was most pervasive. During the Gilded Age, these citadels of the marketplace dominated national growth. In 1860, six million Americans lived in cities. By 1890, the figure was 22 million. When the Civil War began, one American in six dwelt in an urban area; by the turn of the century, the figure reached two out of five. Paeans to rural virtue notwithstanding, city mores anticipated national ones as urban mass markets became the arbiters of American taste. In the cities were concentrated the fans who could make a baseball team profitable, and the customers who would buy tennis rackets, footballs, and boxing gloves.

Sports also changed under the impact of new technologies. Pneumatic tires facilitated both distribution of commodities and the bicycle craze of the 1880s and '90s; motion pictures documented worker efficiency studies as well as prizefights; electric light bulbs illuminated downtown business offices and new sporting arenas. In the two decades before the turn of the century, newspapers made sports pages part of the day's news, and the media reinforced the new cult of the sporting personality with published interviews and product endorsements. Sport was also beginning to experience some of the tensions of America's business culture. In baseball, for example, conflicts between management and players had already resulted in strikes, blacklistings, and combinations to restrain trade. Team owners in the National League (founded in 1876) eventually wrested control of the game from players, destroyed rival clubs, took over the apprenticeship system by seizing the minor leagues, and instituted the reserve rule, denying employees the right to sell their labor to any other franchise.

The process was never uniform, but in countless other ways American sports took their initial steps toward becoming profitable, highly rationalized institutions. Regular schedules were established, national rules promulgated, and regulatory bodies formed. Sporting goods became a significant industry, with former major league pitcher Albert G. Spalding leading the way. He acquired a Michigan lumber mill to make baseball bats, advertised his own products in "Spalding's Athletic Library" of sporting books, and bought up or squeezed out competitors. He opened rinks, then sold skates to eager fans; he sponsored croquet tournaments and retailed mallets to participants. By the late 1800s, Spalding dominated, almost monopolized, the sporting goods industry from manufacture to distribution.

Sport was becoming big business. By the late 1880s, professional baseball was a $10 million-a-year enterprise, the Brooklyn franchise alone averaging five thousand paying customers per game. While ownership of horses and stables remained a prerogative of the rich, Thoroughbred racing had become a mass spectator sport, attracting an estimated $200 million per year in wagers, while bookmakers and pool sellers paid $2.5 million annually just to rent betting stalls at major tracks. And in just one decade before the turn of the century, bicycling exploded into a $100 million business.

Even more important than sheer growth was the interlocking of sports with other social institutions. When a great annual event came to town—a regatta, perhaps, or a horse race—local hotels, restaurants, stores, and transportation companies all benefited. Building a stadium meant jobs in construction, maintenance, and concessions. New facilities also demanded development of sales promotion techniques and crowd control. A rural watering hole or suburban country club required a good system of transportation, so railroad and streetcar companies quickly learned that supporting sports was good business. Use of famous names—as in "Lorillard Yacht Club Smoking Tobacco"—glamorized products, transforming them from mundane things to magical objects of desire. Biographies, rule books, compendiums of statistics, and narratives of great events benefited from new methods of book publishing and in turn became a significant part of the print distribution industry. In an economy gearing toward leisure consumption, sports moved ever closer to the beating heart of social life.

In all of these ways, sports reflected the remaking of American society. Historians of sports have often employed the concept of "modernization" to describe these changes. Modernization is a theory borrowed from the social sciences that claims to describe the structural changes that occurred as groups moved from being "underdeveloped" to "developed": from tribes to nations, from primitive economies to international markets, from kin-based clan loyalties to modern bureaucratic structures. Modernization theory was applied most vigorously to the colonized societies of Asia and Africa, but regardless of culture, history, or national heritage, the change from pre-modern to modern was seen as a uniform process governed by its own laws.

The rise of American sports has been interpreted as part of this global transformation of human society. Unlike the ancient Olympiad, for example, or pre-Columbian Meso-American ball games, modern sports are secular; people play for many reasons, but rarely to please the gods or placate spiritual beings. Moreover, since the later nineteenth century, sports have developed sophisticated regulatory bodies such as baseball's National League, the United States Lawn Tennis Association, and the Amateur Athletic Union, and these in turn paralleled the rise of corporate and government bureaucracies. Sports agencies such as the National Collegiate Athletic Association (NCAA) standardized games by establishing uniform rules. Baseball, football, and other team sports also incorporated the specialization of function, advance planning, and rational, goal-oriented behavior generally associated with industrial production. Quantification is central to modern sports, linking them to the scientific worldview with its emphasis on cause-and-effect relationships. Statistics allow comparison of performances separated by time and space, and thereby establish common standards of excellence.

Above all, modern sports are said to be antithetical to ancient notions of inherited social status. Sports represent pure meritocracy, where people earn what they get under conditions of perfect equality. There are no slaves and masters in baseball, no peasants and lords or gentleman and commoners, just .200 hitters and .300 hitters. Organized sports, then, are a creature of modernity, a trademark of advanced industrial societies. It could even be argued that sports not only reflected modernization but probably helped shape it by packaging new and potentially disruptive values in appealing ways. Sports made problematic norms—secularization, specialization of function, meritocracy, quantification—seem natural and enjoyable.

This interpretation of the rise of sports is at once useful and misleading. Bureaucracies, statistics, uniform rules, an ideology of fair play were all important. Yet those who apply modernization theory—to sports, to agriculture, to religious and ethnic identity—tend to see the transformation as inexorable. Resistance to the modernizing juggernaut is depicted as either reactionary (because modernization allegedly benefits all) or unimportant (because the changes are inevitable). Modernization flattens historical experience by slighting the cultural tensions and the conflicts of power that accompany all major social transformations. Certainly there was nothing smooth, simple, or automatic about the rise of sports after the Civil War. Baseball's relationship to the ideal of equality, for example, was troubled. The rules of the game were applied equally to all players, but blacks and women were systematically excluded from professional teams; the sport defined the prerogatives of white manhood rather a cultural ideal of inclusion. Moreover, baseball's infatuation with statistics developed, not out of consensus that accurate and detailed records benefited everyone, but from a variety of particular constituencies—gamblers could handicap games more reliably, owners and athletes could measure the quality of play more effectively in their never-ending labor disputes, journalists could give fans a better feel for the game. And the bureaucratic structure of baseball arose, not out of an abstract modernizing impulse, but from specific power conflicts between leagues and clubs, and between owners and players.

While it is undeniably true that modern sports exalted the ideal of achievement and sometimes undermined privilege, at least as often they helped police the borders of inequality. Sports historians too often view their subject in missionary terms, describing the gospel of sport spreading equality of opportunity and democracy throughout the land. Exclusion of blacks, women, and others is therefore interpreted as a vestige of reactionary thinking that dissolves as time passes. Yet exclusion, not inclusion, was often the very motive for developing sporting organizations. Even before the Civil War, baseball leagues and athletic clubs built high walls of class and ethnic discrimination; a man's status as an accomplished sportsman—in yachting or tennis, for instance—often was achieved within rigidly limited social situations.

Building on antebellum precedents, thousands of informal athletic clubs and sporting organizations sprang up during the generation preceding the turn of the century. Many, like the New York Athletic Club (1866), were founded as havens for local and national elites, and they sponsored exclusive games: polo, tennis, or golf. In professional sports, too, discrimination often increased rather than decreased as sports "modernized." Blacks played on professional baseball clubs during the Gilded Age, but late in the century, vicious new patterns of discrimination caused the major leagues to disallow all blacks in the game. Blacks formed their own "Negro Leagues," and major league baseball remained lily-white until Jackie Robinson *re*integrated the sport in 1947.

Sports merely replicated nationwide racist trends. Champion John L. Sullivan refused to fight black contenders, claiming that he owed it to his fans not to sully the white race, a policy that conveniently kept him from facing the finest boxer of the 1880s, the Australian black Peter Jackson. In other sports, too, segregation became the norm: the fastest bicyclist alive, African-American Marshall "Major" Taylor, was systematically kept off many tracks and harassed by white cyclists during the 1890s, while even horse racing, traditionally a haven for blacks, began to bar black jockeys from competition. There were exceptions to the new racism—a handful of African Americans in the lighter-weight divisions who boxed against whites, black baseball teams playing non-league exhibition games against major league clubs—but the overall pattern of discrimination was clear.

Moreover, while there were growing numbers of women participating, particularly in such activities as bicycling, croquet, and golf for the upper class, professional sports and big-time amateur athletics were male preserves. By the late nineteenth century, sports were intimately tied to the very definition of American manhood. Celebrated strongmen such as Eugene Sandow earned fabulous amounts of money exhibiting not only their strength from a thousand stages but also their physiques, which were said to epitomize masculine form. The values so often attributed to sports—competitiveness, aggressiveness, the will to win, discipline—were male values in a capitalist society.

But even in less pernicious forms, sports rarely upheld, let alone fulfilled, the modern ideal of equal and unlimited access to competition. Countless middle- and working-class clubs based on occupation, neighborhood, class, ethnicity, or other criteria continued to open across the country. Ironworkers' semiprofessional baseball teams, Irish rowing clubs, track meets staged by neighborhood fire companies, office clerks' bicycling associations, informal Italian bocce tournaments—every variety of sporting organization sprang up in these years, and all were as much an antidote to modernity as an expression of it. Informal voluntary associations provided human contact, a sense of community, and a source of tradition and stability amid the chaos of urban-industrial growth. By offering a communal sense of belonging, sporting clubs mediated between the individual and an impersonal society. Club flags, songs, and cheers provided focal points of local pride in an otherwise anonymous urban environment. People of the working class and ethnic groups played the new sports, but did so in their own style, with local ties to kin, neighborhood, and workplace.

The characteristics that historians identify as modern—rationalization, quantification, bureaucratization, mass spectatorship, equality of opportunity, and so on—were important elements of American athletics by the turn of the century. The rise of sports depended on new technologies, institutions, and patterns of thought. Yet we must not remove the complexity from historical experience. Sports often perpetuated older values, even as modern elements crept in. By at once replicating some of the social forces altering America and denying them, by offering both an elixir of modernity and its antidote, late-nineteenth-century sports symbolically reconciled contradictory reactions to contemporary life.

The Rise of Mass Sports: Boxing and Baseball

The most prominent promoter of late-nineteenth-century sports was not a saloon keeper but a journalist, a sign of sports' growing connection to mass culture and entertainment. Richard Kyle Fox immigrated from Belfast, Ireland, to New York in 1874. His meteoric rise was a classic success story, but without the trappings of conventional piety and virtue. A journalist in the old country, he continued his trade in America, eventually working for the foundering *National Police Gazette*. By the late 1870s, Fox took over the *Gazette* in lieu of back wages; then he borrowed heavily to revitalize it. Within a few years, the magazine reemerged. It was printed on large pink pages and covered with lurid illustrations.

As the seventies ended, Fox's goal became clear: he would make his weekly America's leading journal of sport, theater, romance, and scandal. Young women seduced, scantily clad chorus girls, sexual revelations, horrible fires, train wrecks, vicious murders, immoralities of the high and mighty, hangings, and scandals of the stage—these were the stuff of the *National Police Gazette*. Several newsstands refused to carry the tabloid, Anthony Comstock's Society for the Suppression of Vice tried to shut the paper down, and the editor defended himself against a barrage of criminal and civil charges. But invariably Fox sold 150,000 copies a week. Wherever working-class men gathered, especially in barbershops, saloons, hotels, and livery stables, back issues of the *Gazette* were on hand to stimulate discussions and settle arguments. It was from the *Gazette* that such editors as William Randolph Hearst and Joseph Pulitzer discovered the value of sensationalism in selling newspapers, a lesson the editor of every major daily quickly learned. From the *Gazette*, too, they learned the importance of sports.

Fox's great circulation breakthrough came with the Paddy Ryan–Joe Goss fight of May 30, 1880. Metropolitan newspapers gave the battle little attention, assuming that in an era of fixed fights and mediocre pugilists, the public had lost all interest in the ring. Goss's age and Ryan's inexperience resulted in a tepid match, but the *Police Gazette* presses ran for weeks, printing 400,000 copies of the fight edition to satisfy an insatiable national demand. Sports editor William Edgar Harding's prose and the excellent sketches by a team of artists provided the nation's only

Ratting was a popular blood sport in the antebellum urban underworld. Richard Kyle Fox's *National Police Gazette* helped keep it alive during the late nineteenth century with coverage of matches such as this one in Newark, New Jersey *(William Schutte Collection)*

full coverage of the event. The *Gazette*'s vivid descriptions and graphic illustrations took readers ringside as no publication ever had.

While this early success was unexpected, Richard Fox knew a good thing when he saw it. Rather than wait for spectacles to occur, he spent money lavishly over the next two decades promoting a variety of sporting contests from long-distance running to drink mixing, from bicycle racing to haircutting, from ratting to water guzzling. He campaigned to legalize blood sports, but pugilism was where Fox had his greatest success. He eliminated much of the prize ring's chicanery; promoted fights honestly; defined the categories of light, middle, and heavy weights; and offered championship belts in each division. By using his money and power to become the single most important fight promoter in the 1880s, Fox ended the corruption and the fixed fights that had nearly destroyed the ring in the previous decade. Baseball, football, horse racing all made the *Gazette's* cover, but the paper was most truly in its element with the old sports of the urban underworld. To ensure the best possible coverage, Fox hired some of America's finest journalists, most of whom took pen names when writing for him. A staff of artists brought sporting action home with bold illustrations, and by the nineties, photographs became a regular *Gazette* feature. All of Fox's innovations were done in the name of profit, and sales of the "Barber's Bible" more than made up his costs. By 1883, Fox had new headquarters built for his empire, a seven-story, quarter-million-dollar structure, one of the most striking on New York's skyline. Slender, mustachioed, elegant in silk hat and Prince Albert coat, the editor was as much a landmark on the streets of New York City as the *Gazette* tower.

Fox used aggressive marketing and sophisticated technology in the cause of some very archaic, some might say atavistic, activities. Put another way, the *Gazette* was always a hodgepodge of modernity and anti-modernity. Modern sport and the ideal of social equality might go hand in hand, but Fox was virulently racist, nativist, and anti-Semitic. In addition to virtually every ethnic group, he publicly reviled clergymen, doctors, college youths, and corporate leaders. While the *Gazette* carried news of all sporting events, its real distinction lay in covering the old fancy life swirling around theaters, sporting houses, and bordellos. The *Police Gazette* was filled with advertisements for contraceptives and aphrodisiacs, coverage of juicy scandals, stories reeking of glamour and sin. *Police Gazette* publications included manuals on boxing, cock training, dogfighting, and ratting. In a word, Fox encouraged archaic sports with highly modern means.

In the face of lingering Victorian strictures, Fox also contributed mightily to the growing eroticization of culture, including the eroticization of sports. For example, in 1894, the *Gazette* vividly covered an exhibition given by the famous late-nineteenth-century strongman Eugene Sandow. A scantily clad Sandow posed before a large New York audience; he flexed his muscles, lifted enormous weights, and did acrobatic tricks such as turning somersaults while holding heavy dumbbells. After he satisfied those in the crowd, he went backstage for a private showing. Sandow bathed in ice water, put on fresh briefs, then proceeded to a special room offstage. There he lectured to a small group of about fifteen people about his body. "As I step before you," he declared, "I want each of you to pass the palm of your hand across my chest." The men caressed his pectorals with astonishment and admiration. But one woman hesitated, the *Gazette* reported, so Sandow gently coaxed her: "These muscles, madam, are hard as iron itself, I want you to convince yourself of the fact." He took her gloved hand and ran it slowly across his chest. "It's unbelievable," she gasped before fainting.

Both Sandow's exhibitions and the *Police Gazette* itself were emblems of a new ethic of pleasure emerging at the end of the century. A generation earlier, cabaret entertainment and burlesque shows were considered lower-class dissipations, part of the life of saloons, gambling dens, and whorehouses centered in neighborhoods like New York's Bowery. Late in the nineteenth century, however, some owners of nightclubs began cleaning up their establishments a little in order to cater to a growing demand for excitement among bored bourgeois Americans, many of whom now longed to break out of old Victorian restraints. Especially for the growing class of white-collar workers, after-hours pleasures became a necessary palliative to the dull routine of life. Places like Harry Hill's saloon in New York City, with its tantalizing serving girls, stage shows, and sporting events, were deliciously deviant yet relatively safe, and they garnered a wide clientele. Richard Kyle Fox's publication and Harry Hill's saloon were still beyond the pale for many Americans, but their growing popularity was a sign that the new ethic of pleasure and consumption was becoming more acceptable.

In the midst of this cultural thaw, boxing and baseball emerged as the predominant professional sports before the turn of the century. Boxing's rise, as always, was a checkered one. Even with patriotic fervor stirred by the Sayers-Heenan bout of 1860, prize-fighting was not the sort of thing that respectable men discussed in polite company, though certainly interest in the ring had spread well beyond the old bachelor subculture. During the Civil War, countless men watched others spar, or even put on the gloves themselves. Yet immediately after the war, lasting until Richard Kyle Fox tapped that deep well of interest in the 1880s, prizefighting went into a steep decline.

From the beginning, boxing was the property of the urban underworld. Great champions like Tom Hyer, Yankee Sullivan, John C. Heenan, and John Morrissey (who served as a United States congressman in the late 1860s, then as a New York State legislator in the 1870s after making a fortune as the proprietor of several gambling parlors) were tough street fighters whose personal ferocity and gang connections served the world of illicit pleasures and political corruption. After the war, boxing careened toward anarchy. Fights dissolved into mob violence: "the referee failed to be killed" became a cliché of sporting journalism and it expressed the very real problem of police intervening to break up riotous situations. Equally threatening to the sport were fixed matches that grew common.

So Richard Kyle Fox entered the scene at just the right moment. To sell newspapers, he needed to make sure that there would be good matches to cover, and by systematizing the weight classifications and providing the stakes himself, he took away control of the ring from the old sporting fraternity. But there were other changes occurring that would help redeem boxing during the 1880s and '90s. Fox broke the hold of the urban underworld on boxing just as middle- and upper-class men became increasingly interested in sports. Gentlemen came to distinguish debased prizefighting under the bare-knuckle rules from "scientific" sparring with gloves. Declared Civil Service Commissioner Theodore Roosevelt in 1890, "A prize-fight is simply brutal and degrading. The people who attend it and make a hero

of the prize fighter, are . . . to a very great extent, men who
hover on the borderlines of criminality . . . The prize fighter
and his fellow professional athletes of the same ilk are, together
with their patrons in every rank of life, the very worst foes with
whom the cause of general athletic development has to contend."
Yet Roosevelt loved boxing, and he even sparred in the White
House with former professional fighters. He reconciled the contradiction by rejecting bare-knuckle prizefighting and extolling
scientific boxing under the Marquis of Queensberry rules.

By the 1880s, famous and powerful men—among them editor
Charles A. Dana, Senator Roscoe Conkling, the Reverend Henry
Ward Beecher, and magnates William K. Vanderbilt and Leonard
W. Jerome—were seen at ringside for indoor glove fights. Others
sparred in college or took lessons at exclusive athletic clubs from
professional fighters like Mike Donovan in New York, James J.
Corbett in San Francisco, and Jake Kilrain in Boston. By the end
of the century, distinguished painters such as George Bellows
and Thomas Eakins, as well as writers such as Richard Harding
Davis, Frank Norris, and Jack London, gave the ring artistic
expression. The founder of modern psychology, G. Stanley Hall,
was an open advocate of pugilism. He confessed in his autobiography, "I have never missed an opportunity to attend a prize
fight, if I could do so unknown and away from home, so that I
have seen most of the noted pugilists of my generation in action
and felt the unique thrill at these encounters." The natural world
was filled with the struggle for survival, Hall argued, so men
should rejoice in noble strife. Hall virtually invented the concept
of adolescence, and he argued that boys in that stage of life should
learn to fight. He advocated boxing lessons to help youths become
aggressive, manly, and self-controlled.

Soon respectable journals like *Lippincott's Monthly Magazine*
and *Outing* encouraged men to learn boxing. Duffield Osborn
wrote in the *North American Review* in 1888 that civilization
degenerated into "mere womanishness" as it grew overrefined.
But the unflinching courage of boxers upheld "high manly qualities" that counteracted the "mawkish sentimentality" which
threatened to transform America into a "race of eminently re-

spectable female saints." Osborn and others advocated reforming the prize ring so that it might serve as a model of manly fortitude. To fight championship battles under the English amateur rules —the Queensberry rules that mandated gloves, three-minute rounds, and the ten-second knockout—would paste a veneer of respectability over the outlaw sport, yet still let it retain the old elemental vitality. Boxing would be reformed in the name of bourgeois manliness.

The new rules changed pugilism profoundly. Timed rounds speeded fights up, and with their hands protected by gloves, boxers could now throw more blows to their opponents' heads (arguably making the sport more, not less, dangerous). But these changes in themselves did nothing to break the hold of the old gamblers and rowdies. The most profound changes were that fighting with gloves was legal, and that by moving the ring onto an indoor stage, the new rules cleared the way for entrepreneurs to charge admission, and to control the audience with police and security guards. The transformation took place gradually during the 1880s and culminated with the first heavyweight championship fight under the Queensberry rules in 1892. Fortuitously, these changes coincided with the rise of a uniquely gifted and charismatic champion, the most idolized athlete of the nineteenth century, John L. Sullivan. It was Sullivan who demonstrated that boxers themselves could benefit from the new order.

When he was a young Irish-American in Boston, Sullivan's pugnacity made it difficult for him to keep a job. He loved the all-male camaraderie of working-class saloons, and his great athletic talent quickly showed itself on the baseball diamond. But he turned down a contract from the Cincinnati Red Stockings in 1879 to pursue his true vocation. For the next three years, Sullivan fought several matches with the gloves against much more experienced opponents, and he won them all. Barely out of his teens, he was a young celebrity with the sporting crowd. At Harry Hill's one night, Richard Kyle Fox sent word for the Boston Boy to drop by his table; Sullivan barked that Fox could come to him if he had something to say. The two men began a long and very profitable enmity. Sullivan began publicly badgering the *Gazette*-backed champion, Paddy Ryan, to meet him in a title match. The illegal bare-knuckle contest was finally arranged, and on February 7, 1882, the challenger faced Ryan in Mississippi City, Mississippi. "When Sullivan struck me," the former champion said after the fight, "I thought that a telegraph pole had been shoved against me endways." The fight generated tremendous press coverage, and while Fox's man lost, the *Gazette* presses ran for days with an illustrated special edition.

During the next ten years, Sullivan earned more than a million dollars, not by fighting bare-knuckle battles (he appeared in only a few of these, the most he ever made was $20,000, and he spent much of that on legal fees to avoid imprisonment under the laws against prizefighting), but through a series of Queensberry fights, most of them limited to four or six rounds. Sullivan toured the country, stopping at a new town each night, challenging the house, fighting some local hero, and usually dispatching him in the first round. Occasionally he met competent boxers, but they were generally no match for him. Rather, his greatest difficulties were with alcohol, the police who occasionally broke up the glove battles when they grew too rough, and those fans who believed that only a bare-knuckle fight was a real contest.

The endorsement by Sullivan, the unchallenged king of the ring, of the Queensberry rules helped legitimate the new order. He declared in his 1892 *Life and Remembrances of a Nineteenth Century Gladiator* of glove matches:

> . . . The contest usually takes place in a hall of some description under police supervision, and the price of admission is put purposely high so as to exclude the rowdy element, and a gentleman can see the contest, feeling sure that he will not be robbed of any of his valuables or in any way be interfered with . . . Fighting under the Marquis of Queensberry rules before gentlemen is a pleasure; to the other element, it becomes a brawl.

If the ring never became as pure as Sullivan claimed, enough people believed in boxing's redemption that fights now took place

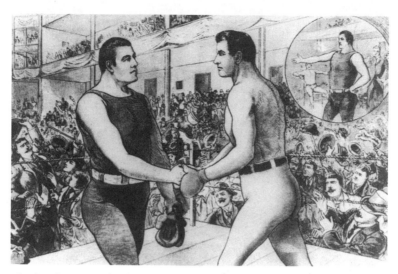

The first heavyweight championship prizefight held under the Queensberry rules. Before ten thousand fans, John L. Sullivan lost his title to James J. Corbett. From the *National Police Gazette*, September 24, 1892 *(William Schutte Collection)*

with the blessings of the law and gate receipts from the fans. Sullivan's success opened the way for the ring's revival.

After the last bare-knuckle championship fight—Sullivan defeated Jake Kilrain on July 8, 1889, in a spectacular seventy-five rounder that lasted more than two hours in hundred-degree Mississippi heat—the Boston Boy went back to touring. But almost three years later, taunted by young fighters, he agreed to a new championship battle, this one to be fought according to the Queensberry rules. His opponent was James J. Corbett, eventually known as "Gentleman Jim" for his clean-cut image. In contrast to the working-class Irish persona Sullivan relished, Corbett had been a bank clerk and boxing instructor; his trainer, William Brady, a show-business entrepreneur who intended to have Corbett tour in a play called *Gentleman Jack* if he won the title, raised the stake money from members of the New York Athletic Club.

The two fighters signed articles of agreement at the headquarters of Joseph Pulitzer's *New York World*, a newspaper that had condemned the ring ten years earlier and now called itself "fistiana's authority." For a $50,000 prize they fought on September 7, 1892, before ten thousand fans, many of them in formal evening wear, in a grandly lit New Orleans arena. William Lyon Phelps, a professor of English at Yale, recalled in his *Autobiography* that next day he read the newspaper to his elderly father, a minister. "I had never heard him mention a prize fight and did not suppose he knew anything on the subject, or cared anything about it. So when I came to the headline CORBETT DEFEATS SULLIVAN, I read that aloud and turned the page. My father leaned forward and said earnestly, 'Read it by rounds.' "

Sullivan's rise to national celebrity status bespoke the changing role of sports in American society. No longer was boxing mainly the preserve of the old bachelor subculture, that collection of men who lived as outlaws from bourgeois respectability. Prizefighting had moved toward the cultural mainstream. Although it would always retain the seamy scent of the underworld, the ring's displays of prowess were becoming commodities for sale in mass entertainment markets. The old urban fancy—the outcast sporting fraternity—had been replaced by fans, respectable seekers of entertainment.

The transformation of sports into entertainment was even clearer in baseball, the acknowledged national pastime by the late nineteenth century. The clubs of the antebellum era continued to proliferate after the Civil War. More than ever, hard-fought games in local leagues were seen as demonstrations of skill and manhood. The game particularly attracted members of ethnic groups—especially the children of immigrants—because a player's ability or a fan's knowledge marked him as possessing something singularly American. But if baseball quickly moved beyond the circle of old-stock Americans to the Irish, the Germans, the newly freed slaves, and others, men from these groups often formed their own teams and leagues. Pure discrimination accounted for some of this, but minority groups also chose to maintain their boundaries, and baseball clubs helped mediate an acceptance of American culture with the desire for a strong group identity. Fourth of July picnics, for example, were often minority events, with Irish or black or French-Canadian teams playing before ethnic audiences.

Young men, too, were disproportionately interested in Gilded Age baseball. As Ronald Story has argued, the game was a veritable youth movement. Young men played anytime and anywhere they could, often in the face of considerable parental disapproval. Baseball offered them opportunities for public displays of toughness and aggression, and such an openly physical game—with its show of sweat and muscle—was implicitly sexual, something still rare for the Victorians of the 1870s. As Story points out, not only did rapid urbanization during the Gilded Age uproot people when they first entered the city; most families moved over and over again for several years thereafter. Teams gave young men an almost instant feeling of community, even as they sought individual recognition for their daring play and manly skill. The baseball diamond also provided a sense of order. Amid the game's fierce competitiveness, batters still came up one at a time, defensive players worked their own territories, yet all pulled together as a team. As Story argues, in the face of a brutal economic cycle, violent street culture, bitter labor disputes, and overburdened families, baseball gave young men a way to create their own well-ordered space.

Even more striking than the proliferation of informal teams and leagues, baseball rapidly became a spectator sport in which professionals set standards of play for all. In the early 1860s some teams charged admission to games, and even paid players. But the Cincinnati Red Stockings of 1869 were the first avowedly professional team. Staffed with athletes tempted away from Eastern clubs, they won fifty-eight games and tied one, making them the only team in baseball history to go through a season undefeated, drew nearly 25,000 fans for six games in New York, took the brand-new transcontinental railroad to compete against California clubs, and in all traveled 12,000 miles to play before 200,000 fans.

Equally significant, in 1876, eight teams—Boston, Chicago, Cincinnati, Hartford, Louisville, New York, Philadelphia, and St.

Louis—came together to form the National League of Professional Base Ball Clubs. The National League quickly tried to establish itself as a cartel. The league constitution gave owners control over rules and regulations. By 1879, a "reserve clause" was instituted that bound players to their teams for life unless they were traded, sold, or released. The league limited teams to one per city, and new clubs had to be approved by the members. The National League also outlawed Sunday games and gambling at the ball park, while retaining exclusive rights to make schedules, hire umpires, and set admission prices. In other words, the National League was an economic arrangement designed to restrain competition, keep player salaries down (they averaged around three times the wages of blue-collar workers), and drive out potential rival teams.

Intentions and realities are not always the same. For the first few years, William Hulbert, president of the Chicago franchise, led the new league. He cracked down on player gambling, insisted on a fifty-cents-per-game admission charge, and forced Cincinnati out of the organization for selling beer and playing Sunday ball. A new league formed in opposition. The American Association of Base Ball Clubs, with teams in Baltimore, Cincinnati, Louisville, Philadelphia, Pittsburgh, and St. Louis, played its first season in 1882. The new teams lured National League players with high salaries, sold beer at the ball parks (several team owners were also brewers), and charged twenty-five cents admission for a game. Within a year, however, the two leagues came to an agreement that lasted through the 1880s, restoring the reserve rule and each team's exclusive territorial rights.

With competition again quashed, owners of both leagues blacklisted players to ban them from the game, they instituted a uniform salary structure, and they enforced the reserve rule. Teams prospered under these cartel conditions of the 1880s, but the athletes rebelled. They resented a new $2,500 salary cap imposed by management and the owners' buying and selling of player contracts. The Brotherhood of Professional Base Ball Players, a fraternal organization, threatened first to strike, then to set up a rival league if management continued its practices. When the owners refused to budge, the Players' League was born. For a year, seven cities had two teams each, and the Players' League teams generally outdrew their National League rivals. Most athletes jumped to the Players' League, and the new teams were joint-ownership ventures between rich backers and the players themselves. Former pitcher, now sporting goods manufacturer, and part owner of the National League Chicago franchise, Albert G. Spalding denounced the players as anarchists and revolutionaries. Insofar as players (workers) attempted to take back control of their labor from owners (capitalists), theirs was indeed a radical step. The old owners, however, had deeper pockets than the athletes; they outlasted their former employees, and when the dust settled, both the American Association and the Players' League collapsed, allowing the consolidation of the National League into a twelve-team organization.

Fans experienced the ball park as an arena of play so long as owners quietly ran their businesses like paternalistic plantations or benign company towns. Men such as Albert Spalding could speak of baseball as a democratic game only if no one noticed the power of management to blacklist, buy, sell, fine, and suspend players, to dictate salary terms to them, to regulate their behavior with temperance pledges and private guards. The point is not that baseball was somehow more pure during the golden days of the amateur clubs. The best amateur teams played to win, and they played well because of practice and discipline. The problem was not that players expected to be paid for excellence or that the game was becoming too serious. Rather, management's desire for profits, for manipulating markets, for paternalistic control constantly rankled the players, and the feuding between athletes and team owners intruded on the fans' ability to lose themselves in the game. Baseball replicated the conflicts of capitalism, a fact that the fans preferred not to notice.

Still, for those men skilled and lucky enough to make it, playing ball for a living must have been glamorous work. Most came from (and returned to) urban blue-collar families; disproportionate numbers were descendants of German or Irish immigrants. Despite the efforts of some owners to impose Victorian

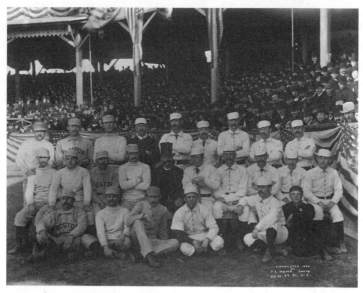

Opening day, 1886: New York versus Boston at the Polo Grounds *(Library of Congress)*

strictures on the game, many players retained their reputations for carousing. Throughout the nineteenth century, the conflict remained whether baseball would be a model of manly decorum (especially for teams that charged fifty cents per game, banned beer, kept the Sabbath, and welcomed female fans to shame men into proper behavior) or more of a raucous working-class game. But the larger trend was clear. By the end of the nineteenth century, baseball had become much like today's game, with four balls for a walk, overhand pitching, the mound sixty feet six inches from the plate, and many of the techniques of offense and defense that a modern fan would recognize. Equally important, the game now appealed across a wide social spectrum. Knowledge of teams from various cities, knowing who the great ones were in New York and Philadelphia and St. Louis, having opinions on how the season would turn out, purchasing a ticket and going to the ball park—all had become hallmarks of the consumer culture. Sport spectatorship was now part of the very definition of being a man in America. And fans who also played ball for informal clubs or on sandlots reinforced the kinship between spectators and players and made the connections clear between athletics, consumerism, and manhood.

Elite Sports

Blue- or white-collar workers watched and played sports for the pleasure of it, but lack of means limited their involvement. The upper classes, on the other hand, now had the time, money, and inclination to enjoy new recreations. This was especially true for children raised after the Civil War, and colleges were an important site of change. Austere, church-affiliated institutions, antebellum colleges had served their all-male student bodies a diet of classical learning. Faculties divided their charges' time between prayer and study; they allowed little room for the extracurricular activities such as singing, sports, and informal get-togethers that students arranged themselves. Colleges produced genteel scholars, not career-oriented professionals; teachers gave young men a general education that prepared them for law, the clergy, or belles lettres.

The trickle of college athletic activities during the antebellum era grew to flood tide in the postwar years. Students organized a variety of new activities, especially informal, interclass matches, often against the wishes of their mentors. In the late 1870s, poor eyesight kept young Theodore Roosevelt from competing in most Harvard team sports, yet he participated passionately, even rabidly, in all sorts of athletic events, including boxing, wrestling, rowing, swimming, and sailing. The scale of events expanded rapidly during the last quarter of the nineteenth century, and intercollegiate competition grew increasingly prominent in college life.

Sporting events became serious affairs, and students trained hard to uphold their schools' prestige. The occasional rowing matches held before the Civil War turned into ritual events dur-

Harvard versus Oxford in their 1869 regatta. Oxford won by one and a half boat lengths. From a Currier and Ives lithograph *(Library of Congress)*

ing the seventies and involved several Eastern colleges. By 1875, the annual Harvard-Yale regatta received prominent coverage in national magazines and leading newspapers. College baseball followed a similar pattern. Little more than a decade after the first intercollegiate contest between Amherst and Williams, the Harvard nine played a forty-four-game schedule, plus a twenty-six-game postseason tour against professional teams around the country. By the end of the seventies, Harvard, Brown, Dartmouth, Princeton, and Amherst had formed an intercollegiate baseball league. The development of sports during the 1870s culminated with the founding of the Intercollegiate Association of Amateur Athletes of America, an umbrella organization for several Eastern schools.

Football, the consuming collegiate passion of the late nineteenth century, originated in informal matches. Young men played both the soccer and rugby versions in pickup games and interclass rivalries, such as Harvard's annual "Bloody Monday." During the 1860s, Boston's Oneida Football Club gave prep school student Henry Cabot Lodge a chance to play alongside other

By 1890, when this stylized drawing by Charles Dana Gibson appeared in *Harper's Young People*, football had become the focus of college extracurricular life *(Library of Congress)*

privileged boys. Soon young men with old Brahmin names like Bowditch, Forbes, Wolcott, Lawrence, and Peabody were ready for college games. Princeton and Rutgers's 1869 match marked the first between colleges; Harvard and Yale played their inaugural game in 1875; and the next year, four Ivy League institutions formed the Intercollegiate Football Association to standardize rules. Harvard's Rugby School style of play won out over Yale's soccer style, and before long, new rules added such familiar features as blocking, alternating ball possessions, fixed numbers of downs, and other hallmarks of the American game. By the 1880s and '90s, football was a central feature of college social life. Most important, football originated with students and, until the last decade of the century, was run by them. Student captains—often the team's most gifted athletes—trained and disciplined their squads, while other undergraduates held fund drives and raised subscriptions to support the team. In football as in the other sports, it was the students themselves who formed clubs, fraternities, and sporting associations to mitigate dull curricula.

Most of these developments occurred at all-male, elite colleges; the collegiate athletic movement was part of a larger process of redefining bourgeois masculinity. But in several women's colleges, too, the tentative steps taken during the antebellum years had turned, by the 1890s, into a confident stride toward baseball, bowling, track, croquet, swimming, tennis, basketball, and many other sports. The calisthenics of antebellum years was replaced by competitive sports, and women students expressed great excitement over playing and watching games. By the 1890s, interclass baseball and basketball, under somewhat modified rules, were important parts of campus life at Smith, Vassar, Berkeley, and other colleges. Shortly after basketball was introduced at Wellesley, the 1898 yearbook declared: "The grimy and generally disheveled appearance of the players, as they emerge from the fray, fills our athletic souls with pride." The old Victorian association of femininity with delicacy could still be heard. Dr. Arabella Kenealy, for example, wrote that athletic women strengthened their muscles at a cost to their internal organs, especially their reproductive systems. But others in the late nineteenth century argued that sports gave women strength to compete in the professions which were just now opening up to them. Some writers even declared that athletics made women beautiful, healthy, and feminine. For many women at elite colleges, interest in sports was part of a larger determination to be active outside the home; sports were part of their commitment to energetic and productive public lives.

Sports for the priveleged were not confined to colleges. During the last third of the nineteenth century, old Brahmin and new industrial elites became fascinated with sports, and they joined together in a variety of exclusive athletic organizations. The founding of the New York Athletic Club in 1866 marked the single most important step in this movement. By the 1870s, the NYAC had built America's first cinder track and was sponsoring national amateur championships in swimming, boxing, wrestling, and track and field. Similar metropolitan clubs quickly proliferated. There were one hundred fifty of them by 1883, and many of them promoted elaborate annual athletic meets. New umbrella organizations arose, among them the National Association of Amateur Athletics of America (1879), the Amateur Athletic Union (1888), and the National Collegiate Athletic Association (1905), to regulate competition and enforce the code of the gentleman amateur. The athletic club movement grew so rapidly that in 1888, the Boston Athletic Association built a new clubhouse that cost $300,000; a speaker at the dedication estimated that a dozen years before, men could not have raised half that amount of money.

For many athletic-club members, the movement's mission was to promote not just health but social status. Besides building new facilities and hiring instructors in fencing, swimming, handball, gymnastics, boxing, even baseball and football, the clubs' larger goal was to promote sports for the elite, to employ athletics as a marker of class distinctions. This impulse led the movement in two apparently opposite directions, toward the amateur ideal on the one hand, and toward sport as a means for displaying wealth on the other.

The amateur ideal purported to defend sport as a realm of pure competition that money-grubbing professionalism threatened to spoil. True sport was sullied by those who played for pay, because they were not motivated by uncontaminated love of the game. Amateurism, of course, was a luxury to working-class people, and the amateur ideal was used to bar all but the wealthy from participation. But the elite quest for status sometimes threatened to overwhelm spartan amateur sports in a sea of conspicuous consumption. Sporting events provided an opportunity for the rich to show off to one another and to all who might envy them. When the Tuxedo Park Country Club opened in Orange County, New York, late in the century, for example, a few amateur athletes wondered aloud if sports were not being subordinated to social display. Exclusivity, however, was always the main driving force behind the amateur ideal. Elite clubs, and later colleges, did not hesitate to bring in "ringers" (professionals) when big games were on the line; but these men were hired help, not members of the club. The apparent conflict between austere amateurism and sport as conspicuous consumption was

The first national lawn tennis tournament, New Brighton, Staten Island, 1880, from *Harper's Weekly*. Tennis was considered one of the most elite of amateur sports *(Library of Congress)*

no contradiction at all; both grew out of the same elitist impulse.

The quest for status through athletics extended beyond the athletic-club movement. Saratoga, Newport, and other rich watering holes became centers of elite sport. Country clubs, yacht clubs, bicycle associations, tennis tournaments, jockey clubs, opulent new Thoroughbred tracks such as Belmont and Pimlico, golf courses, and polo grounds offered participants a chance to display their wealth and status. New federations—the American Association of Amateur Oarsmen (1872), the United States Lawn Tennis Association (1881), the League of American Wheelmen (1880), and the United States Golf Association (1894)—bound local clubs together with uniform rules and entrance requirements. They also sponsored annual events at exclusive venues where elegant clothes (female spectators often wore furs and jewels) and expensive athletic equipment converted otherwise simple sports into grand pageants. Under the auspices of athletic clubs, country clubs, and related institutions, playing sports could become a mark of privilege and a source of distinction for those who sought recognition as part of a social elite.

Most of the early athletic clubs were entirely male, but some women refused to be excluded. In a few cases they formed their own clubs, or pressured men to admit them. Charlotte Perkins Gilman helped found a club for women in Providence, Rhode Island, and she maintained a lifelong interest in athletics. But it was in the exclusive country clubs rather than the urban athletic clubs that women made their greatest inroads. Tennis, golf, and croquet were the sports of choice for the upper-class women who entered these elite institutions. Many of them were fine athletes, such as Eleonora Sears, of a prominent Boston family, who became a renowned tennis and squash player.

But sport itself was often lost in the quest for social exclusivity. One observer declared that the Philadelphia ladies' tennis championships "are social functions of the highest class, and none enter their names but those of assured social position . . . all our first lady tennis players belong to the best families." The new athleticism certainly was a metaphor for the more active role that women like Charlotte Perkins Gilman took in American life. However, because these new sports were associated with exclusivity, glamour, and fashion, the message of women as active agents in their own lives was submerged in a sea of goods; sports became one more place where women were identified as consumers. No one noted the quality of Ava Willing Astor's play on the Newport tennis courts in 1893; rather, her scandalous decision to wear bloomers in defiance of her mother-in-law—that arbiter of social taste Caroline Astor—caught public attention. Inspired by slender, athletic golfers and tennis players, Charles Dana Gibson created his "Gibson Girl" in 1890, an advertising prototype for a quarter century. So the presence of women on the playing fields of late-nineteenth-century America was double-edged. They broke out of the stifling Victorian role of wife and mother for a more active life; yet the emphasis on wealth and fashion in the country-club setting threatened to reduce women themselves to the status of baubles.

Sports were associated with the rise of the liberated "new woman." They were also part of the commercialization and eroticization of American culture. From an 1887 lithograph *(Library of Congress)*

Exclusive sports organizations such as urban athletic and country clubs were part of a larger process of upper-class organization building. In an era of labor strife and powerful radical movements, the elite segregated their neighborhoods, built walls, hired guards, and stocked armories as never before. Just as vast factories and bureaucracies divided labor from management, making strangers of employers and employees, so the upper class isolated itself on its own playing fields from the perceived rowdiness, vulgarity, even militancy of its inferiors. Sporting clubs tightened bonds of cohesion and strengthened identity among social elites by excluding "undesirables." At the turn of the century, the names Bennett, Lorillard, and Forbes were famous in yachting as well as business; Vanderbilts, Stillmans, and Astors signed the register of the Newport Country Club; Rockefellers, Carnegies, and Tafts chased golf balls on the links; Whitneys, Harrimans, and Belmonts evoked smiles of recognition at tracks and stables. To retain such exclusivity, athletic clubs policed their borders against social inferiors. Many of them obtained corporate charters, then required initiates to buy shares of stock in the club; others demanded that potential new members present letters of reference from old ones; failing this, individuals could be blackballed, and expulsion for unbecoming conduct winnowed out those who slipped through.

In all of these ways, the athletic movement was part of the larger impulse, which began before the Civil War and deepened during the Gilded Age, of creating prestigious institutions for a new capitalist elite. Sports clubs were enmeshed in an interlocking directorate of exclusive organizations. In New Orleans, men of the best families belonged at once to elite athletic associations and top-flight social clubs. In Boston, Cabots, Lowells, Adamses, and Peabodys joined the Somerset and Union Clubs as well as the Brookline Country Club. In New York, William R. Travers was president of the New York Athletic Association and a member of twenty-seven other social organizations, including the august Union League and Century Clubs. Sporting organizations were part of a complex network of elite connections, a network that allowed whole families to live and die, work and play, marry and reproduce within the "right" social circles.

The code of the amateur athlete became the reigning gospel of elite sports and an ideological form of wall building. Borrowed from English athletics, the amateur creed rejected all commercialization. The professional sportsman, amateur ideologues argued, held no loyalty higher than his pocketbook, sold his services to anyone, and debauched himself with gambling and drinking. Professionalism in sport, the profit motive, and the subordination of play to business threatened the amateur code by placing ends ahead of means, winning over playing well. In colleges, in exclusive sporting clubs, and in such organizations as the AAU and NCAA, the gentleman's code helped justify elitist practices, even while the desire to win caused many clubs hypocritically to employ ringers as major competitions drew near. Baseball players and boxers especially felt the wrath of amateurs. When it was discovered in mid-1883, for example, that Joseph Killion (soon to be known as Jake Kilrain) had boxed professionally, the National Rowing Association took away both his junior sculling championship and his amateur standing for future rowing competitions.

In practice, the amateur ideal was more of an excuse for discrimination than a philosophical commitment to the value of play. College teams and athletic clubs hungered to win at all costs. Ultimately, the gentleman's code was little more than a tool for shoring up social boundaries, one technique among many for an upper class to distance itself from an increasingly restless, even militant working class. The amateur code flattered wealthy Americans that they stood above sullying themselves with base lucre. But how many workingmen, if they were athletically gifted, could afford not to sell their skills? How many, in an era of wage cuts, chronic unemployment, and brutal anti-labor policies, could heed Theodore Roosevelt's advice to take a month's leave of absence from work and spend it playing frontiersman in the woods?

"The Strenuous Life"

The historian John Higham has argued that America in the 1890s experienced a broad cultural reorientation, a sharp departure from the old values of Victorian culture. Through sports and similar activities, Americans sought to break through the constraints of genteel Victorian life. Theodore Roosevelt's peripatetic career, his espousal of the "strenuous life," his love of hunting, mountain climbing, and boxing captured the frenetic energy of the age. The nation's quickened beat manifested itself in such diverse phenomena as muscular sports, realistic literature, up-tempo music, a cult of Napoleon, renewed interest in wilderness, and a jingoist foreign policy.

The surge of energy also expressed deep spiritual longings. Time clocks, cities, factories, and stuffy manners made Americans hunger, in Higham's words, "to break out of the frustrations, the routine, and the sheer dullness of an urban industrial culture. It was everywhere an urge to be young, masculine and adventurous." Competitive, often violent athletics were a prime example of this impulse, but, more than any specific set of activities, the new cultural orientation was an ethos, best understood metaphorically. American culture demanded a series of substitutions: virility for impotence, strenuosity for ease, power for sentimentality, action for intellection. In a word, Americans were desperate to break out of the Victorian straitjacket.

By focusing on the nineties, Higham dates this cultural shift too precisely, for it began much earlier. Besides, it affected diverse groups in different ways. One suspects that steel workers were rarely troubled by the "soft spirit of the cloistered life," that miners worried little about the "base spirit of gain," to use Theodore Roosevelt's words. Despite the presence of some great athletes, the increasing discrimination African Americans felt in their daily lives was replicated in sports. Many women, however, welcomed their first athletic activities as a further step into the public sphere that men had previously dominated.

Workers, immigrants, members of minorities, and women became spectators and players to the extent that they could because the commercialization of leisure offered unprecedented opportunities. Professional athletes were generally working-class and ethnic heroes who fulfilled the American dream of success through talent and hard work. For those less gifted, sport offered temporary relief from the daily grind. Baseball, especially, with its spontaneity, pre-industrial rhythms, and open-air ball parks, was a working-class sport. For those whose skills were being eroded by increasing division of labor, athletics could give a sense of competence and wholeness missing from the workplace. Because sports promised an escape from poverty, public playgrounds and even schools with athletic programs attracted parents eager to keep their children out of trouble and to improve their lot in life. And no doubt the growing connection between conspicuous leisure and the wealthy reinforced the inclination of working people to associate sports and play with success.

Most American workers and immigrants preserved recreational traditions as vital elements of their cultures, so their adoption of late-century sports was often more a matter of learning additional pastimes than changing their behavior. Besides, working people often bent sports to their own outlook; amateur baseball teams, for example, might represent particular neighborhoods, or ethnic groups, or trades, all reflecting a working-class communal consciousness. But the Victorian middle class, especially the upper-middle class, had spent decades learning to control every impulse and deny the worth of play. Their conversion to sports—one is tempted to say wholesale conversion, but voices of opposition such as that of *The Nation*'s editor E. L. Godkin remained—is more puzzling.

While the amateur ideal was indeed an attempt to maintain class boundaries, it also expressed an underlying unease with the materialism and moral emptiness of American business life. This was especially true for the post–Civil War generation, men who were born too late to share in their fathers' wartime glory, but who were incessantly reminded by parades, speeches, and dinnertime stories of their elders' heroic sacrifices. It was not coincidental that within a decade after Appomattox, college men such as Theodore Roosevelt began testing themselves in violent sports on college "fields of battle." As we have seen, even before the war a handful of men began to express their sense of a crisis in American masculinity. By the late nineteenth century, confusion over the meaning of manliness grew acute, and sports became a venue for addressing such fears.

The historian George Fredrickson has argued persuasively that sport as a moral equivalent of war became a very popular idea by the 1890s. Athletics offered an opportunity for young men to get their first taste of glory, and for older men to renew the tingle of heroic combat. Thus, Henry Lee Higginson contributed the money to build Harvard's "Soldiers' Field," in the name of half a dozen young Brahmins killed a generation earlier on Civil War battlefields. Privilege, Higginson told a dedication-day audience in 1890, carried moral obligation, and his martyred friends had demonstrated the utmost selflessness. Soldiers' Field not only kept alive their memory but forged symbolic links between war and athletics, privilege and duty. Higginson's speech slipped effortlessly from discussing sacrifice on the battlefield to self-testing on the playing field. Far from a plaything of the rich, sports renewed the commitment to service.

Oliver Wendell Holmes, Jr., a Supreme Court justice and the son of the celebrated "Autocrat of the Breakfast Table," made these connections even more explicit. In his 1895 Memorial Day address, "The Soldier's Faith," he bewailed the ascendancy of soft commercial values. Idleness, wealth, security now supplanted patriotism, he told Harvard's graduating class; pleasure and ease replaced self-sacrifice. Yet America of the nineties was a fool's paradise, for at bottom, struggle, not comfort, was the way of the world. Holmes welcomed strife not just as a painful fact of life but as the font of human virtue. And war was the ultimate form of strife:

> I do not know what is true. I do not know the meaning of the universe. But in the midst of doubt, in the collapse of creeds, there is one thing I do not doubt, that no man who lives in the same world with most of us can doubt, and that is that the faith is true and adorable which leads a soldier to throw away his life in obedience to a blindly accepted duty, in a cause which he little understands, in a plan of campaign of which he had no notion, under tactics of which he does not see the use.

With all faiths besieged in a Darwinian world—faith in a Protestant God, in beneficent progress, in man's ability to conceive and control his earthly fate—the one remaining rock of meaning was faith in man's honor, in his willingness to happily sacrifice all for a cause.

Rugged sports, Holmes believed, with their stern self-testing, could substitute for battle. Because they were structured and conducted with war as a model, sports helped remind Americans that routine commercial life was "merely a little space of calm in the midst of the tempestuous untamed streaming of the world." To learn heroism, one must practice heroism, and an occasional broken neck—no rarity in collegiate sport—was "a price well paid for the breeding of a race fit for headship and command." Like war, sports demanded duty, sacrifice, and the straining of every nerve and muscle to feel "the passion of life at its top." Here, then, was Holmes's creed:

To ride boldly at what is in front of you, be it fence or
enemy; to pray not for comfort but for combat; to keep the
soldier's faith against the doubts of civil life, more besetting
and harder to overcome than all the misgivings of the battlefield; . . . to love glory more than the temptations of
wallowing in ease, but to know that one's final judge and
only rival is oneself . . .

Not the transcendent Victorian universe but each man's personal
battle for dignity must now give significance to life.

Holmes never meant that his young Harvard audience should
withdraw into a world of sport for sport's sake. His reference to
building a race "fit for headship and command" revealed a central
preoccupation of elite sports. Athletics became part of the process
Christopher Lasch has called the "rehabilitation of the ruling
class." In America, Theodore Roosevelt declared, the worst variety of professional athlete was a rich man's son who did nothing
but cultivate athletic skills. Sport should be a teacher; its lessons
in self-discipline, teamwork, and leadership prepared men for
future responsibilities. Holmes, Roosevelt, and others of their
class hated decadence, feared cloying prosperity. The right attitude toward sports, they believed, would lead the rising generation to take up the reins of power. As it turned out, fears of
an idle leisure class were unfounded; while a few men from elite
families lost themselves in frivolity, most assumed positions of
authority in law, government, business, and corporations. They
took to heart Francis Walker's 1893 Phi Beta Kappa address at
Harvard, entitled "College Athletics": "Man is not a pilgrim but
a citizen. He is going to tarry nights enough to make it worth-
while to patch up the tenement and even look into the drainage.
This world is a place to work in; activity and development, not
suffering and self-repression, its law."

As the bourgeois Victorian world eroded, as huge new concentrations of power altered social relationships, rugged sports
helped men slough off defeatist attitudes, replicate the heroism
of their fathers, and gear up for battle in new arenas. Athletics
provided metaphors for action and antidotes to the spiritual emp-

tiness of the age. The existential doubts articulated by Holmes plagued many late-Victorian intellectuals. The old style of certitude and didacticism still lingered, but assertions of Victorian values took on an ever more strident tone as ideals became divorced from their religious and social moorings. The children of venerable families often complained of being cut off from the vitality of life; they felt stunted, stultified, and overcivilized. What, after all, was left to do after the wilderness was tamed, fortunes made, and rebellions put down? For most men, engaging in active public life—leading corporations, entering government service, and participating in vigorous, purposeful sports—provided a solution.

Not only men but women felt these pressures, and the rise of women's sports seemed an especially radical departure from Victorian propriety. In the antebellum period, a few influential women, among them Catharine Beecher, Angelina Grimké, and Lydia Sigourney suggested that physical activities—rowing, swimming, walking, riding, or calisthenics—would strengthen women's constitutions. Lydia Maria Child drew the all-important Victorian distinction between public and private space when she suggested that even some "boyish sports" were fine for girls if practiced in an enclosed garden or court, thus avoiding the appearance of vulgarity. Although working- and even middle-class women performed arduous labor during this era, the cult of domesticity drew the line at all that seemed excessively aggressive or competitive. A woman too strong or athletic was simply written off as unfeminine.

For many males, Darwinism merely confirmed the Victorian assumption that men were by nature active, women passive; primitive man was a hunter and fighter, early woman cared for the home, declared Luther Gulick, who founded the Camp Fire Girls, as well as other youth programs. But women of the late nineteenth century broke out of these stereotypes in significant ways, and sports were part of the entrance of women into the public sphere. By late in the century, working-class women sometimes appeared in shows and carnivals as weightlifters, bodybuilders, and prizefighters, and no doubt the mostly male audiences reacted by feeling at once titillated and threatened. But women in country clubs and colleges were also becoming much more visible as athletes, and the omnipresent Gibson Girl, racket or golf club in hand, helped legitimate the ideal of feminine athleticism.

Perhaps upper-middle-class women believed—as some men claimed—that sports would "unsex" them, that is, destroy their domestic natures and render them masculine. But a significant and growing minority chose to participate in a variety of athletic activities. Especially eager to avoid the trap of stifling domestic roles were those highly educated daughters of prosperous patriarchal households. As a sizable number of them rejected the cult of true womanhood, rejected the image of themselves as nurturing, pious, and frail, they turned to vigorous new activities. Like the world of paid work into which many middle- and upper-class women now ventured, sports offered a way to embrace the fullness of public life, to escape imprisonment in cloistered, overstuffed, bric-a-brac homes.

Men as well as women faced the crisis of Victorian gentility. Men were taught to value not just success but the process of becoming successful. The success ethic, however, always contained contradictory elements that became painfully evident as the nineteenth century ebbed. Men cultivated virtues that both developed character and produced wealth. While money might signify moral success, it was also a source of corruption. Fear of luxury, softness, and privilege was an age-old American obsession dating back to pre-Revolutionary republican thought. This problem became painfully real as generations of wealth piled up. Simply put, sons might inherit their fathers' fortunes without their fathers' good characters. The effeminate and dandified rich boy who became a stock character in nineteenth-century fiction symbolized the fear that, across generations, hard work, honesty, and self-discipline might degenerate into slothful self-indulgence.

Here was a deep cultural conflict: the worship of success commingled with contempt for corrupting materialism. The historian David Brion Davis has argued that a late-nineteenth-century fascination with risk-taking and self-testing provided a cultural means of resolving the conflict. Dangerous sports such as football, mountain climbing, and boxing offered a route to renewal. The amateur stress-seeker gave testimony that money was not the measure of all value, that heroic struggle remained a vital part of American life. Rugged sportsmen proved to themselves and others that the wellsprings of the pioneer, nation-building, empire-creating spirit still flowed strong and deep. The strenuous life allowed Americans to deny the ennui of daily bourgeois routine, even as they grew ever more enmeshed in it.

The surge of sports participation and spectatorship at the end of the century was part of a vigorous reassertion of masculinity. Working-class men had been active in sports before the Civil War, but the Victorian bourgeoisie—including the industrial elite, white-collar workers, and managers—had to reject their genteel heritage in favor of new forms of action. Despite the growing presence of women in athletics—perhaps because of the increasing prominence of women in public life—sports were becoming an expression of a male culture that in part transcended lines of class, though certainly not boundaries of race. Spectator sports became largely a *private* male space, filled with heroic competition and virile deeds. The sports hero (and his counterparts as cultural icons, the cowboy and the soldier) symbolically negated fears of emasculation. Cities denied men the heroism of pioneer ancestors, boys in school grew soft, white-collar workers pushed paper in impersonal bureaucracies, all labor became ever more specialized even as the hope of economic autonomy faded. But on the gridiron, in the ring, on the diamond, physical excellence still mattered and individual heroism carried the day. Sports reaffirmed that strength, aggressiveness, and the will to win—*male* values—were the fundamentals of life.

All of these threads intertwined in the person of young Theodore Roosevelt. The son of one of America's wealthiest families—ten millionaires resided in New York City in 1864, and Roosevelt's grandfather was one of them—Theodore grew up in a socially, morally, and physically active household. His father encouraged the asthmatic child to strengthen his anemic physique through a variety of athletic activities. Theodore Senior even sent his son to the sparring rooms of John Long, a former prize-fighter, where, with lithographs of great champions—Yankee Sullivan, John C. Heenan, and Tom Sayers—staring down at him, the aristocratic fourteen-year-old learned how to box. Moreover, the Roosevelts summered on Long Island, where all swam, rowed, and sailed, where the forests invited fishing, shooting, and riding, and where the Roosevelt boys competed in running, jumping, wrestling, and boxing. Although he was not athletically gifted, by his late teens young Theodore's sickliness had given way to incredible endurance.

In 1876, Roosevelt entered Harvard, and his interest in athletics deepened. He boxed, rowed, and wrestled on inter-class teams. His sparring abilities led him to the Harvard Athletic Association's lightweight boxing finals (which he lost). Roosevelt also spent long vacations hunting in the Maine wilderness with a backwoodsman named Bill Sewell. The young Brahmin and the mountaineer took unbelievably grueling treks through the wilderness. Riding, hunting, and sparring were habits that stayed with Roosevelt throughout his life; he was especially proud when he held his own with ex-prizefighters and rugged woodsmen. But for all the democratic leveling implied in such acts, Roosevelt was an independently wealthy man. During his college days, the earnings on his trust funds were half again more than the salary of Harvard president Charles Eliot, and young Roosevelt enjoyed his legacy. He associated only with the cream of Harvard society. While nineteen men in his class finished with higher grades, Roosevelt declared that only one of them was a "gentleman." He belonged to prestigious clubs, dressed stylishly, drove the finest carriages, and attended the most elegant dinners. His love for rugged sports, in other words, coexisted with rather dandified tastes.

A man does not climb a mountain because he feels patriotic or row across a lake to relieve his status anxieties. But personal and social motivations never stay entirely distinct, and by about 1890, a decade after leaving Harvard, Roosevelt began articulating an ideology of sports. Breaking through restraints, asserting dominance, displaying power—these, he declared, were the things that counted among men and nations. Roosevelt argued in an essay entitled "The Value of an Athletic Training" (1893) that the sports of youth help cultivate such qualities:

> In a perfectly peaceful and commercial civilization such as ours there is always a danger of laying too little stress upon the more virile virtues—upon the virtues which go to make up a race of statesmen and soldiers, of pioneers and explorers by land and sea, of bridge-builders and road-makers, of commonwealth-builders—in short, upon those virtues for the lack of which, whether in an individual or in a nation, no amount of refinement and learning of gentleness and culture, can possibly atone. These are the very qualities which are fostered by vigorous manly out-of-door sports.

All of the "masterful nations" in history, Roosevelt declared, encouraged rugged sports. Athletic training could help revitalize commercial America and build a new Anglo-Saxon super-race.

Courage, resolution, and endurance were by-products of manly sports, and these qualities were essential in the struggle between men as well as between nations. Because leaders needed good character above all else, and because most college men were destined to go into law, politics, and business, college athletics were as important as academic studies. Roosevelt despised the idle rich who spent all their time on yachts and polo ponies, as much as those whose wealth begot effeminate softness. Vigorous sports were training for life's hard struggles, not for self-indulgence. "If you are rich, and are worth your salt," he admonished, "you will teach your sons that though they may have leisure, it is not to be spent in idleness . . . We do not admire the man of timid peace. We admire the man who embodies victorious effort; the man who never wrongs his neighbor, who is prompt to help a friend, but who has those virile qualities necessary to win in the stern strife of actual life." Here was the full flowering of bourgeois masculinity for a mature industrial nation: not the wild old machismo of bare-knuckle fighting but the purposeful athleticism of modern sports. And for bourgeois women, Roosevelt offered a version of heroic motherhood, in which female vigor was claimed by those who gave birth to many children, who outbred women of "inferior" races.

Conflict would intensify during the twentieth century, Roosevelt predicted, demanding bold intervention in domestic and international affairs. Gripped by the Darwinian assumptions of his day, he believed civilization hung in the balance. Already American cities were filled with Eastern and Southern European immigrants, men and women of inferior racial stock given to radicalism and violence. Lest foreigners without or labor agitators within prove more virile than Americans, this nation must prepare for a death struggle. The self-testing of athletics helped future leaders shoulder moral responsibilities. The world of sport thus provided telling metaphors for the world of work. In a 1900 essay, "The American Boy," Roosevelt advised young men: ". . . In life, as in a foot-ball game, the principle to follow is: Hit the line hard; don't foul and don't shirk, but hit the line hard."

Roosevelt came of age in an era when durable social ideals such as self-reliance and piety withered as corporate bureaucracies destroyed personal autonomy, and creeping secularization eroded moral convictions. But Roosevelt's strategy was to ignore the fact that Victorian certitude was cracking under the pressure of modernity. In this sense, he was more representative of his era than intellectuals like Henry James, Henry Adams, and George Santayana. Roosevelt *knew* what words like "duty," "purity," and "morality" meant. Clear-cut victories and defeats on the playing field mirrored the equally precise boundaries between good and evil, right and wrong. Americans responded to the assaults of modernity in complex and contradictory ways. Roosevelt and many other men of good families recast Victorian values to fit the new order.

Life was not just hard work, it was struggle, survival of the fittest, dog-eat-dog. Sports taught the character values necessary to cope with such an existence, and, equally important, they made the new Darwinian worldview palpable. Before one's eyes on a college football field, struggle, glory, pain, victory, and defeat took shape. The old Victorian emphasis on earnest hard work was still quite serviceable, but all that was romantic, sentimental, or feminine had to go. Men who seized the day and took command of their fate needed masculine metaphors to counter the feminine weakness that threatened to overwhelm the nation. Commercial values were feminine ones, implying passivity, avoidance of strife, consumption of life's fruits. Far from an enemy of business, Roosevelt believed businessmen must be saved from their own timidity, for their desire for secure profits blunted their will to mastery. The Gilded Age extolled progress, praised rationality, craved equilibrium, yet witnessed class strife, labor violence, and anarchic market competition. Roosevelt declared that virile but inferior races, aggressive foreign foes, and reckless labor radicals all menaced the nation. Teaching rough and manly sports to the sons of wealthy families helped stave off feminine softness, for just when a plethora of goods tempted men to sloth, sports demonstrated that life was a battlefield and taught the will to win.

In 1898, for the sake of Cuba's freedom and America's power, Colonel Theodore Roosevelt led his Rough Riders up San Juan Hill in a glorious little imperialist war. Alongside cowboys and frontiersmen charged a Yale quarterback, Princeton's tennis champion, a renowned polo player, and athletes from Boston's Somerset Club and New York's Knickerbocker Club.

PART II

· ·

Sport and Its Discontents:
The Twentieth Century

4 / Sports with a Mission: Football and Basketball

. . . .

Walter Camp and the Bureaucratization of the Strenuous Life

Theodore Roosevelt related the strenuousness of college football to the masculine and martial virtues young upper-class Anglo-Saxon men would need in order to govern themselves, their country, and the world. Inspired by a similar vision, and by his growing sense of the value of corporate organization, Walter Camp built Yale football into a powerful bureaucratic structure which, year after year, produced winning teams and toughened college men. Not only an organizer and tactician for Yale, Camp served as football's most prominent national spokesman, its premier promoter, and the person most responsible for the enormous popularity of the game in the late nineteenth and early twentieth centuries. For more than a hundred years, Walter Camp has been widely and accurately acknowledged as the father of American football.

Football never overtook baseball as the national game during these years. Many millions more played and watched baseball, from the major and minor leagues down to workplace or small-town nines. But the advent of college football represented a crucial institutional innovation in the late nineteenth century, with dramatic consequences for the history of twentieth-century sports.

In the 1870s and '80s, college football teams, like other student activities, were run by the students, who selected, coached, trained, organized, and financed the squads. A student captain —often the school's most gifted athlete—trained and disciplined his men, while other undergraduates held fund drives and raised subscriptions to support the team. As football grew in popularity and brutality, however, faculty and administration committees intervened in the organization and oversight of the game, while leaving direction of on-field play in student hands.

Prior to 1880, the game resembled English rugby much more than today's football. Play was more or less continuous unless the ball went out of bounds, while almost any physical means of stopping the ballcarrier was permitted and encouraged. There was no line of scrimmage, no series of downs, and no forward passing. Touchdowns were scored only by running. Early football differed far more from the modern game than did early baseball.

From today's vantage point, it is hard to imagine such a game catching on. But it quickly became extraordinarily popular, especially among the middle and upper classes, first in the Northeast and then across the country. The annual Thanksgiving Day championship game between the two best college teams—usually Yale and Princeton—in New York City kicked off the winter social season and by the early 1890s drew as many as forty thousand spectators. Wealthy patrons paid up to $150 for boxes, were driven up Fifth Avenue in elegant liveries, displayed their jewels and finery, and wagered hundreds of thousands of dollars on the game's outcome.

Even so, the game provoked an enormous amount of controversy, on and off campuses, throughout the late nineteenth century, essentially for three reasons. First, the game was extremely brutal: serious injuries were routine, while at least a handful of players in the country were killed each year. Second, the games took on a win-at-any-cost attitude that many observers—particularly college faculties—found disturbing. Player and alumni emphasis on victory led many colleges to engage in what are now illegal recruiting practices but were then only shady or dishonest. The historian Frederick Jackson Turner, for example, denounced the way faculty members had to play "a game of hide and seek with the man who sells his athletic skill for personal gain." Finally, the amount of energy and sheer hoopla surrounding intercollegiate football led many educational traditionalists first to question, then to lament the new and overweening importance of what one historian has aptly called the "intercollegiate football spectacle." While there were other college sports, football, according to historian Ronald Smith, came to stand for them all. And within that world, Walter Camp was dominant.

Walter Camp's football career began at Yale in 1876, in the middle of those controversial and formative years, and ended fifty years later, when his game had become a revered national institution. After graduating in 1880, he stayed on for two years as a medical student and continued to play football. Like his contemporary Theodore Roosevelt, he had transformed childhood physical weakness into adolescent and adult physical strength and athletic prowess. In addition to starring at football, he crewed and participated in intercollegiate tennis, track, and baseball.

As a football player, strategist, tactician, and innovator, Camp was unmatched. Nor can the importance of his service to the Yale team be overemphasized. He first represented Yale at the game's annual rules convention in 1877, but it was in 1880 that he offered one of the most far-reaching rules changes in the history of the sport. The new rule establishing the scrimmage began to transform English rugby into American football. Two years later, again under Camp's leadership, came the series of downs to gain a set number of yards (initially five), new styles of blocking (or interference, as it was known at the time), and tackles below the waist.

Because low tackles reduced the effectiveness of open-field running with the football, the offense retaliated by developing what were known at the time as mass plays—large numbers of players driving into the defense in order to gain the necessary five yards. During the 1880s and '90s, as the game grew more popular with alumni and students, gridiron brutality escalated. Reformers, moralists, academics, and the occasional politician attacked football morality. Their calls for "reform" of the game occasionally met with public approval, but they had little impact on the conduct of the game itself. Walter Camp, sometimes pictured as a rock-ribbed standard-bearer of Victorian honor in the midst of corruption ("Be each, pray God, a gentleman," ran one of his published refrains) saw no contradiction between honor and brutality. He defended—nearly always successfully—the game he loved against all efforts at significant reform; he remains one of the central figures whose efforts increased the game's violence.

When he left medical school in 1882 (thereby ending his playing days) and went to work for the New Haven Clock Company, Camp maintained a close connection to the football team. His precise role is a matter of some disagreement, but nearly all observers confirm that Camp was the "czar," official or unofficial, of Yale football for several decades. Because football programs were structured differently from today's, so was Camp's involvement. While he worked at the clock company during the day, his wife (the former Alice Graham Sumner, sister of Yale's famous social Darwinist William Graham Sumner) attended the Yale practices and took careful notes. Each evening, the student coaches would huddle with the Camps to analyze the team's work, and Camp would give directions. This system endured in more or less the same form into this century. During the years that Camp played or ran Yale football (1876–1909), his alma mater lost only fourteen games, fewer than one every other year—an astonishing record that has never been matched.

But Camp played an even greater role as a football innovator, defender, and propagandist. When the game came under attack during the 1893 season (the year the dangerous flying wedge was introduced) it was Camp who, as the key member of a blue-ribbon commission charged with investigating football brutality,

In the late nineteenth and early twentieth centuries, intercollegiate football was so violent that athletes like these from Yale and Princeton could be seriously injured and even killed during games. In the early 1880s, rules allowed a player to hit another three times with closed fists before he could be ejected. From the *National Police Gazette (Library of Congress)*

selected the data to publish in his *Football Facts and Figures* (1894). He concluded, predictably, that "Harvard, Yale, and Princeton players during the previous eighteen years had an 'almost unanimous opinion' that football has been a 'marked benefit' both physically and mentally." When Camp became secretary of the intercollegiate rules committee that assumed authority over the game that year, football's future was secure. The group eliminated the flying wedge and some other dangerous mass plays, and the game returned to its earlier level of brutality.

Again, in 1905, another year of crisis for the game, Camp intervened decisively. So many players had died that season that President Theodore Roosevelt was moved to call a White House conference of football's Big Three—Yale, Harvard, and Princeton—to "persuade them to play football honestly." It is impossible not to think of Roosevelt convening the leaders of

American industry to insist that their business be pursued honestly. No more than the leaders of the trusts intended to reduce their control over the American economy did the Big Three intend to give up control of their successful and popular sport. By then known as a defender of the status quo, Camp helped design a mild statement promising to "eliminate unnecessary roughness, holding, and foul play." Roosevelt, who had made a career out of talking tough and accepting what he was offered, went along. Camp had won.

Camp's contributions over the next several decades ranged from prolific writing about football and other college sports, to consistent involvement in changes in the rules, to innovations in public relations. He led the way in developing the game's scoring system for touchdowns, safeties, field goals, and extra points. Throughout his career he manifested a shrewd understanding of the art of promotion, one example of which was the All-America team, an annual rite begun by Camp and the prominent sportswriter Caspar Whitney back in 1889.

Meanwhile, Camp's career with the New Haven Clock Company prospered, and he rose to become president and chairman of the board. That a clock manufacturer should have been the leading spirit in college football is for a number of reasons an intriguing coincidence. Camp frequently noted the connections between the structure of football and the world of business, as in the following comment, which he wrote around 1920:

> Finding a weak spot through which a play can be made, feeling out the line with experimental attempts, concealing the real strength till everything is ripe for the big push, then letting drive where least expected, what is this—an outline of football or business tactics? Both of course.

Convinced that "American business has found in American college football the epitomization of present day business methods," Camp claimed that the game "has come to be recognized as the best school for instilling into the young man those attributes which business desires and demands."

Camp modeled his teams on the structure of industrial production. The late-nineteenth-century workplace saw complex manufacturing processes reorganized into a multitude of small, repetitive tasks, in which workers themselves saw only a tiny piece of the whole. Employers increasingly arrogated to themselves the task of managing, measuring, organizing, and timing the production processes as a whole. This was precisely the pattern Camp employed in managing Yale football.

As he shaped his teams and provided a powerful example for programs across the country, Camp paralleled the work of such industrial reformers as Frederick Winslow Taylor, the father and chief theorist of the scientific management movement. Michael Oriard, in his *Reading Football*, has pointed to the very striking similarity between Taylor's "four elements of scientific management (Science, Harmony, Cooperation, and Maximum Output)" and Camp's principles of "team work, strategy, and tactics." Such parallels are more than coincidence. Walter Camp's professional life was lived in a modern manufacturing enterprise. At the same time, he constructed a sport that was probably the fullest expression of industrial organization—on the playing field and at the training camp—that the world of play had ever seen.

It is difficult to look at Camp's football system and not see military organization as well. The very language of football— drills, training camps, strategy, and tactics—drew on military life and experience. And of course, the play of the game itself consisted of organized violence and the capture of territory. While comedian George Carlin has a well-known routine comparing the military ethos of football (bombs, hits, helmets, territory) with the bucolic images of baseball (pastures, parks, circles, home), the distinction is not recent. From its earliest years, college football was run by a merger of military and industrial organization.

Camp brought bureaucracy to Yale football, institutionalizing regular practice and training. Such innovations resembled captain Harry Wright's preparation for the Cincinnati Red Stockings' legendary undefeated season in 1869 (the sportswriter Henry Chadwick called the club the first "regularly trained" all-professional nine). A generation later, even a Harvard magazine had to acknowledge that Camp's system deserved "full credit for organizing and maintaining the most remarkable athletic system ever seen in an American or an English university." But such a system had its costs. Owen Johnson's popular novel of 1890s Ivy League student life *Stover at Yale* (1912) provides a revealing look at Yale's version of the sport. "What has become of the natural, spontaneous joy of the contest?" asks one of his characters. "Instead you have the most perfectly organized business systems for achieving the required result—success. Football is driving slavish work." Football coaches usually drove their men harder than professional baseball managers did theirs, acting almost as though they were drill sergeants in boot camp. Camp would not have disagreed. In *The Book of Football* (1910), he argued that the game taught "obedience to authority," specialization, and self-control. Owen Johnson likened Yale teams to the beef trust, which also had "every by-product organized, down to the last possibility."

One of those by-products, of course, was time. Football was the first American spectator sport in which the clock played a major role. Walter Camp manufactured clocks, sometimes the very ones that entered American offices and factories in the 1890s. (Again, Frederick Taylor, stopwatch in hand as he conducted his time and motion studies, symbolized the rationalization of work during this era.) The reorganization of industrial production, mirrored in Walter Camp's restructuring of football from virtually continuous play to a series of downs, produced a different rhythm of life in the early twentieth century, one presided over by the importance of measured time.

Baseball had been different. Popularized toward the end of the heyday of craft production in the third quarter of the nineteenth century, the national game offered an on-field vision of individually performed craft in the service of a collective ideal (making outs, scoring runs). A baseball nine's success depended on the entire team, of course, but the very positioning of the players and the play of the game focused attention on one player, perhaps two or three, at a time. And no time limit was ever placed on the length of a baseball game.

Football, on the other hand, demanded allegiance to a machinelike system. Except for the few heroes—running backs who scored touchdowns, ends who caught long passes—the great majority of players were to find their fulfillment in the collective, orderly functioning of the system. "Football players seem to be peculiarly unselfish in this respect," Camp claimed. And many of the young middle- and upper-class American men who attended college apparently absorbed this ideology almost without question. According to James Church, a player of the 1890s, what most characterized the game at the time was its *"clock-like regularity."* It was far better, he added, "to expect moderately rapid work with *system* than fast play which savors of individuality and is confused."

During the late nineteenth and early twentieth centuries, Yale's football squads regularly beat Harvard's. The differences between the rival colleges may be instructive. According to Peter Dobkin Hall, Harvard remained, even in the late 1800s, the university principally of the northeastern elite. Its buildings named for old Massachusetts families, its students drawn primarily from New England, Harvard's city was Boston, the Hub of colonial America. Yale on the other hand, oriented more toward New York City since the early nineteenth century, cast its net farther across the continent. Much more than Harvard, Hall contends, Yale became the college and university of the national elite, drawing its students and money from all over the United States, providing an experience of socialization that knit together geographically disparate students into a national upper class.

If we look at Harvard and Yale as symbols as well as institutions, then we can draw some significance from Yale's domination of football for most of the late nineteenth and early twentieth centuries. Yale football flourished under Camp's system, while Harvard football remained individualistic and disorderly. The distinction between these two colleges' football programs was emblematic of the new direction of upper-class

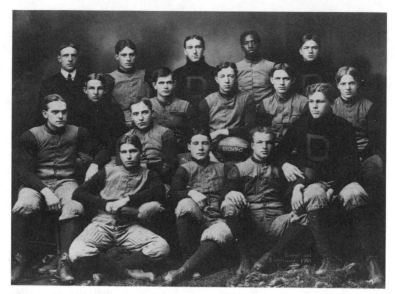

The 1901 Dartmouth football team poses with the game ball after defeating Brown 22–0 *(Library of Congress)*

culture in the late nineteenth century. Not only was the Yale system most effective and most widely copied, but, after decades of being thrashed by Yale, the Harvard Athletic Association in 1908 finally hired Percy Haughton to reorganize its rather slap-dash football program. Haughton instituted a thoroughly military system of command and drills, which soon paid off: Harvard lost only one game to Yale in an eight-year span. As Camp's system was copied across the country, his vision of the future triumphed.

What, we might ask, did football mean to the men who played it? It built camaraderie among men who were expected to take up leadership positions in their communities. The intense emotional identification fostered by football bound men to one another and to their class long after their gridiron days had passed. The shared experience of violence made these bonds especially strong. The risk of serious injury run by each player, the degree to which he depended on his fellows to protect him, the relief at

surviving danger, and the sense of having gone through something together that others could not share gave football players
the feeling of being special, distinct, and worthy. Such feelings
are also perhaps the defining characteristic of the bonds between
combat veterans of military units.

Especially for young men, football was a means of defining
and testing physical and psychological masculinity, a kind of
initiation ritual. Though football carried fewer risks than military
combat, players invested it with many of the same feelings.
Theodore Roosevelt's son Theodore Junior wrote to his father
after playing for the Harvard freshmen in 1905: "I feel so large
in my black sweater with the numerals on. Saturday's game was
a hard one, as I knew it was bound to be. I was not seriously
hurt at all. Just shaken up and bruised. I broke my nose."

If surviving violence was one side of this coin, attraction to
other men was the other. As is suggested by the popularity of
Eugene Sandow's exhibitions, there has always been a strong
element of homoeroticism in masculine sports, dating in this
country at least from the loving descriptions of boxers' bodies
offered in the sporting press in the early nineteenth century.
When men spent so much time with one another in situations
that involved physical strength, as young men did in the brawling
bachelor subculture of antebellum cities, it should hardly be surprising that their physical relationships were at least tinged with
erotic attraction. Upper-class football players, like working-class
urban gang members in the 1830s and in the 1980s, and like
soldiers everywhere, depended heavily on each other's strength,
courage, and loyalty. Their primary identifications were with the
team, with the eleven, and with the coach, the ever-present Pop.
Brothers and comrades, athletes were lovers perhaps rarely, but
men who identified with men nearly all the time. After all, the
big football campuses were all-male. Swimmers in the Yale University pool, for example (until women undergraduates were
admitted in 1969), were *required* to swim nude. And in coeducational institutions, college athletics, whether intercollegiate or
intramural, were entirely segregated by gender.

Finally, since the late nineteenth century, men's memories of college sports have produced powerful emotional responses. Long after their youth, as men watch, discuss, or participate in sports, they are able to tap into a reservoir of feelings buried since childhood. Through the strength and influence of alumni associations and college reunions, the intensely felt experiences of college sports are kept very much alive. Such memories and identifications have had important consequences for higher education in the twentieth century.

Football, Alumni, and the Control of the University

By and large, football worked. It effectively built connections between young men that went well beyond a single season. It helped construct a culture and a set of institutions—in which college players were connected to multitudes of fans—that served a remarkable range of social purposes. In fact, the more closely we look at college football in the late nineteenth and early twentieth centuries, the more disparate strands of modern American education and middle- and upper-class culture we find intertwined in the sport. Perhaps most important, college alumni associations were founded to help control and promote college athletics, which for the most part meant football. Athletics in general, but football in particular, were the arena in which alumni associations gained increasing influence at colleges and universities around the turn of the century.

Far more than academic achievement, the experience and culture of football linked different generations of American leaders in a collegiate socialization process that helped provide class cohesion for the children of the American upper classes. Not all colleges, of course, were Ivy League (and it is important to remember that the origin of this term, which nowadays refers only to a group of elite northeastern, formerly all-male colleges, lay in the football association linking these schools). But regional colleges and state universities filled many of the same functions, if for a slightly lower class. Elites sent their sons to local and regional colleges and universities, where they underwent experiences that paralleled the Ivy League's. Football, and alumni involvement in it, played as central a role in the culture of Wisconsin and Michigan, Berkeley and Stanford, and other institutions as at Harvard and Yale.

Though we tend to assume that the tail of football began wagging the dog of college only recently, the historian Frederick Rudolph argues that by 1900, football's importance as a public relations tool had already become well understood and established. College football's appeal extended to many citizens who would never attend an institution of higher learning. At the same time, the sport helped transform power relations within the academy.

In the 1890s, when alumni gained virtually complete control over college sports, the chief prize was football. As long as football continued to dominate collegiate publicity and make money (it was the major revenue producer after tuition, and, according to Rudolph, the *only* moneymaking activity of most colleges), those who controlled it exercised enormous influence over college and university policy. Yale's yearly football receipts grew to $100,000 by the end of the nineteenth century, which equaled one-eighth of that institution's total income, and more than the university's expenditures on law and medicine.

Dartmouth College had been fielding mediocre teams, but in 1902 the alumni requested and were given authority to manage the college's athletic program. The alumni athletic committee began to produce winning teams and even built an athletic field. Not long after, a member of this committee became president of Dartmouth. In the midst of the 1905 football crisis brought on by the violence of the game, the faculty tried to take back some control over the athletic program, but were completely rebuffed by the board of trustees. Here is a prime example of how power was shifting in colleges around the turn of the century. Alumni came to control colleges because they were becoming the principal fund-raisers, and football was crucial to fund-raising.

The explosive growth of college athletics, particularly football, helps explain the nature of the overall undergraduate experience in the twentieth century. The rise of college social life, the growth of sports, and the increase in alumni influence (beginning with athletics) foreshadowed the modern alliance between alumni and students—against the faculty—to manage the college and university as a site of fun and socialization as much as of academic pursuit. As one young college graduate wrote in a national magazine in 1890, "You do not remember whether Thorpwright was valedictorian or not, but you can never forget that glorious run of his in the football game."

By the 1890s, students were bored stiff by the classical, scholarly curriculum. Faculty and students faced each other across what one historian called an "awful chasm." On the other hand, there was extraordinary student enthusiasm for the "extracurriculum"—clubs, fraternities, athletic associations—which students much preferred to their studies. For many students and alumni during this period, social life came to hold far more importance than academic pursuits. "The work of the college," according to Princeton president Woodrow Wilson in 1909, "the work of its classrooms and laboratories, has become the merely formal and compulsory side of its life, and . . . a score of other things, lumped under the term 'undergraduate activities,' have become the vital, spontaneous, absorbing realities for nine out of every ten men who go to college." A century ago, according to historian Laurence Veysey, the motto "Don't Let Your Studies Interfere with Your Education" graced dormitory and fraternity walls across the country.

This attitude will be familiar to today's college students. The modern equivalent may be the standard pre-college pep talk given by recruiters to high school juniors and seniors: "Ninety percent of your learning will take place with your fellow students, not in the classroom." Such an attitude is an exceptionally clear statement about the place of academic learning—of the curriculum—in college life. Moreover, many of the alumni who took over the reins of higher educational institutions did so in the service of class socialization and cohesion, and of character-building and "preparation for life." If the saying "It's not what you know—it's whom you know" is true, then colleges had become important places for young men of elite families to meet the "right" people.

College life in the late nineteenth century was centered less and less on academic pursuits in favor of the "extracurriculum" of societies, social events, and, above all, athletics. With the caption "Education. Is there no middle course?" *Harper's Weekly* (November 30, 1879) worried about the educational consequences of a student's choices being limited to a discredited classical curriculum and a brutish athletic life *(Library of Congress)*

Of course, colleges had not previously been simply pristine sanctuaries for the life of the mind. Veysey reminds us that conflict between professors and students has a long history; it has included student riots, the stoning of professors' houses, and at least a couple of professorial murders. But by the 1890s, as leaders of the American upper classes worried about the flood of immigrants from Southern and Eastern Europe, the growth of the nouveau riche, and the apparent decline of Anglo-Saxon dominance, they feared that the academic college experience was contributing to the decline of American manhood. Christopher Lasch has described this development as a crisis in the 1890s among the ruling class, one that was addressed frontally and successfully by Theodore Roosevelt and his more foresighted peers. In the years around the turn of the century, college life changed to serve children of the new business class as much as the traditional arbiters of taste and culture. Victorian religious, cultural, and intellectual leadership gave way to those whose status came from their corporate, managerial, or financial power. As Lasch argues, the ancient curriculum of classical sciences and humanities seemed irrelevant to young men who would soon lead expansive private and public bureaucracies. Clannishness and snobbery notwithstanding, children of old Victorian and nouveau riche families found common ground in the turn-of-the-century colleges.

The new extracurriculum facilitated this social mixing. Future leaders of American politics and industry needed less an ethos of genteel learning than lessons in the art of power. They also needed a congenial social atmosphere that produced lifelong friendships and valuable social contacts. In a process that was not always conscious, sports helped transform colleges from bastions of Victorian provincialism into socializing institutions for a new elite based on professionalism, business efficiency, and technocratic expertise. Colleges became places to acquire social contacts, business credentials, and upper-class style. They were both a path to respectable society and a route to corporate success, a way to have the old polish and the new power. As Walter Camp and others argued, the new games—especially football—emphasized institutional loyalty and teamwork, valuable assets in a corporate world.

At the same time, college athletics helped restore, both for participants and spectators, a sense of vigor and strength to youthful upper-class masculinity. As we have seen, the growth of college football, indeed of all college sports around the turn of the century, was connected to the martial, jingoistic, and exceptionally masculine spirit of that time. John Higham points to a new group of impatient, anti-genteel, sexually charged epithets that became popular during these years: "sissy," "pussyfoot," "cold feet," "stuffed shirt."

College football, as a consuming phenomenon in institutions of higher learning, stood at the center of the cultural transformations of the late nineteenth and early twentieth centuries. It assisted in the redefinition of American middle- and upper-class masculinity; it helped reorganize American colleges and universities into institutions controlled by alumni in the service of class socialization and character-building at the expense of academics; it provided a public spectacle of upper-class display; and it furnished an experience of corporate, collective, quasi-military physical combat for sons of national and local elites.

Progressives, Play, and Basketball

But college students and alumni were not the only ones whose passion for sports grew. Indeed, college teams in the Midwest, the far West, and the South developed loyal regional fans who never experienced a day of higher education. It is hard to overstate the degree of ferment and new interest in recreation during the Progressive Era. Unprecedented numbers of Americans threw themselves into sports, games, and organized play. While the growth of football held the most significance for the future of the sports and entertainment business (and for the development of higher education), the entire culture experienced a phenomenal upsurge in recreation and outdoor activity. The rush toward active sports and pastimes that began in the late nineteenth century became a stampede by the early twentieth century.

Middle-class Americans in particular reacted to the growing bureaucracy and confinement of their work lives, and to the remarkable crowding of their cities, by rushing to the outdoors, on foot and on bicycles. Hiking, bird-watching, camping, rock-climbing, or simply walking in the new national parks—participation in all of these activities soared in the years around the turn of the century. The invention of the safety bicycle, with wheels the same size and pneumatic tires, and a substantial drop in price, led to a cycling craze. Ten million bicycles were on the

Along with tennis, golf was the sport most associated with elite social status and the country club movement. In general, upper-class women faced fewer obstacles to participation in athletics than their less-well-off sisters. From *Harper's Weekly*, July 1889 *(Library of Congress)*

roads by 1900 (ten times the figure seven years earlier); countless enthusiasts joined bicycle clubs, read cycling magazines, and attended races. Women participated fully in the bicycle fad of the nineties, and the image of the vigorous "new woman" on a bicycle shattered the old ideal of the delicate Victorian lady.

In cities, recreation took on new importance. The settlement-house movement was partly responsible, as it sought to organize the time and energy of immigrant youths crowding the slums of America's largest cities. The Young Men's Christian Association continued to play a key role in promoting organized play in the city. Under the vigorous leadership of Luther Halsey Gulick (designer of the "Mind-Body-Spirit" symbol of the YMCA), the organization provided gymnasiums, instruction in physical education, and, as we shall see, a new game for the cities.

The recreation movement found its intellectual and scientific foundation in the work of psychologists, principally G. Stanley

In the 1890s, bicycle riding (here along New York City's Riverside Drive) became an immensely popular recreation for middle-class men and women. From *Harper's Weekly*, June 15, 1895 *(Library of Congress)*

Hall and his students, whose "discovery" of adolescence and the educative role of children's play proved enormously useful to reformers and play advocates. The movement garnered many of its best advocates in the young middle-class professionals—above all, social workers—who sought to soften the distressing conflicts and everyday brutalities of immigrant children's lives. Social workers thought they could bridge and defuse the class conflict tearing much of American society apart if only they could reach the children. Organized play seemed to be one means to that end.

Reformers thought of themselves as being on an exciting new mission, Americanizing children by helping them to have fun. With varying degrees of empathy for their new "clients," playground reformers sought to clean up American streets, confine play to designated recreational spaces, and use their professional expertise to teach "respectable" athletics. With its professional associations, popular magazines, and social-science foundations, the playground movement caused the amount of attention given to organized play to shoot upward during the Progressive Era.

But the development destined to have the greatest impact on urban sport and recreation took place at the YMCA training school in Springfield, Massachusetts, in the early 1890s. There three young men, missionaries, really, only they didn't realize it—Amos Alonzo Stagg, James Naismith, and the school director, Luther Halsey Gulick—created a unique laboratory for American physical education and athletic training.

Stagg, after starring at Yale as a baseball pitcher and right end on Walter Camp's 1888 football squad, had given up the ministry for Christian physical education. A stutter had convinced him that his preaching could be better done "on the football field." Stagg began his coaching career with the faculty-student team of Springfield. Later, at the University of Chicago, he became one of the most successful and influential college football coaches in the twentieth century. As an undergraduate at McGill University in Montreal, and then at its affiliated Presbyterian College, James Naismith had prepared for the ministry but felt even more drawn to the athletic field. Upon graduation, he made a momentous choice, leaving the ministry for the doubtful new career of physical education, then flourishing most impressively at Springfield. Luther Gulick had gone a step further on the same journey. The son of missionary parents, Gulick had found his commitment to the ministry seriously faltering at college; he "converted" to the new gospel of physical education when, as he recalled later, he became convinced that "good bodies and good morals" could be mutually reinforcing. Gulick joined the YMCA the next year, first in Michigan, then in Springfield, and soon acquired a medical degree. At Springfield he had found a perfect niche for his inexhaustible zeal in the service of physical education.

These three—Stagg, Naismith, and Gulick—lived for athletics, but they combined their athletic work with a concern for health and Christianity that, like much of Victorian culture, seems exceptionally earnest from our vantage point today. For them muscular Christianity was an exciting, even liberating set of ideas.

Naismith, for instance, had consistently felt a little guilty about his inability to stay away from athletics. He took ribbing from his seminary classmates and felt the sting of the disapproval of his sister, who worried that athletics were "the Devil's work." When Luther Gulick tried dutifully to follow in his father's ministerial footsteps, he ended up with migraine headaches; now, as director of the YMCA's training school and its chief theorist of play, he found his mission. All three young men were proselytizing for athletics and creating careers for themselves in physical education that a previous generation could not have understood and would have distrusted.

Under Gulick's leadership, the Springfield physical-education curriculum abandoned the repetitive gymnastic drills of the late nineteenth century. The director's fascination with the socializing aspects of physical education led him to focus on play and team sports. Naismith added creativity to Gulick's philosophy. In December 1891, faced with the ennui of wintertime (with no organized sports between the end of the football season and the beginning of baseball), and a particularly difficult group of students in an adult gymnastics class, he invented the game of basketball.

Primitive by today's standards (Naismith *really* nailed peach baskets to gymnasium balconies), but thoroughly recognizable from the beginning as the game we know today, basketball quickly spread across the country, first through YMCA networks but soon far wider. YMCA missionaries carried the game abroad, while colleges in this country took it up. Women first played the game at Springfield and then elsewhere, not always to the approval of male audiences, or even to that of the game's inventors. Nevertheless, college women in particular adopted basketball; the first national rules for women were published in 1901. Gulick was ecstatic at basketball's popularity. In October 1892, before the game had marked its first birthday, he enthused, "It is doubtful whether a gymnastic game has ever spread so rapidly over the continent as has 'basket ball.' It is played from New York to San Francisco and from Maine to Texas by hundreds of teams in associations, athletic clubs and schools."

Invented in 1891 at Springfield College, basketball soon became the most popular team sport among women. "Girls' " basketball team, 1912, Monroe, Wisconsin (*Library of Congress*)

Because basketball did not require the large field needed for baseball and football, it was ideally suited to urban recreation programs, to settlement houses and playgrounds, to schools and churches. During these early years, most basketball games took place in supervised environments. (In this respect the game differed markedly from baseball, which was played as stickball in precisely those less orderly urban environments that made play reformers and settlement-house workers nervous.) So basketball, unintentionally, became a major sport to recruit new members for the YMCA. Even though basketball had been invented to meet a precise set of needs and circumstances, and James Naismith had never intended it to change the shape of urban recreation, the game he invented probably made possible the extraordinary expansion of organized, supervised play in the early twentieth century.

Basketball served as the foundation on which social workers

The new game also became the prime athletic recruiting tool of the YMCA: the "city game" of supervised playgrounds and gymnasiums. The Carnegie Playground, Fifth Avenue, New York City, 1912 *(Library of Congress)*

and reformers built huge intellectual and bureaucratic structures. Without a game so suitable for the cities where the largest number of immigrant children were concentrated, and where settlement-house workers saw the greatest need for social work, the movement for organized play might very well have sputtered out soon after its birth. Instead, basketball became one of the two most important new American sports. Football, as we have seen, served upper-class revitalization and the attendant restructuring of college life. Basketball became part of the Progressive, professional, middle-class effort to channel, guide, and Americanize immigrant youth through elementary and secondary extracurricular activities.

This history helps explain why, through much of this century, basketball has been the preferred sport of working-class ethnic communities. That is where it was first played, where it was promulgated, where local institutions took the game to heart.

Urban settlement-house teams and leagues, frequently located in immigrant enclaves, furnished the finest players in the country. In New York, for instance, Jewish players at Clark House and the University Settlement dominated local tournaments. Irish neighborhoods in New York served as home base for the Celtics basketball club, which, founded in 1914, became the leading professional team of the next decade. Well into the twentieth century, basketball organization and interest followed ethnic lines. Chicago hosted an annual exhibition between the B'nai B'rith and Catholic Youth Organization All-Stars, while there were national Serbian, Lithuanian, and Polish championships in the 1930s.

Following the lead of the YMCA, cities across the country founded Sunday school athletic leagues in the decade before World War I. Luther Gulick, who had left Springfield and become director of physical training for New York City public schools in 1903, founded the Public Schools Athletic League that same year, with the financial sponsorship of some of America's most prominent bankers and industrialists. One reason this effort received such praise and support (it was copied in seventeen other cities within seven years), and why some observers have raised questions about its political purpose, was that it promised to channel the chaotic, frequently delinquent, occasionally criminal activities of immigrant children into wholesome, orderly, "Americanizing" play. While this critique has much merit—the PSAL explicitly stressed the values of "Duty," "Thoroughness," "Patriotism," "Honor," and "Obedience"—it probably overstates the reformer's real impact. As Benjamin Rader points out, two-thirds of New York City's teenage boys did not even attend school.

The Playground Association of America attacked the issue of urban recreation from a slightly different angle. Organized by the indefatigable Gulick and his friend and mentor Henry S. Curtis (a student of G. Stanley Hall), the association lobbied municipalities to build playgrounds for urban youth. Its early leadership came from urban reformers, mostly settlement-house workers, including Lillian Wald and Jane Addams. Jacob Riis, the crusading photojournalist of urban poverty, served as honorary vice-president, while President Theodore Roosevelt, who had given a ceremonial approval to the group at the White House in 1906, was named honorary president the following year.

With a theory (the developmental importance of children's play), a game (basketball), and several key constituencies (urban immigrants and reformers), the movement for organized play took off in the next decade. Playground appropriations increased in cities and the association itself ballooned. Between 1911 and 1917, the number of playgrounds in hundreds of cities reporting to the PAA more than doubled, from 1,543 to 3,940.

By the eve of World War I, however, the movement began to flag. Playgrounds weren't drawing enough children, advocates felt. But children weren't the only problem. There was neither land nor money enough to build and equip playgrounds throughout the crowded neighborhoods of American cities. For Gulick and Curtis, the real solution to "the play problem"—that is, society's inadequate attention to the need for widespread organized play—was the public school, which could quickly absorb and organize play activity, guarantee attendance, and solve the funding difficulty. Their hopes were realized, oddly enough, as America entered World War I.

World War I: The Great Unifier

America's big wars—the Revolution, the Civil War, the two World Wars, Vietnam—all helped create new cultural patterns. The material and emotional preparation for war, the frightful business of fighting and dying, the organizational changes and ideological battles produced an unusual intensity in American life that accelerated and redirected cultural change. The First World War drew together the strands of Progressivism into a cultural tapestry that delighted some Americans and horrified others. Never before had so many social engineers joined the federal government. Never before had the rhetoric of Americanization and socialization taken on such urgency, even stridency. Never before had new middle-class professionals been involved in such an overarching and exciting effort of worldwide significance. The military draft provided a treasure trove of raw material for the human engineers—social scientists, psychologists, efficiency experts, and physical educators—who joined the great crusade. All those young men needed to be sorted and classified, trained and equipped to serve.

And once in uniform, they needed to be protected from themselves. Secretary of War Newton D. Baker was determined not to expose the troops or his Administration to the embarrassing publicity that had accompanied General John J. Pershing's Mexican "expedition" in pursuit of Pancho Villa in 1916. Then newspapers had made much of the drinking and prostitution that had served to entertain an army with time on its hands. The War and Navy Departments each created Commissions on Training Camp Activities that called on public and private agencies to assist them in guaranteeing decent and healthy living conditions for the servicemen.

A host of organizations responded to the patriotic call, including the YMCA (by far the largest), Knights of Columbus, Jewish Welfare Board, American Library Association, and the renamed Playground and Recreation Association of America. Two familiar figures enlisted in this effort. James Naismith, now on the physical-education faculty of the University of Kansas, had served for a while as chaplain with a Kansas regiment on the Mexican border. There he had closed down saloons and brothels while offering athletics as a substitute. This approach was taken up by the new commissions, while Naismith himself went on the circuit for the Y's sex education program, traveling the country to lecture young soldiers and sailors about clean living and the dangers of venereal disease. And Walter Camp, by now nearly sixty, joined the Navy's commission as athletic director. What better field for his organizational talents?

Soon athletics became central to the operations of army and navy bases. President Woodrow Wilson declared, "I hope that sports will be continued . . . as a real contribution to the national defense," and continued they were. For the first time in American history, sports were formally linked to military preparedness;

athletics now would be sanctioned and even financed by the federal government. Recreational experts assured the nation that by playing baseball and football, by boxing and exercising, young American men would be fit enough for war. As we have seen, American men had previously played sports in the military—a USS *Maine* baseball team went down when that battleship was blown up in Havana harbor in 1898, and there are stories of Civil War soldiers who kept baseballs in their knapsacks. But not until World War I were athletic training and competition systematically adopted for troop morale, hygiene, and physical readiness for war. Recreation professionals greeted these developments enthusiastically. The editor of *Outing* magazine offered to help publicize athletics and predicted that "5,000,000 men in service by July means 5,000,000 converts to the out-of-doors after the war."

As American troops were deployed overseas in 1917, they were accompanied everywhere by twelve thousand YMCA workers who brought sports along with them. Raymond Fosdick, appointed to head the federal Commissions on Training Camp Activities for both the War and the Navy Departments, joined General Pershing's staff as an adviser on morale. When the war ended the following year, policymakers were faced with a dilemma. Frightened by the threat of Bolshevism in postwar Europe and therefore unwilling to bring troops home immediately, they needed to address the age-old problem of soldiers in large groups not fighting a war. The YMCA stepped into the breach, proposing and organizing an immense series of athletic competitions leading up to American Expeditionary Forces championships. Pershing himself observed that "the results of this type of athletics are sure to create a higher type of athletics at home. Two million men are going to carry back home a better notion of what clean sport should be." The celebration went even further, as the AEF championships slid over into the Inter-Allied Games (also known as the Military Olympics) in Joinville, France, in the summer of 1919, an astonishing extravaganza staged in the midst of postwar devastation which nevertheless drew something like half a million spectators over two weeks.

After the war, physical educators rightly anticipated a boom in their discipline; draft statistics had indicated that somewhere between a quarter and a third of American recruits were physically unfit. The war had made physical fitness and athletic ability patriotic virtues. On the heels of a national meeting called by the U.S. Commissioner of Education, representatives of youth, health, and education agencies founded the National Committee on Physical Education. The committee undertook an ambitious campaign to have physical education adopted as a requirement in public schools. The National Collegiate Athletic Association acted as the foremost advocate of college athletics. Meanwhile, the Playground and Recreation Association of America turned its attention to the secondary-school curriculum and to lobbying state legislatures on behalf of organized physical education. From 1919 through 1921, seventeen states adopted physical-education requirements; by 1930, thirty-six had done so. Gulick and his colleagues had accurately foreseen that public schools held the key to reaching American youth with the gospel of athletics. At the committee's urging, both national political parties in 1920 adopted platform planks calling for a federal physical-education program.

"The effect of all this work upon the future citizenship of the United States is incalculable," Raymond Fosdick exulted in 1919. He had much to be proud of. His commissions had not only educated and trained hundreds of thousands of young men in athletics; their efforts would help reshape the very experience of American youth for decades. Sports and physical fitness would not receive another such official boost until World War II, and then from the physical fitness boom fostered by President John F. Kennedy in the early 1960s.

The Great War made the nation more conscious of organized play—and of its potential as an educational force—than ever. Two distinct streams in American sports history joined forces for the war effort, creating a powerful vocabulary and set of experiences for the coming decades. Walter Camp's systems for producing teamwork and toughness on the gridiron proved themselves in training camps and on battlefields. If Theodore Roosevelt had provided the idea and demonstrated the appeal of the strenuous life, it fell to Walter Camp, Percy Haughton, and their colleagues in higher education to translate those ideals into effective, workable programs. Football's lessons—the importance of physical toughness, of unquestioning teamwork, its military metaphors—helped train a generation of American leaders for war.

The labors of Luther Gulick, James Naismith, and their comrades in the settlement-house movement also fed the war effort. For several decades, they had been stressing the importance of play and physical education in the development of children and adolescents. Basketball may have been the ideal sport for small urban spaces, but it also brought millions of young immigrants indoors to be supervised in their play and instructed in "American values." Urban middle-class social workers and working-class children developed a commitment to athletics through the large networks of the YMCA, public-school athletic leagues, and playground associations. Their experience helped organize the mass training camps and overseas athletic activity.

These two streams that merged in World War I accomplished far more together than they ever could have apart. They brought participation in organized athletics to millions of American men. In so doing, they democratized sport and created a newly powerful constituency for the leisure movement. For the first time, organized athletics and physical education were linked in the minds of leaders and participants to patriotism and military preparedness. By demonstrating the value of mass organized athletics as a builder of bodies and morale, wartime sports laid the groundwork for public schools to adopt sports programs. And finally, by providing a mass experience of participant and spectator sports for the troops, the war helped prepare the nation for the sports boom of the 1920s.

Many of these developments continued to bear the signs of their wartime origins. The occasionally manipulative, heavy-handed efforts of sports promoters and organizers have never managed to contain the play impulse in athletic activity completely. Nevertheless, to those concerned about Bolshevism abroad and radicalism at home, youth sports appeared to hold much hope. During the 1920s, the American Legion began to sponsor a baseball program, part of its campaign to make sure that all citizens stayed "100 percent American." Legionnaires had harassed and intimidated radicals and union members just after the war, and they decided in 1925 to launch an athletic program that would afford "the best possible medium through which to teach the principles of Americanism. Under cloak of a sport code, we would inculcate more good citizenship during one year than would be possible in five years of direct appeal." More than one hundred thousand boys in the next three years took what one Legionnaire called the "bait" of Junior Baseball. Whether they also swallowed the "hook" of Americanism may be harder to tell, though the general cultural respect accorded the American Legion today (a group founded in frequently violent opposition to immigrants and radicals) suggests the size of the achievement.

Between 1890 and the early 1920s, then, organized sports had expanded dramatically throughout American society. The sporting scene, and the widespread popular attention devoted to it, was still dominated by baseball and football, but basketball had become established as a central urban, ethnic, working-class sport. Strictures on recreation that had concerned middle-class Americans in the previous century had mostly disappeared, as many millions filled their increasing leisure time with athletics, sports, and games of all kinds. Children learned sports in school, as the college extracurriculum became institutionalized in the primary and secondary curriculum. Walter Camp and James Naismith could hardly have predicted such a triumph for their ideas.

5 / Play, Business, and Space: Sports and the Public Sphere

. . . .

Home Teams

The movie *Major League* (1989) opens as the camera slowly explores the monuments, neighborhoods, and industries of Cleveland, Ohio. In the background, Randy Newman's sarcastic song "Cleveland: City of Light" recounts the time when the pollution-choked Cuyahoga River caught fire. Sunlight oozes through the smog, and we can almost smell the odor of toxic decay and urban failure. Yet this is a movie about baseball, the sport of green fields and childhood nostalgia, a movie about the trials of a barely major league team with a chronic losing history which, in an amusing reversal, is being deliberately molded to be the worst team in the game.

The series of connections implied by the opening scenes are easily made. The decay of the city is matched to the dismal fortunes of its baseball team. And yet, despite our knowing contempt for Cleveland and the Indians, we cannot but feel there is something evil and mercenary about the plan of the new owner (a wealthy young widow) to move the ball club to Miami. A team, we know, belongs to its city, no matter how far either of them has fallen. After its forgettable first half (a string of so-so jokes and baseball profanity), *Major League* picks up; once the hapless team decides to start winning, the movie conveys beautifully the intensity of a team and town caught up in pennant fever. The depressingly empty ball park metamorphoses into a stadium filled to capacity, overflowing with roaring, stomping mass love for the Indians, particularly for the offbeat young parolee pitcher known as Wild Thing.

The close relationship between the city and the team, interestingly, had never been in question. Even when the Indians were losing, residents cared deeply. That all of their baseball conversations concluded with "They stink!" merely confirmed their emotional involvement with the team. The hostility a fan directs toward a losing team is largely self-directed; such feelings gnaw at, even poison, many fans' deeper feelings about themselves and the place they live. So when the club starts winning, the outpouring of emotion has a joy to it that we rarely see in civic affairs.

People's relationships to sports teams are powerful, complicated, and revealing. Even a movie like *Major League* draws on significant cultural currents during its thin hour and three-quarters. One of these is the sense of place. From Cleveland the perpetual loser, the industrial dinosaur dying on its feet, to the Cleveland of winners and full stadiums and new heroes—this is a transformation to which audiences respond. Sports may be the most powerful setting Americans have had in the twentieth century for expressing their relationship to place. They are also central to the way we define and experience the public world. For the past hundred years, more people have gathered in large numbers on a regular basis to watch sporting events than for any other reason. The closest competitors—religious revivals, rock concerts, plays, movies, and political rallies—are either substantially smaller in attendance, much less frequent, or irregular. Because most sports—even children's games of Little League baseball—invite spectatorship, they are not purely private matters but part of the public realm.

For better than a century, people have more or less accepted the view that a sports team can "represent" a neighborhood, town, or city. In the case of the first baseball teams, in the 1850s and early 1860s, this notion had some validity. Most baseball clubs drew members from particular urban neighborhoods, workplaces, or volunteer fire companies. The Brooklyn Eckfords, for example, one of the powerhouses of the New York baseball world in the 1850s and '60s, were based in the Henry Eckford shipyards. The New York Mutuals, similarly, were named for, and drew members from, the Mutual Hook and Ladder Company No. 1 in New York City.

By the later 1860s, however, the better baseball players moved around from club to club—or "revolved," as the press dubbed the practice—in search of better teams or more congenial colleagues or better pay. By the time the all-professional Cincinnati Red Stockings began their famous undefeated season in 1869, baseball fans had already made the adjustment to rooting for players who wore the home-team uniform but who were not in fact from the neighborhood, shop, or even city. On that Red Stocking team, the majority of the players had come from northeastern clubs (captain Harry Wright himself and his younger brother George had been fixtures of the New York sporting scene for years), a circumstance that accounted for the national (which is to say New York) press attention they received. At the same time, these outstanding and successful ballplayers accustomed the sporting public to the generally harmless notion that professional athletes could "represent" a city to which they had no other connection.

There are times, of course, when fans and owners tire of maintaining the fiction, but they usually wait until the team starts to lose games or money, as the Cincinnati Red Stockings did in 1870. Then—and only then—did the club directors discover the evil of what was called "importing" ballplayers from far away to represent the home club. As long as the club was winning or drawing spectators, the importation of first-rate athletes served club purposes admirably. Losing, or, in the Red Stockings' case, merely joining the ranks of mortals who lose now and then, broke the spell of Harry Wright's magic, and the club directors abandoned the professional arena. They needed an excuse, however, and they used what modern fans will recognize as timeworn ones: the players were dissipated (something their manager, Harry Wright, would never have tolerated) and insubordinate. Worse, the athletes kept insisting on higher pay, proof, the owners said, that they were not particularly loyal to the home team, that they would play, which is to say work, for whoever offered the highest salary. The Cincinnati directors anticipated the laments of club owners and directors for the next century and more. The Red Stocking players, though, had the greater impact, because they demonstrated just how good a professional, imported team could be. Henceforth cities that wanted a winning club knew how to get one.

What of the fans in this process? How did followers of a local team respond when they were asked to identify with their hometown "representatives"? Generally, fans made an uneasy accommodation to what had become the realities of professional sports in the late 1800s. After all, few nineteenth-century Americans lived their entire lives in one town, especially in the larger cities, many of which were just becoming big enough toward the end of the century to support a professional sports franchise. How could recent arrivals to Fort Wayne, say, or Buffalo or Chicago worry very much about the birthplace of ballplayers when many—if not most—fans had themselves been born elsewhere, even in foreign countries? It is sometimes overlooked that the sense of place in American cities simply cannot have been terribly strong for most of their residents in the late nineteenth and early twentieth centuries. As early as 1855, more than half New York City's population was foreign-born. Chicago's million-plus residents in 1890 were more than 80 percent foreign-born or born in the United States of foreign parentage. Forty years earlier the town had been a commercial crossroads numbering barely 30,000 souls. If ballplayers came from halfway across the continent, some of their fans hailed from halfway around the world.

Though fans complained about players being too mercenary, or not having strong feelings for their clubs, they were nearly always expressing dissatisfaction with the players' or team's performance. The language of "disloyalty" was handy. Few fans ever objected to gaining a talented player from another team. The issue was whether the import would live up to expectations, or, doing well, abandon his new "home" in a season or two.

What is fascinating about baseball's rise to sporting preeminence in the late nineteenth century is that a game which so idealized the notion of home should have become the favorite sport of a country in which most people had only transitory homes. Could it be that the game appealed simultaneously to immigrants, migrants, and settled native-born Americans precisely because it incorporated such a powerful emotional center —home teams, home plates, home runs—for its spectators?

Ronald Story has suggested that baseball became popular among young men of the late nineteenth century because it provided a more attractive family life—at once individualistic and collective, allowing physical and emotional release—than the actual family experience available to young men living in urban tenements. Carrying this loyalty into adulthood, these grown-up youths became the well-known "cranks" and fanatics, "fans," of the nineties and early twentieth century.

The fact that these young men organized an elaborate structure of play around a highly specific "home base" shows just how much they needed such a concept in their daily lives as well, one to which they returned for their entire lifetimes. Warren Goldstein has argued, in *Playing for Keeps*, that baseball's popularity in the late nineteenth century was partly due to the play of the game itself, which incorporated notions of home and away, visitors and the home team, us and them, in the midst of exceptionally frequent and necessarily disorienting geographical mobility. Playing and watching baseball became participation in, and perhaps metaphorical control over, the process of incessant migration and physical movement during these years. After all, on the baseball field, all movement ultimately circled the familiar diamond; it invariably began in the identical place, to which it regularly returned: home plate. Baseball's anthem, "Take Me Out to the Ball Game," plays with the same set of ideas.

> *Take me out to the ball game,*
> *Take me out with the crowd.*

> *Buy me some peanuts and cracker-jack;*
> *I don't care if I never get back.*
> *Let me root, root, root for the home team;*
> *If they don't win it's a shame.*
> *For it's one! two! three! strikes you're out,*
> *At the old ball game.*

The identification of a "home team" moves the private conception of a home, as in the Victorian family circle, for instance, into the public realm. Sporting language may have been one bridge by which Americans connected their family lives to the larger social world, and to a publicly proclaimed sense of place. A relationship to a home team connected millions of uprooted Americans to a sentimental language and cluster of values and feelings for which they hungered.

Though many Jewish immigrant parents frowned on their sons' baseball playing, Abraham Cahan, editor of the *Jewish Daily Forward*, advised a father, "Let your boy play baseball, and become excellent in playing the game." Cahan appreciated the game's contribution to health, but he also had another aim in mind: "Mainly," he wrote, "let us not raise the children that they should grow up foreigners in their own birthplace."

Sports Heroes and Mass Culture

The 1920s saw a redefinition of the public sphere in America. The sudden flowering of mass culture gave new prominence to a wide range of heroes, from Charles Lindbergh to Babe Ruth, Rudolph Valentino, and Mary Pickford. Increasingly, the public world came to be populated by celebrities with national reputations and appeal. Sports both contributed to these changes and felt their effects.

The relationship between sports fans and their heroes has always had significance far beyond the realm of athletics. Particularly in matters of class, race, and gender, these relationships have had tremendous political and cultural import. Jack Johnson and Joe Louis, Jackie Robinson and Muhammad Ali were tremendous folk heroes to African Americans. So were Joe DiMaggio and Rocky Marciano to Italian Americans; Hank Greenberg and Sandy Koufax to American Jews; Mildred "Babe" Didrikson and Billie Jean King to American women. But what has it meant to have folk heroes, or role models (to use the modern term)? More precisely, how have heroes influenced the way ordinary people perceive and experience the public sphere?

Popular icons became a new, powerful force in the early twentieth century. The nineteenth century had its sporting heroes, of course, and John L. Sullivan was probably the greatest of them all. But without the mass media—the metropolitan press, movies, and radio—of the early twentieth century, the reach of these men was limited. Social theorists worried that the growth of American society around the turn of the twentieth century had created a mass society in which few ordinary citizens could rise to greatness. In fact, Herbert Croly, in *The Promise of American Life* (1909), and Walter Lippmann, in *Public Opinion* (1922), were both convinced that ordinary individuals were losing their identity in the mass of humanity crowding into American cities. They despaired of the democratic potential of ordinary citizens and argued for the redemptive power of those individuals who were transformed into larger-than-life heroes by the machinery of mass culture. Croly thought that his good friend Theodore Roosevelt was the archetype of the new hero for mass society, a figure through whom masses of people could imaginatively live out a life that had not been bureaucratized, standardized, and diminished by the sheer size and power of the modern industrial state.

And in fact, the new professions of advertising and public relations that flourished in the 1920s mastered the techniques of selling particular products by connecting them with virile or glamorous or successful celebrities. Through market research, citizens were labeled by demographic profiles; individuals were reduced to their buying habits. The public's fascination with fame and glamour enabled celebrities to command higher fees for lending their names and faces on behalf of products. In the teens and twenties, as American society turned from an economy and culture centered on production to one grounded in consumption, its heroes changed as well. Not only did Americans come to know what products movie stars and boxers, socialites and football players were alleged to use; those heroes helped mold the taste of their fans.

Leo Lowenthal's famous study of popular biographies captures this development. Early in the century, the subjects of magazine biographies—scientists, artists and writers, business leaders—had all achieved prominence (and had frequently overcome adversity) through hard work, persistence, skill, or courage. Lowenthal called them "idols of production." Forty years later, popular heroes had become famous less by what they had achieved than by something happening to them, by the society accidentally singling them out. Since there was nothing readers could do to imitate these figures, Lowenthal argued, "there is no road left . . . for an attempt to emulate their success." Recognizing this vacuum, the biographers filled it with information about the celebrities' consumption habits, which ordinary mortals could imitate, at least in part.

In the world of sports, we can see the cultural shift implied in the turn toward consumption by looking at the two greatest baseball players in the history of the game: Ty Cobb and Babe Ruth. Tyrus Raymond Cobb's extraordinary career spanned nearly a quarter century (1905–28), during which time he set records that stood for more than fifty years; only recently have some been challenged and broken. Cobb still holds the record for the highest lifetime batting average (.367) and runs scored (2,245). Although they stand no longer, for more than a half century his career hits (4,191) topped the all-time list, while his stolen base total (892) ranked highest in the modern era. As a player, Cobb thought, calculated, and maneuvered his way around the base paths. The greatest hitter of the dead-ball era, Cobb mastered what at the time was called scientific baseball. Before the home run became so important, baseball offense relied on place hitting, sacrifices, and speed on the base paths, what Bill James has called long-sequence offense. It could take three successful at-bats—walk, hit-and-run, and sacrifice fly, for example—to produce one run. Cobb was a master of all of these tactics. He was known and feared even more, perhaps, for his manner, for his nasty, mean-spirited, bullying, vicious demeanor on and off the field. A notorious brawler with a hair-trigger sense of "honor," Cobb practiced a belligerent, at times physically brutal style of play.

Cobb's personality and baseball-playing style demonstrated a baseball version of the culture of production. Acquisitive, calculating, aggressive, he made the most of his lean build and terrific speed and took instant advantage of every opportunity. Cobb got what he wanted: the intimidation of his opponents, respect as a ballplayer, the hatred of his fellows. He was the very model of the loner, the introvert, furious at the world (and perhaps even his game), mastering its rules, slashing at his opponents' mistakes, barreling through their weaknesses. He described baseball as warfare, as a Darwinian "survival of the fittest" to which he brought his remarkable talents. Financially astute as well, Cobb died a millionaire several times over, mainly from having invested in Coca-Cola stock when he was young. There exist few better indications of Cobb's emotional impact on the baseball world than the attendance at his 1961 funeral, which included hundreds of children who knew him only as a past baseball star, and just three adults from organized baseball. Cobb survived the culture in which he flourished, and lived long enough to become a lonely relic of an era long past.

The greatest player in the history of baseball, George Herman Ruth never quite grew up, and was probably more comfortable with the young people he called "the kids" than with anyone else. A player of power rather than calculation, Ruth was that rare "natural" who seemed to have been born with an instinctive knowledge of the game; unlike Cobb, he never appeared to think about strategy, or guard or control his strength. He was the central figure in the transformation of baseball to a game centered on the home run—the sudden explosion of base-clearing force—rather than the one-base-at-a-time "scientific" baseball of Ty Cobb and John McGraw, longtime New York Giants manager. Many of the records he set did not last as long as Cobb's, partly because the style of baseball he championed, far different from Cobb's, was bound to produce challengers to his statistics. Ruth's personality fit the new game and the new era. In fact, he helped create both. Left to his own devices, Ruth spent what he had, in all senses of the term. He consumed prodigiously. As the new advertising industry sought to undermine people's fears of spending too much, to encourage them to buy on credit, and to urge consumers to seek status symbols, it could not have found a better walking billboard. Ruth was huge, with a belly that displayed his penchant for gargantuan eating bouts. It was said that he could gobble up dozens of hot dogs and gulp down quarts of beer at a single sitting. He would throw away silk shirts after wearing them once. His sexual appetite and capacity were deservedly legendary. He frequently forgot people's names as well, including those of his own teammates, and relied on the all-purpose "kid."

Ruth also became the first sports star to be represented by a press agent, Christy Walsh. Walsh, who began by ghost-writing columns for Ruth describing each of his home runs, later built Ruth's persona into a lucrative business. The Babe earned large sums from "writing," but Walsh also engineered profitable vaudeville tours, off-season barnstorming circuits, celebrity appearances, and product endorsements. For fishing equipment and alligator shoes, Packards and Cadillacs, and much, much more, Ruth's image was for sale. Estimates of Ruth's career baseball income range as high as $1.5 million, but he earned about as much outside the game, somewhere between one and two million dollars. While the business created by Walsh and Ruth depended on free-spending consumerism, Walsh was shrewd enough to prevent Ruth from falling victim to it. He got the Bambino to put enough money away to be able to retire in style in 1935.

Babe Ruth was far from the only athletic hero of the 1920s. The twenties, in fact, have become known to cultural historians as the era of heroes. The fighters Jack Dempsey and Gene Tunney, the college and professional football player Harold Edward "Red" Grange, golfer Bobby Jones, and tennis player William T. "Big Bill" Tilden received a degree of publicity and adulation rarely matched before. Nowhere was the new profession and industry of advertising more visible than in the promotion of sporting champions. What we think of as the Age of Heroes, or the Golden Age of American Sport, could be known equally as the Golden Age of American Sports Promoters, since it was in that decade that the boosting and selling of sports became a powerful force.

Boxing may have been the sport most heavily dominated by its promoters. George Lewis "Tex" Rickard, known accurately as the King of Ballyhoo, among other titles, raised the art of packaging sports figures and events to an unprecedented level. He manipulated the careers of boxers to build up phony reputations for them, he played the press as a virtuoso plays the violin, he kept politicians in his corner, and he cultivated New York's elite. Rickard made millions for himself and his fighters, especially heavyweight champion Jack Dempsey, and played a key role in transforming the way Americans perceived and experienced professional sports.

At the same time, Red Grange, a nationally admired running back at the University of Illinois, turned his amateur success into a golden commercial career under the guidance of his agent Charles C. Pyle, known as "Cash and Carry" and "Cold Cash" Pyle. Pyle negotiated Grange's first professional football contract, as well as endorsements, public appearances, barnstorming tours, and a movie contract for his client. Grange's off-field activities —endorsing products, selling chocolate bars, acting in a movie —made him into a "personality." Like Babe Ruth and Jack Dempsey, whose "personalities" had been fashioned by a remarkable publicity machine, and the public's apparently limitless appetite for its novel products, Red Grange cashed in on the new entertainment culture. He also pioneered a new pattern among professional athletes. After his playing days in pro football ended, he enjoyed a successful career as a sportscaster, first on radio and later on television.

Because these new sports celebrities were creations of national publicity, their fame was at odds with the sense of place fostered by sports teams. Consider, for example, the nicknames of the great 1920s heroes. Except for Jack Dempsey, still known as the Manassa Mauler, they made no reference to locale, city, or region: the Fighting Marine (Gene Tunney); the Sultan of Swat,

The great Red Grange, "the Galloping Ghost," carries the ball for the University of Illinois in a game against Michigan. The 1920s have often been called the Golden Age of Sports—and sports heroes—because of unprecedented interest by fans and the media's creation of athlete-celebrities *(Library of Congress)*

the Bambino (*Babe* Ruth); the Iron Horse (Lou Gehrig); the Galloping Ghost (Red Grange); the Brown Bomber (Joe Louis). Ty Cobb, in an earlier era, had been the Georgia Peach, and John L. Sullivan, the Boston Strong Boy.

For publicity to pay off, it needed national scope: only with a nationwide market could an athlete be worth a great deal of money for putting his face next to a bar of soap. The enormous productive machinery called into being by World War I helped increase the capacity of industry and communications to produce and distribute to a national market. After the war, it was the marketing potential of a championship boxing match or college football game that created the nationwide radio hookups necessary to exploit the immense audience effectively. As an example of the new mass nature of sports entertainment, consider the second Dempsey-Tunney matchup at Chicago's Soldier Field in 1927. While more than 104,000 people attended, some 50 million Americans were estimated to have been reached by the seventy-three stations of the NBC radio hookup. Such numbers showed broadcast executives, as never before, the potential of mass marketing through electronic media.

While these national extravaganzas undercut the importance of locale and region on which most people's sense of place depended, it is likely that the nationalism fanned during the war and early postwar years caused increasing numbers of Americans to see their public world in nationwide rather than local terms. The fights Tex Rickard arranged for Dempsey against Frenchman Georges Carpentier (the Orchid Man, Rickard's people named him) and Louis Firpo (the Argentinean known as the Wild Bull of the Pampas) played on this nationalistic sentiment. Boxing may also have gotten a special boost from the war because personalized one-on-one combat easily lent itself to Manichaean visions of good and evil, light versus dark, enlightenment against irrationality, and often enough, white against black.

The twenties ushered in a brave new public world, a more homogenized, consumption-oriented culture. In this emerging mass society, public relations experts and publicity agents, reporters and promoters, hustlers and go-betweens all looked to promote and profit by sports heroes. Paul Gallico's *Farewell to Sport* (1938) describes the bitter departure of a longtime sportswriter from just this world. The shady nonstop hucksterism had finally convinced him that he was no longer covering "sport," that, instead, he was participating in a shoddy entertainment spectacle. For Gallico, top-flight sports had lost their connections to communities, to ordinary fans' loyalties and emotions.

If Gallico's cynicism overstated the case, he was not far off the mark. Increasingly, big-time sports became a whirl of personality and promotion, cash and corruption. F. Scott Fitzgerald recognized this new world and portrayed it beautifully in *The Great Gatsby* (1925). Sport pervades the novel, from Tom Buchanan's football days at Yale to his Long Island polo-playing, to Jordan Baker's golfing and Gatsby's annoying term of endearment, "old sport." Fitzgerald's Jazz Age was organized around duplicity, image manipulation, and fakery. At Gatsby's parties, celebrities merge into one glamorous cacophony: symphony conductors dance and drink alongside Broadway sensations, professional athletes, and film directors. Sports and entertainment have become indistinguishable.

At the heart of *The Great Gatsby* is a tension between different places and what they represent. Adjoining Long Island villages embodied conflicting sensibilities: "West Egg," representing the sound and solid Midwest, was enticed and done in by the "East Egg" mix of greed, power, glamour, and corruption. When the story's narrator, the apprentice bond salesman Nick Carraway, has lunch with Gatsby in New York and meets Meyer Wolfsheim—the epitome of Eastern corruption, the Jewish gambler looking for "gonnegtions," and "the man who fixed the World's Series back in 1919"—Nick is astonished. He muses that it "never occurred to me that one man could start to play with the faith of fifty million people—with the single-mindedness of a burglar blowing a safe." For if sports are one important way we think about public space, then the 1919 Black Sox scandal—in which professional gamblers paid members of the Chicago White Sox to lose to Cincinnati in the World Series—and Nick's odd encounter with the man who put in the fix showed how the public's open, honest, sunlit world could be sabotaged and manipulated from restaurants and hotel rooms. The anguish felt by baseball fans when the scandal was exposed came partly out of the shock that outsiders—criminals—could intervene powerfully and for ill in their relationship with their team, with their game. How did such evil men get here, people wondered; what were they doing here?

The most powerful public response to the crime was to immortalize the apocryphal plea of a little boy to Shoeless Joe

Jackson, one of the accused players: "Say it ain't so, Joe." That the scandal was conceptualized then and is even remembered today as a pleading confrontation between a distraught boy and a child-man, unlettered and unsophisticated, suggests how far we are from being able to think about sports in adult categories. Seventy years after the Black Sox scandal, when Pete Rose's gambling became public knowledge in the late 1980s, newspapers across the country ran headlines pleading "Say It Ain't So, Pete." The little boy continues to speak for sports fans because we still react to such affronts with the hurt feelings of childhood. For it is in childhood that the bond between fans and sports is born and nurtured. By increasing the distance between ordinary fans and the "stars" of the ball park or gridiron, the mass culture of advertising and consumption also invited fans to fantasize more about their favorite players. But increasingly, the machinery of image creation and distribution for national markets undermined the possibility of either group—famous athletes or fans—actually knowing the other. This development helps explain why sports so often appear to take place in public, but in a world none of us recognize as a real place.

Gender and Sport

The history of women's sports in the twentieth century is both a story of struggles over the meaning of public femininity and of women's efforts to obtain a rough equality on the many playing fields of organized sports. Before the end of the nineteenth century, most women felt athletic activity to be irrelevant, if not antithetical, to their concept of their role as women. But even for the first three-quarters of the twentieth century, few observers remarked on or questioned women's lack of participation in most organized sports. So deep had been the assumption that sports were for men—that sports defined masculine identity—that women's absence has often gone unnoticed. True, women were welcome in the social world of sporting exhibitions, a world highly conscious of different roles based on gender. They were prized ornaments in the realm of big-time college athletics, parades, dinners, dances, and attendance at the games. But compared to men, relatively few women were encouraged to play.

When women left the grandstands and stepped onto the playing fields, they did so as their role in American society was being redefined. As we have seen, the 1890s witnessed the emergence of the "new woman" of the middle and upper classes, characterized as much by energetic physical activity as her Victorian mother had been by a languid fragility. As women agitated for the vote and joined temperance societies and municipal reform leagues, they also headed out of doors to their bicycles. But the long dresses of middle-class women interfered with comfortable bicycle riding, which led Amelia Bloomer to invent "bloomers," a kind of baggy pants that made it possible for women to ride and pedal with modesty as well as comfort. Many men and women were aghast when gender boundaries were breached in such powerful, symbolic ways. Crudely put, how could men wear the pants in the family if women were wearing them, too? The "bloomer controversy" simmered all over the United States in the nineties. A telling incident took place in Riverhead, a rural county seat on eastern Long Island. A woman cyclist wearing bloomers pedaled into the village; word spread, a crowd gathered, and she was soon run out of town on her bicycle. How women were allowed to dress in public has much to do with what part of the public sphere they could inhabit.

So women's sports have always been connected to broader developments in feminism and public conceptions of gender roles. Wealthy women generally had the most choice. In the 1880s, for example, women at Vassar and Smith, Mount Holyoke and Wellesley, played, not softball or rounders or some gentler version of the game, but baseball. There is an important parallel here between women's higher education and women's sports. At elite schools, out of the public eye, women could gain an education, value their own minds, and have their intellectual development praised. In such segregated environments, women's mental *and* physical ability flourished.

If sport was common in women's colleges, elsewhere it was considerably less accepted. Most women did not burn to play

College women had taken up baseball and other athletic activity in the 1880s. In the early twentieth century, basketball reigned supreme. Games such as this 1913 contest at Vassar became a common sight at women's colleges *(Library of Congress)*

sports, and if they had begun showing up en masse, their presence would probably have puzzled—even enraged—male and female spectators. Still, exceptions abounded. Women's baseball teams sprang up all over the country, frequently to loud disapproval and intimations of impropriety. Some legitimate teams—the Chicago Stars of 1902, for example, and the St. Louis Stars and Boston Bloomer Girls of 1903—traveled and played male clubs. Others were roving brothels assembled by "promoters" who made money from the very pornographic notoriety so loudly denounced by the guardians of morality. Women ballplayers frequently wore bloomers to play games, which publicly linked the issues of sexuality, dress, and women's sports. According to Harold Seymour, a women's baseball team had been planning to play a game in Freeport, Long Island, and was prevented by an uprising of the town's "respectable" women, who informed their husbands that attending the game would jeopardize their marriages.

Women's baseball teams dotted the United States during the early twentieth century. Their games could draw spectators as well as moralizing disapproval. Note the "bloomers" worn by the "New York Female Giants," July 11, 1913 *(Library of Congress)*

Given prevailing attitudes and obstacles, the fact that some women fought to be accepted within the public world of sport is all the more remarkable. Those few females who entered the male arenas attracted quite a bit of attention from women as well as men. In the late 1890s, Lizzie Stroud (known as Lizzie Arlington) played briefly for the Reading, Pennsylvania, baseball club in the minor Atlantic League. After the turn of the century, Bloomer Girl teams were common; these could include men, frequently wearing wigs, while others were all-female. Some prominent suffragists and female reformers, Charlotte Perkins Gilman and Crystal Eastman among them, were advocates for women's sports and athleticism, and women's teams occasionally put on benefits for women's rights.

The finest woman ballplayer of this period was Alta Weiss of Ragersville, Ohio, whose pitching talent had brought her countywide fame by the time she was fourteen. She pitched successfully on a local semipro team in her late teens, attracting attention throughout northern Ohio. Her father, a doctor and ballplayer, soon built a ball park for the town team, and the following year formed the Weiss All-Stars, a traveling semipro team featuring Alta as pitcher. Weiss was so well known in the Cleveland area that some sportswriters suggested—perhaps not entirely seriously, but in vain nevertheless—that she be given a tryout with the major league Indians. Though she had set her sights on teaching college physical education, and continuing her athletic career in another form, her father persuaded her to join his medical practice instead. Even the finest female athletes soon ran out of places to display their talents, and cultural pressures brought them back to more acceptable behavior. It is interesting that in Alta Weiss's case, her "settling down" was as a doctor; she was the only woman in her medical-school class when she graduated in 1914. Her athletic skill and, we must assume, personal determination, combined with her father's encouragement to pursue unconventional paths, had effects beyond the confines of the ball park. For most working-class girls and women around the turn of the century, however, even those inclined toward athletics, public criticism and ridicule exacted too high a price, and they turned away from sports.

Following World War I, many American businesses sought to blunt labor conflict by combining active hostility to unions with efforts to provide recreational activities for their employees. As a result, women's baseball gained more sponsors than ever before, as local industrial teams and leagues dotted the United States. Harold Seymour uncovered a good deal of evidence that girls and women could receive some instruction and practice in baseball, gymnastics, and other sports throughout the 1920s and 1930s. Private girls' schools, not surprisingly, led in these developments, but a field day in 1925 at a public high school in Paterson, New Jersey, featured girls' baseball, photos of which appeared in *The New York Times*. And there were women's college baseball clubs into the 1930s, as well as the occasional barnstorming team.

Despite substantial competition from basketball and softball, women's baseball refused to die out until the 1950s. As is now well known, thanks to the popular movie *A League of Their Own*, the All-American Girls Professional Baseball League provided for an eleven-year period (1943–54) the most significant opportunity in modern sports history for women to play organized professional baseball. But the trend has been away from baseball and toward softball since the 1930s. In fact, *Time* estimated in 1935 that some 2 million Americans were playing the newer game, on sixty thousand organized teams. Philip K. Wrigley, owner of the minor league Angels in Los Angeles (and later founder of the All-American Girls Professional Baseball League), discovered that within a hundred-mile radius of his stadium there were some nine thousand softball teams, a thousand of which were all-female. The real "leagues of their own" existed in softball throughout the United States, but with important differences: players were not paid, and the publicity for the games remained overwhelmingly local.

In the 1920s and 1930s, as women athletic heroes burst into the public arena, it was the stars of individual, non-contact sports that rose to prominence: Babe Didrikson in golf and track and field, Gertrude Ederle in swimming, Suzanne Lenglen in tennis. It is true, of course, that the publicity machine preferred individuals, so promoters and advertisers could concentrate on the personal: looks, biography, love life, banquet appearances, makeup preferences, and the heroic story of one person's struggle for victory. The need of a mass society for detailed portraits of outstanding individuals helped create within modern sports a heavy emphasis on personal achievement.

But perhaps, too, the worlds of sports and of public relations —both overwhelmingly controlled by men—preferred individual women to women in groups. If female sports heroes raised uncomfortable questions about the role and abilities of women, the reach of these questions was limited by the ease with which individual examples could be explained away. In *The Great Gatsby*, F. Scott Fitzgerald even felt the need to make his character Jordan Baker, a professional golfer and "new woman" of the twenties, into a cheat. Baker's "boyish" figure, androgynous name, and doubtful morals suggest Fitzgerald's discomfort with

The new look for women in the 1920s—slender and athletic—is captured in this 1928 photo of a "tennis girl" *(Library of Congress)*

the crossing of gender boundaries, and with the newer roles for women.

Without diminishing the extraordinary athletic achievements of Babe Didrikson (who received her nickname from the many home runs she hit as a baseball player), it is important to note that her accomplishments had a limited effect on how men and women perceived women's overall athletic potential. Despite her national, world, and Olympic records in a range of events, her amateur women's championship basketball team, her exceptional skill as a golfer, and her all-around athletic excellence, Didrikson's career did not open doors wide for other women athletes. Too few women or men were encouraged by the dramatic revision of gender roles suggested by Didrikson's mannish appearance and decidedly unladylike manners. Paul Gallico called her a "muscle moll."

If they have been more easily assimilated by public relations and public culture, single women athletes have also been viewed as threatening. Questions raised about an unmarried female athlete have nearly all been concerned with sexuality. Unmarried male athletic heroes were (and are) understood to spend a good portion of their leisure time consorting and cavorting with beautiful members of the opposite sex; sporting culture thrives on legends of male athletes' sexual exploits. The double standard has made such behavior from a woman an invitation to scandal. By their very existence, female athletes pose questions of sexuality. Through their intense experience in the world of the body, they demonstrate a public involvement with their own physiques that still scandalizes a broader sexual culture which, if superficially libertine, is in fact built around prudery and repression, especially for women.

So the sporting world, including, of course, fans and reporters, breathes more easily when women athletes marry, or come on the scene already married. The romance and engagement of the professional tennis players Jimmy Connors and Chris Evert in the 1970s received enormous press attention. The eagerness with which the pairing was celebrated revealed the public desire for "Chrissie" to be connected. Connors's pugnacious style and boorish behavior may have cried out for domestication, but his marital status attracted much less attention than Evert's. In the 1980s, Martina Navratilova could live relatively openly as a lesbian, even in the limelight of top-flight tennis, at least partly because of her longtime companionship with Judy Nelson. Her "domesticity" helped neutralize what would otherwise have been an excuse for critical public treatment.

In the last generation, women, in their struggle to gain equality in the sporting world, have not only contended with cultural prejudice but also grappled directly with sexual discrimination in education and employment. Their political high-water mark was reached in 1972, with passage of the innocuous-sounding

Title IX of the federal Education Amendments. Title IX holds that

> no person in the United States shall, on the basis of sex, be excluded from participation in, be denied the benefits of, or be subjected to discrimination under any education program or activity receiving federal financial assistance.

The most far-reaching federal regulation having to do with women's sports, Title IX provided the legal basis for a structural change in girls' and women's physical education and athletics at all educational levels, from elementary grades through colleges and universities. Although efforts to implement Title IX have been the subject of interpretive battles, political conflict, and litigation, by now we can chart some of the tremendous effects this regulation has had on male and female athletic experience and education.

Most significantly, Title IX established in law the understanding that girls and boys in schools have the same rights to athletic facilities and programs, coaches and instructors, uniforms and transportation. Even though few schools have genuinely equivalent programs (there is still no female counterpart to football as the premier high-school and college sport), the principle now exists. Doubtless this state of affairs can be considered a glass half-full or half-empty; both perspectives have force and validity. On the one hand, a mechanism for change exists; on the other, if full gender equality in school sports is the goal, it remains very far away. The achievement is perhaps best measured in the contrasting experience of women in the field before Title IX, and of those after. They barely speak the same language, and older women are bemused at the number of things taken for granted —basketball court time, pool time, coaches' salaries, locker-room facilities, the assumption of legitimate female competition—by their younger sisters.

Ironically, the equalization of school coaching salaries has meant that many more men coach women's and girls' sports than ever before. So as women's and girls' athletics have moved more into the public sphere, with the rewards that accompany public life, men have capitalized on this development, both for themselves and for their charges. As coaches, men have been less content to allow women to practice on distant fields or with inferior equipment. Indeed, coaching girls' sports has changed the consciousness of some men who would not ordinarily think twice about issues of women's rights or equity. (The film *A League of Their Own* captures a similar development as the manager played by Tom Hanks is transformed from a misogynist boor to a fierce champion of his female ballplayers.) So if by identifying with females, male coaches have become feminists of a sort, women's athletics are now less controlled by women than they used to be. The contradictory movement is that as women have moved into the public sphere, they have lost some control over an activity that—though always within the constraints of segregation—they used to shape and direct themselves. Perhaps most important of all, and representing the real and symbolic power of male sports on nearly every coeducational campus, football and, to a lesser extent, men's basketball reign supreme.

There are more ironies. Over the past century, women have been both invited into and barred from sports stadiums. Wives, mothers, and sweethearts cheered on boats in intercollegiate regattas in the early nineteenth century, and Southern women attended the gentry's horse races as a matter of course. The carriages of upper- and middle-class men and women adorn all mid-nineteenth-century baseball and cricket illustrations. Early baseball players earnestly sought the patronage and approval of women for their fledgling sport. Women's attendance at ball games served to legitimate the sport in the eyes both of the ballplayers and of the larger culture. Just as women were supposed to preside over the emotionally calm and nurturant domestic hearth in middle-class Victorian homes, they were encouraged to bring their domesticating influence to bear on the occasionally raucous scene on the ball field. Reporters went to great lengths to mention women's attendance at games, and players' off-season activities—soirees, balls, outings—frequently included "the fair sex." Ladies' Days date from the years just following the Civil War, and clubs sometimes built special grandstands to attract more of their members' sisters, wives, mothers, and sweethearts. Later in the nineteenth century, the National League labored to make the stands more hospitable for women and families by banning swearing from its parks (it had previously banned the sale of alcohol). That the effort failed is not surprising; that it was made indicates the extent of the desire to have women in the stands.

Yet when they step out of circumscribed roles—cheerleaders at a football game, "bimbos" at a prizefight, household guardians of family values at baseball games—hostility toward women in sports surfaces easily. And when girls or women attempt to play Little League baseball, or high-school football, or to wrestle, or to play on a boys' basketball team, or to officiate in male contests, the level of male opposition often rises to a shrill pitch. It has taken twenty years of lawsuits for most Little Leagues to be integrated by gender. Most other young people's sports (with the important exception of soccer) remain gender-segregated.

The other major public achievement of women's sports in the twentieth century has been realized through the efforts of the successors of the 1920s and '30s heroines. Women's tennis, golf, track and field, and gymnastics now receive sizable purses and headline coverage in daily newspapers and on television. Such developments are due not only to the outstanding female athletes of the past twenty-five years but to the political and public relations savvy of one particular star, Billie Jean King. King shone both on the tennis court and as an organizer of women athletes. She put together the first successful women's professional tennis circuit in 1971 and negotiated better deals for women players in the biggest tournaments. She accepted the limelight with skill and humor and enlarged the circle of publicity for women's tennis. With King's outspoken feminism, the women's movement of the 1970s joined the struggle for girls' and women's rights on the playing fields of organized sports. The combination helped produce a near revolution in professional women's sports, one important measure of which was the degree to which female athletes now inhabit the fully public—if not entirely integrated—world.

One of the odder modern battles over gender and sports has

taken place off the playing field. As women sportswriters have sought and received access to male locker rooms, a minority of sportswriters, owners, and athletes have reacted as though the last bastion of all-male sports culture had fallen to prying women. Then–Commissioner of Baseball Bowie Kuhn argued in 1978 that "to permit members of the opposite sex into this place of privacy, where players, who are, of course, men, are in a state of undress, would be to undermine the basic dignity of the game." But locker rooms have been public spaces, workplaces, really, for male sportswriters for more than a century. Women felt that they needed access in order to do their jobs. Realities collided. As women sportswriters took on the interpretation of male sports for a predominantly male audience in the late 1970s, they laid claim to a piece of the public sphere that few men had considered up for grabs.

Over the course of the twentieth century, sports have continued to define masculine gender identity. Sports metaphors abound in politics and business, as men discuss their "game plans," or their ability to "take hits," or complain about "Monday-morning quarterbacking." For all classes of men, work has become more routinized, more bureaucratized, more integrated into immense impersonal systems of production and exchange.

Sports offer participants and spectators understandable, satisfying experiences that still engender feelings of competence, excitement, tension, emotional commitment, beauty, and joy. Along with the ceremonies and conduct of war, sports in the public arena are the only place in which men are expected or permitted to express vulnerable emotions. The popularity of Robert Bly's *Iron John* and other men's-movement books and workshops suggests that many American men are deeply dissatisfied with the emotional aridity of their everyday lives. Since being an avid sports fan can provide both emotional release and connection—what Roger Angell has called the experience of "caring—caring deeply and passionately, really *caring*"—it is at least understandable that men would hold on to their exclusive sporting world with a powerful grip.

The irony, of course, is that sports encourage the very machismo that makes the expression of emotions so difficult for men. But whether as sites of emotional brotherhood or stoical manliness, twentieth-century sports have been arenas of male privilege that men have relinquished to women only partially and grudgingly.

Racial Integration

Because sports usually attract audiences, attitudes toward them have always been mingled with notions of proper public behavior, of how communities and complex societies ought to identify and present their public faces. We have seen how the propriety, even legality, of sports was a subject of controversy between Puritans and Anglicans in seventeenth-century England. Prizefights were illegal through most of the nineteenth century, while moral reformers condemned as idle and profligate everything from horse racing to ice skating. During the twentieth century, settlement-house workers sought to remove children's play from the loosely defined but nevertheless very public realm of the street into enclosed playgrounds where it could be supervised, managed, and organized into discrete units, specific games, healthful exercise.

Throughout the late nineteenth and early twentieth centuries, proponents of middle-class Protestant recreational morality battled with immigrant groups, most of whom still shared the "Continental Sabbath"—derived from Catholic, European peasant cultures that tolerated drinking and rough play. In America, baseball became embroiled in this conflict. The frequently boisterous and drunken behavior of early baseball spectators, as we have seen, led entrepreneurs to close off ball grounds for big matches and charge admission fees that commentators hoped would exceed the reach of the poorer and rowdier fans.

Later in the century, the National League barred alcohol from its parks, charged a much higher admission (fifty cents) than the rival American Association (twenty-five cents), and observed the Protestant Sabbath by not scheduling games on Sunday. Long after the American Association had dropped its claim to major league status and the National and American Leagues ruled the pinnacle of organized baseball, Sunday games remained a controversial issue in American cities. Not until the 1930s was Sunday ball finally established beyond controversy.

Attention to public space helps us understand the history of racial segregation and integration in sports. African Americans played sports from the beginning of American history—from the time of slavery. Occasional black stars emerged from obscurity. The boxer Tom Molineaux, for example, achieved all of his brief early-nineteenth-century boxing fame in Britain and remained relatively unknown in his native country, even though he almost won the championship of England. African Americans did found early baseball clubs in the mid-nineteenth century, called "colored clubs" by the press. They played both among themselves and, at least occasionally, against white teams. There may also have been some integrated clubs, although the evidence is unclear. Nothing in the baseball literature prior to the Civil War suggests any attempt to exclude blacks or to segregate the baseball fraternity.

Things changed in October of 1867, when the African-American Pythian Base Ball Club of Philadelphia was denied admission to the Pennsylvania Association of Base Ball Players at its state convention. Despite what the Pythians' delegate described as the personal "courtesy and kindness" of individual delegates, he was powerless to affect the outcome. Then in December of the same year, at the convention of the mushrooming National Association of Base Ball Players, the color bar became explicit; the Nominating Committee's report to the convention included the following:

> It is not presumed by your committee that any club who have applied are composed of persons of color, or any portion of them; and the recommendations of your committee in this report are based upon this view, and they unanimously report against the admission of any club which may be composed of one or more colored persons.

Although the convention accepted the report, these actions (ridiculed as "cowardly" by the *New York Tribune*) did little to stop the growth of black baseball, which appears to have flourished alongside the white game from the late 1860s on. What Ronald Story suggests for baseball as a whole very likely described black baseball as well. For each club or professional player whose name showed up in newspaper box scores, there must have been hundreds, if not thousands, of others, black as well as white, playing the game in a less well organized manner. Newspapers noted black baseball in passing, but gave little space to the games of black clubs, even when they played white ones.

The segregation of professional baseball did not become complete until the end of the century. In the 1880s, according to Jules Tygiel, perhaps two dozen African Americans participated in organized professional baseball, including the brothers Moses and Welday Walker, who played briefly with the American Association Toledo team in 1884. The active and very public racism of future Hall of Fame first baseman and manager Adrian "Cap" Anson helped create a generally hostile climate toward blacks by the end of the eighties, and by 1892, the color bar had become open policy in baseball. It took a few more years before the professional game purged itself of relapses; by 1900, Jim Crow reigned supreme.

Baseball was, in the late nineteenth century, a mass leisure movement, and the exclusion of African-American athletes from the white sporting culture had a serious impact on black culture. It meant being excluded from a public space where equality might be demonstrated. It meant humiliation, and it meant banishment from a key public stage where blacks could see themselves, and be seen, on display, proud and successful.

Even so, African-American ballplayers were well-known figures in black communities across the United States. Negro League baseball, first in the 1920s, but far more in the thirties and forties, became an institution central to African-American life. Opening day, for instance, had as much ritual significance in black baseball as in white. Black newspapers' society pages covered baseball regularly. The Chicago *Defender*'s account of opening day in

Kansas City in 1937 describes a parade of "500 decorated cars, the Lincoln High School Cadets, two fifty-piece bands, a group from the Veterans of Foreign Wars, and the Kansas City Monarchs Booster Club." Celebrities and politicians threw out opening-day balls, and women and girls dressed for the occasion as though it were Easter.

As Donn Rogosin notes astutely in *Invisible Men*, Negro League baseball represented a powerful and complex response to the realities of racial segregation in American life, especially as the Jim Crow laws hardened in the 1890s. It is not only that the great Negro League ballplayers deserve to be rescued by historians from the ghetto to which they were consigned by Organized Baseball; we also need to recognize that Negro League ball challenged racial discrimination in many ways. Black entrepreneurs and ballplayers fought racism constantly as they sought to draw crowds, put together schedules, and locate available ball parks. While their "official" season consisted of playing against the other teams in the Negro Leagues, their baseball experience consistently breached the boundaries of locale, the leagues, and segregation itself. Negro teams barnstormed across the United States, playing local white as well as black teams. They also played against white major leaguers often enough for each group to know the kind of players the others were. When they barnstormed in Canada, black ballplayers momentarily lived free from Jim Crow laws. When they played winter ball in Latin America, they lived in a multiracial environment and played on integrated teams. They knew that segregation was wrong; they experienced integration and saw, firsthand, that it could work—helped make it work; and perhaps most important of all, they knew that they were the athletic equals of white ballplayers. They knew, consequently, that they deserved to be in the white major leagues —and never thought otherwise.

Black audiences supported the Negro Leagues for a variety of reasons, ranging from the quality of play (which was very high, judging from the consistency with which black teams beat major league opponents in exhibitions) to a desire to support such an important showcase for black entrepreneurial and athletic talent. Excluded from the public world inhabited by whites, black communities nevertheless created their own public worlds, in which they could see and delight in their own achievements.

Black audiences thrilled to the exploits of Oscar Charleston, Cool Papa Bell, Josh Gibson, and Satchel Paige; African Americans mourned en masse the passing of Rube Foster, the entrepreneurial genius behind the Negro National League; blacks referred to the great Pittsburgh Crawfords as the "Yankees of Negro baseball." But in 1946 and 1947, Jackie Robinson became the first black man in organized (white) baseball in the twentieth century, and quickly everything changed. One of the most dramatic and powerful episodes in twentieth-century cultural history, the Jackie Robinson saga had an immense impact on the shape of modern sports, on the development of modern race relations, and on the way Americans consider, occupy, and conceptualize public space.

The story has been told many times, most thoroughly by Jules Tygiel in *Baseball's Great Experiment*. It represents the intersection of such large-scale historical forces as the "great migration" of African Americans from the rural South to the cities of the North, and the conflagration of World War II, with the aspirations of two extraordinary individuals, Jack Roosevelt Robinson and Branch Rickey. For years, black sportswriters had waged a dogged campaign to get white teams to offer tryouts to black players. No one paid attention before Brooklyn Dodger general manager Branch Rickey. One of the most farsighted organizers and shrewdest businessmen in American sports history, Rickey had already guaranteed his future fame by inventing the farm system, the tying of minor league teams to a major league parent club, designed to provide talent for the major league clubs. But by 1945, this stogie-chomping showman and occasional Methodist moralist had decided to break baseball's clear but unwritten Jim Crow code. Doubtless affected by the times as well as his personal convictions (black Americans had poured into National League cities during and after World War II; African-American soldiers had distinguished themselves during the war), Rickey also hoped to reap a bonanza at the box office.

He undertook a nationwide search for the "right" pioneer and chose Robinson, an army veteran and former four-sport All-American at UCLA, where he may have been the best college athlete in the country. A visceral opponent of racial prejudice, Robinson had been court-martialed—and acquitted—for challenging an illegally segregated army bus at Fort Hood, and was now playing baseball with the Negro League Kansas City Monarchs. Robinson agreed to be Rickey's candidate, and Rickey exacted a promise from Robinson not to respond to the provocations they both expected. As the story goes, Rickey, in a test, leveled a series of increasingly offensive racial insults and taunts at Robinson, to the point that Robinson shot back, "Mr. Rickey, do you want a ballplayer who's afraid to fight back?" At that point Rickey is reported to have answered, "I want a player with guts enough not to fight back!" Robinson played the 1946 season with the Dodgers' Montreal AAA farm club, burning up the International League, and then came up to the parent club in 1947.

Jackie Robinson honored his agreement with Rickey and for two seasons refused to respond to torrents of vilification, to repeated provocation on the field and off. The sports world has probably never seen such an example of turning the other cheek, even more impressive because Robinson had a fierce temper, a hard-driving playing style, and an extremely combative personality. Branch Rickey, who understood the primacy of public relations in conducting public entertainment, attempted to manage not only Robinson's entry into baseball but the perceptions of that entrance as well. He did better with the former than the latter, but not for lack of trying. Even he had a hard time predicting the effects of his daring.

Rickey went to black leaders and asked for their public restraint. Before the 1947 season, Rickey addressed a black middle-class audience in Brooklyn and warned them, in terms that today seem patronizing and racist, not to "spoil Jackie's chances." Rickey argued that "the biggest threat to his success—is the Negro people themselves." He told these leaders that every one of you will go out and form parades and welcoming committees. You'll strut. You'll wear badges, You'll hold Jackie Robinson Days . . . and Jackie Robinson nights. You'll get drunk. You'll fight. You'll be arrested. You'll wine and dine the player until he is fat and futile. You'll symbolize his importance into a national comedy . . . and an ultimate tragedy.

Rickey's listeners applauded and promptly organized a master committee to spread far and wide the slogan "Don't Spoil Jackie's Chances!" The black press tried to cooperate, as in this typical warning from the Chicago *Defender*: "Let's not make him a race problem; he's just a ballplayer."

African Americans' own battle to integrate baseball was a double-edged effort to control public space: to establish their right to it in the person of Jackie Robinson, and to make sure that Robinson's tenure in the spotlight was not spoiled by "unrespectable" behavior—despite the hostility of the white world. Three-quarters of a century after early baseball promoters struggled to clean up ball parks and suppress rowdy behavior, black fans and community leaders fought a similar battle, with far more success. The black presence at ball parks, so uniformly remarked upon as respectful and self-controlled, helped legitimate the "experiment."

In the midst of such self-control, however, there was an excitement around Robinson the pioneer and Robinson the ballplayer that is hard to recapture. African Americans simply flocked to watch Robinson play baseball, first in the International League and then with the Dodgers. Because of the way baseball focuses attention on a single player at a time, Robinson probably had a greater impact on racial perceptions—white and black—than if he had played any other sport. Watching Robinson on the field turns out to have been one of the most important experiences of the twentieth century for black Americans. (There is some evidence that it was nearly as important for white Americans as well.) The African-American press covered Robinson and the Dodgers to an extraordinary extent, and in city after city, ticket

Jackie Robinson's greatest impact was on African Americans. Here a young black child reads the latest issue of *Negro Heroes* with the cover story "Jackie Robinson: Rookie of the Year" *(Library of Congress)*

offices were overwhelmed with black patrons. Black baseball fans in Kansas City, home of the Monarchs, a first-rate Negro League team for which Robinson had played, chartered buses to travel six or seven hours across the state to St. Louis to watch Robinson perform when the Dodgers came to town. A "Jackie Robinson special" train ran all the way from Norfolk, Virginia, to Cincinnati, stopping to pick up fans along the way. A white Dodger fan recalls visiting relatives in St. Louis in the late 1940s, and going to the ball park to see the Brooklyn club. As Dodger fans stood up for their team at the top of the seventh inning, she remembers seeing only African Americans among the standees —a thousand miles from Brooklyn.

Jackie Robinson's greatest impact was on the lives and aspirations of African Americans, standing, as we know now, on the threshold of the civil rights movement. During his first year with the Dodgers, Robinson received a letter written on the stationery of the Eaton Hotel in Wichita, Kansas:

> Mr. Robison
> Saw you play in Wichita in [?] An also in St. Louis about 30 ds ago. An decided I wanted to name my expected child for the first Negro in League Baseball. An above that a good sport an Gentleman something our race needs as bad as they do a square deal. Littl Jackie Lee was born the 8-15-47 2 pm. A girl at St. Francis Hospital.
>
> Yours for many years,
Big League Baseball.
An, Fine, Fine, Sportmanship
>
> T.S. WASHINGTON.
> Bell boy at Eaton Hotel.

No longer would African-American baseball fans have to cheer their heroes in separate ball parks, unnoticed by the white press. Robinson and Rickey integrated not only baseball but the public space of American sports. Not that prejudice or discrimination ever disappeared. Leaders of the sports world, including team owners, maintained an elaborate series of defenses against racial equality. But the precedent had been set.

Whites feared that black athletes, if not rigorously limited, would outshine whites. And given the rush of African Americans into professional sports since World War II, those fears were not unfounded. Between 1947, when Jackie Robinson exploded into the National League, and 1959, black ballplayers made up a minuscule percentage of the league's players, but nevertheless won nine of the NL's thirteen Most Valuable Player awards (Roy Campanella three times, Ernie Banks twice); in that same period, they garnered an equal number of Rookie of the Year awards. (There is a structural parallel here between black achievements in the 1940s and 1950s and players' salaries following the onset of free agency in the mid-1970s. In both cases, what had been artificially held back for generations surged forward to astonishing levels.)

When blacks were accepted in white leagues, they received substandard equipment, play, and facilities, and their numbers were limited. It is sometimes forgotten that it took twelve years after Robinson's debut with the Dodgers before the Boston Red Sox finally ended their status as the last all-white major league club. When numerical limits more or less disappeared in the 1970s, African Americans were largely kept out of positions requiring the most understanding of their games: quarterback, catcher, and pitcher. Even today, as black talent spreads more evenly through all sports leagues, black salaries below the superstar level range below those of statistically comparable white players. African-American athletes still need better statistics than whites to be retained by their teams, and relatively few blacks hold positions as managers or top front-office officials. There are no African-American owners of major league sports franchises.

Theorists and pundits have spent much energy wondering whether sports "mirror" or "represent" fundamental aspects of American society. The search for an adequate model for understanding sports has also consumed whole fields in academic sports studies. Even a brief look at the history of race and sports, however, shows how closely linked sports are to the rest of American culture, society, and politics. For if the Jackie Robinson saga was a sports-world version of the early stage of the civil rights movement—restrained, self-sacrificing, aiming for justice and reconciliation, idealizing integration—the story of Muhammad Ali is just as powerfully rooted in the Black Power and black separatist movements of the late 1960s and early 1970s.

The African-American boxer who first came to public attention as Cassius Marcellus Clay in 1959 and 1960, and who transformed himself into Muhammad Ali, possibly the best-known human being in the world a decade later, carried the emotional and political burden of this dramatic change. While Jackie Robinson stumped for Richard Nixon in the 1968 Presidential election, militant black athletes boycotted the premier track-and-field event in the country, chanting "Muhammad Ali is our champ."

Cassius Clay won Golden Glove and Olympic championships in 1959 and 1960, but he appeared to be little more than a fine boxer. As he approached the heavyweight championship in the next four years, however, he began to flout conventions of the sports world. His style in the ring combined speed, agility, and exceptional energy—"float like a butterfly, sting like a bee," as he characterized it. But Clay also had a fine quick wit, the ability to predict the round in which he would knock out his opponents, and an unabashed talent for outrageous self-promotion. "I am the greatest," he declared *before* defeating Sonny Liston for the heavyweight championship of the world in 1964. By the end of the 1970s, few fans disputed that he was indeed the greatest.

Since the days of Jack Johnson at the turn of the century, the white world had not seen a black hero who cared so little for the niceties of white opinion, who seemed so determined not to "know his place." When, in 1964, the new champion announced his membership in the Nation of Islam and took the name of Muhammad Ali (spurning his "slave name"), he ignited a firestorm of criticism. Black Muslims, as the Nation of Islam was known to whites, preached black superiority and separatism, ridiculed integration and Christianity, and terrified whites, who felt theirs was a radical and violent hate group.

Later in the decade, Ali refused induction into the Army on religious grounds—all members of the Nation of Islam considered themselves ministers of the faith. But Ali had also become famous for saying, "I ain't got nothing against the Vietnamese," and for noting that "no Viet Cong ever called me nigger." The boxing establishment retaliated swiftly, taking away his titles, suspending him from the ring, destroying, without due process of law, his livelihood. Worried about such a high-profile resister, the U.S. government prosecuted Ali as a draft evader.

But precisely because Ali thumbed his nose at the white establishment, he represented, for black Americans in revolt, a powerful public example of black pride, skill, and masculine

The black heavyweight champion Jack Johnson, who held the title from 1908 to 1915, thumbed his nose at white opponents and social conventions. Admired by African Americans, he was pursued on morals charges by the federal government. In a secret deal, Johnson allegedly lost intentionally his title fight with Jess Willard in Cuba in 1915. In exchange, federal charges were dropped against Johnson and he was permitted to reenter America. Having been knocked "unconscious," Johnson shields his eyes from the Cuban sun *(Library of Congress)*

beauty. Ali embodied defiance in the face of massive white pressure. He became a symbol of opposition to the Vietnam War, and of the distance America still had to travel before racial equality became a reality. And he inspired other black athletes in a revolt that culminated when Tommie Smith and John Carlos, two African-American U.S. Olympic medalists at the 1968 Mexico City games, gave the Black Power salute (raised gloved fists) during the playing of the national anthem.

Although he never respected or followed the religion or the tactics of his civil rights elders, Muhammad Ali eventually gained public acceptance in ways they could appreciate. He won his draft case before the Supreme Court and fought his way back to the heavyweight championship. His fearlessness in the face of public disapproval brought an eventual grudging respect from erstwhile opponents, even as his own attitudes softened through the later 1970s. That we cannot imagine Ali making the kind of agreement with his manager, Angelo Dundee, that Jackie Robinson made with Branch Rickey is some measure of the changed climate in the past half century.

6 / Money, Television, Drugs, and the Win: Dilemmas of Modern Sports

· · · · · · · · · · · · · · · · · · · ·

Amateur Ideals and Sporting Reality

Changes in the racial composition of big-time sports are one visible measure of the distance sports have traveled in the past century. But to a nineteenth-century fan suddenly transplanted into our day, the most striking change in organized athletics would doubtless be the vast increase in the amount of money absorbed and generated by professional and "amateur" sports. It is less likely, though, that our time-traveling fan would be surprised by the persistence of conflict over amateur sports. For the question of amateurism in American sports, as we have seen, has had a long history. Almost from the earliest days of organized sports, some version of an amateur ideal has inspired and motivated participants, spectators, and commentators. It is testimony to the ongoing intensity of feelings about amateur play that no amount of money, advertising, or business machinations has been able to extinguish people's attachment to the ideal of sports played for something other than material gain.

Historically, it has been devilishly difficult to define amateur sports to everyone's satisfaction. No matter what set of rules or definitions have prevailed over the past century and a half, they have given rise to controversy. It may even be the case that sporting impulses themselves are necessarily structured by a contradiction: we play sports for fun, but as soon as we organize them, we move onto different terrain. As we consider the historical problem of amateurism and its discontents, we discover some of the roots of the modern dilemmas and problems of organized sports. At the same time, of course, we need to recognize the other side of the impulse: the desire for intense play that has nothing to do with TV contracts or performance-enhancing drugs or recruitment scandals. Despite emotional appeals to the contrary, these two versions of sports are more connected than we might think.

Consider the following letter to a weekly baseball paper written by a veteran ballplayer in the winter of 1868:

> Somehow or other they don't play ball nowadays as they used to some eight or ten years ago . . . I mean that they don't play with the same kinds of feelings or for the same objects they used to . . . But it's no use talking like a father to you fellows, you're in for "biz" now, and have forgotten the time when your club's name stood higher as a fair and square club than it does now.

The language may be quaint, but the sentiment easily leaps a dozen decades. It is possible that the letter writer, who called himself "Old Peto Brine" (a play on the name of Peter O'Brien, a well-known ballplayer from baseball's earliest years), did remember different days in club baseball, but only barely. Ten years earlier, he might even have played in the first series of baseball games—a New York and Brooklyn all-star best-two-out-of-three matchup at the Fashion Race Course on Long Island—for which spectators had to pay admission. Eight years earlier, the Brooklyn Excelsiors had been paying the young pitching phenomenon James Creighton under the table, while the Philadelphia Athletics covertly paid their pitcher Al Reach.

Almost from the moment in baseball history when there were enough clubs to allow for frequent games—the later 1850s—they began specializing their best players at one or two positions, practicing regularly, and developing winning strategies based on skill and cunning. Press coverage of matches between the top clubs offered detailed, opinionated analyses of a nine's strengths and weaknesses and did not shy away from advice or criticism. These clubs, in other words, played to win. They must also have played for the fun of the game, but once on the field, they were expected by everyone—themselves, their fellow club members, the spectators, the press, their "club followers" (as fans were called)—to win ball games.

Emphasis on competition transformed the life of baseball clubs, which had been genuine social *and* ballplaying entities in the 1850s and early 1860s. As more attention focused on the club's "first nine" (its varsity team), other members gradually became little more than glorified spectators. Whether or not to compete for the metropolitan championship became a sensitive issue for clubs, while some in the press questioned the rationale for having a championship. "It is unquestionably for the best interests of the game," intoned the *New York Clipper* in 1863, "that matches for the championship, together with the title of champion, should be entirely done away with, and the sooner the leading men of the fraternity drown this class of matches down the better." Competition and the desire for victory led to too much "rivalry," "ill feeling," and "endless disputes."

Once money, in the form of gate receipts, salaries, and potential profits, entered this highly competitive world, it proved impossible to limit its influence. By the late 1860s, the best clubs in the New York metropolitan area and in cities such as Chicago, Philadelphia, and Cincinnati were paying most, if not all, of their players. Harry Wright, one of New York's finer baseball and cricket players, left Gotham in 1867 for Cincinnati, where he soon would assemble, train, and lead the finest baseball club in the country, the professional Red Stockings, to its legendary, never equaled, undefeated 1869 season.

Like the love of money, the love of victory is extremely hard to limit voluntarily. This is not a matter of "blaming" players and entrepreneurs. Sports structures themselves came to incorporate these goals. If maintaining an organization—a club, say, or a league—depends on gate receipts and victories, individual players or club members have much less genuine choice in the matter. Championship-level baseball followed just this path in the 1860s and '70s.

There was another path that sports organizations might have taken, one common in European countries and nonexistent in the United States in the nineteenth century. That path involved the intervention in and subsidy of sports by the state. State sponsorship of organized sports removes the need for individual clubs and leagues to raise money for operating expenses. If public resources are allocated to acquire and maintain equipment, playing fields, and facilities, or to arrange matches and provide officials, an enormous burden is lifted from the athletes and their friends.

In fact, the United States is nearly alone in the world in leaving most top-flight sports to the private sector, a set of choices with huge consequences. For one thing, this distinction helps explain why some of the best examples of amateur play in the United States today can be found in municipal youth and adult sports leagues, where the presence of paying spectators is irrelevant to whether or not the league finishes the season. Money does not disappear as an issue in state-sponsored sports, of course. Political constituencies vie for public funds in sports just as they do for other municipal services. Nor has public sponsorship of organized sports escaped the racial and sexual prejudice that kept African Americans and women off public playing fields for most of the past century. Still, by removing money as a condition of existence, publicly sponsored sports offered an arena more open to amateur play than any other.

In the United States, the principal municipal involvement in organized sports before 1900 consisted of maintaining baseball fields in public parks. Even here, whether to allow baseball on the Boston Common or in New York City's Central Park became a substantial political issue between those (generally wealthier) people who wanted public parks to provide serene oases from crowds and urban bustle and those (generally immigrant, working-class, and young) people who wanted to use parks for sports. Baseball diamonds came and went in Central Park, in accordance with the city's election returns. The minutes of the Boston Common Council show frequent efforts to ban baseball from the Common, as petitions and counterpetitions were submitted. Political machines, too, understood the importance of organized sports to building their constituencies, as the Tammany Hall leader George Washington Plunkitt pointed out in 1905:

> For instance, here's how I gather in the young men . . . Another young feller gains a reputation as a baseball player in a vacant lot. I bring him into our baseball club. That fixes him. You'll find him workin' for my ticket at the polls next election day. Then there's the feller that likes rowin' on the river, the young feller that makes a name as a waltzer on his block, the young feller that's handy with his dukes—I rope them all in by givin' them opportunities to show themselves off.

While such public and quasi-public sponsorship of sports provided opportunities for thousands to play outside organized professional clubs, it had little impact on the course of top-flight sports in the late nineteenth century. Baseball clubs began operating their own grounds and paying their players; quite naturally, they wanted some return on their investment, either in money or in the prestige attached to a winning record. During this period, the only way for a club to make money was to attract paying spectators who would so much enjoy what they experienced at the ball park that they would return. Constantly at the mercy of weather, the business cycle, and public moods, outdoor entertainment was a trying business in which to earn money. A club's best assets in this struggle were a winning team, attractive accommodations, and publicity, but not even these could guarantee profits. While the Red Stockings' great 1869 tour netted about $1,700, the club only broke even the following year, when they lost six games, an excellent but not legendary record.

A group of baseball traditionalists based mostly in New York tried to form an amateur alternative to the money game in 1871. Asserting that the sport's original purity had been corrupted by the "money-seekers," the men behind the amateur rebellion sought to "restore" a genteel, healthful, harmonious pastime that would "discountenance the playing of the game for money, or as a business pursuit." That the game had never resembled this baseball Eden helped ensure that the effort to "bring it back" would fail. At the amateurs' founding convention, the Star Club of New York City insisted upon the right to continue charging admission to its games. Within the better clubs, professional structures soon emerged, as the great majority of games were played by a very small proportion of the "members." Soon the amateur Beacons of Boston began exploring the idea of a state-wide amateur championship; while in 1874 the Staten Island amateurs toured as far west as Keokuk, Iowa. This version of the amateur ideal could not keep clubs from getting into occasional fights with opponents; nor did it exempt them from the kind of press analysis directed at professional clubs. The amateur arena, in short, differed from its professional counterpart only in not paying players. And the lengthy playing tours suggest that some players were at least subsidized, and perhaps paid.

Players wanted to win, and the entire structure of the game nourished such feelings. Once victory had become important—to players, to club directors, to club members, to fans and reporters—then it could be limited only by the most strenuous effort, an effort that required emotions antithetical to those that had drawn players or spectators to the game in the first place. Profits were probably secondary. It was so difficult to generate a secure income operating a baseball team that most needed wealthy backers even to make the attempt. A look through Harry Wright's correspondence in the 1870s, when he captained and managed—that is, ran the business side as well as the on-field play—the Boston Red Stockings in the first professional league, the National Association of Professional Base Ball Players, shows just how hard he worked to make the game pay. Small wonder that weaker clubs (with smaller populations to draw on, and greater distances to travel) dropped out during all but one of the league's five seasons.

So even before money there was the need to win, a goal that preceded and has nearly always triumphed over notions of "pure recreation" in American sports history. That is not to say that people have played or watched baseball only for money or for victory. Contradictory impulses have existed at different levels of the game, as in informal or children's games, and sometimes even within the most professional levels. But in organized sports, winning has usually held more importance than sportsmanship, amusement, exercise, or patriotism. Even some of those early commentators who bemoaned the decline of baseball due to professionalism found it impossible to resist the pull of the game played at its best.

Twentieth-Century Amateurism

Throughout the twentieth century, there has existed a wide range of less well organized sports in which money has played little or no role. Recreational sports such as tennis, bowling, golf, basketball, volleyball, softball, swimming, diving, and running have existed alongside the big-money, big-time sports for the better part of the century. It may even be that most people's experience of participant sports falls into this category and serves as a reminder of the values people seek in sports: freedom, choice, fun, camaraderie, vigorous physical activity, the display and testing of acquired skills. The intense desire for such experiences serves almost as a counterthrust against a world in which our economic, civic, and recreational lives are increasingly organized by enormous impersonal bureaucracies. At the same time, however, our hopes distort our vision, making it harder to see the ways in which the sports we follow have been in effect colonized by television and the culture of the big time.

The point is not to wail in wounded innocence about the influence of money and professionalism, or to thunder about the abuses of big-time sports. It is rather to outline a framework that can give some historical perspective on modern controversies over amateur sports, education, television, drugs, and money. While details of individual incidents will always be shocking, the case, say, of college basketball prospect Chris Washburn (who despite being unable to give one correct answer on the verbal segment of the 1983 Scholastic Aptitude Test was recruited by more than one hundred colleges) ought to be more comprehensible in this historical context.

By focusing on the most highly structured end of the sporting spectrum—for example, organized college and university athletics governed by the NCAA—we are not suggesting that the amateur sporting experiences of millions of children and adults are irrelevant, or governed by an identical ethos. Most Little Leagues and junior soccer leagues provide fields where children can learn a sport, engage in a healthy amount of exercise, and enjoy themselves. Still, the influence of big-time sports, professional or "amateur," conveyed through television and the press, has a powerful effect on lower-level sports and tends to mold them along the lines of their own big-time structures. By and large, of course, fans and participants are unaware of this power and therefore resist it very little. Their experience and expectations from sports have been shaped by following the big time for many years.

In a Little League game in Riverhead, New York, in 1992, for example, two coaches of nine-to-twelve-year-old teams accused each other of using ineligible thirteen-year-olds in order to increase their chances of winning. One coach pulled his team off the field and forfeited, to the complete bewilderment of the children. Nevertheless, the "winning" team excitedly told their friends that they had won, 13–0. Similarly, African-American parents, sensing that their children's best chances of attending a good college lie in athletic scholarships, encourage their youngsters to play Pop Warner football rather than baseball or soccer, which receive less high-school and college publicity and award fewer scholarships. The children do not dwell on multimillion-dollar contracts (though who could blame them if they did?), and many of them have tremendous fun playing football. But if children—and adults—having fun as they play games is a constant and powerful element of the history of American sports, the structure within which that fun takes place has undergone substantial historical change. A hundred years ago, for instance, a parent or child could not have had the nightly experience of watching superstar baseball players earning millions of dollars make the same plays attempted on the Little League field several hours earlier. Such comparisons can be difficult for a youngster or eager parent. That is why we ought not to lose sight of the fact that players and athletes of all kinds, at no matter what level, are always influenced, at least in part, by the dramatic and powerful pull of professional and top-flight "amateur" sports.

Consider the lead story on the front page of the *Chronicle of Higher Education* for January 15, 1992: "NCAA Votes Higher Academic Standards for College Athletes: Presidents' reform package wins overwhelming support at meeting." The centerpiece of this heralded reform is that, beginning in August of 1995, entering student athletes will be admitted to college only if they have earned a 2.5, as opposed to a 2.0, grade point average in a group of thirteen, as opposed to the current eleven, high-school courses. In other words, until the fall of 1995, freshmen athletes may have earned no grade higher than a C in eleven core high-school courses; thereafter they must earn six or seven B's as well.

While the rules that college athletic program administrators must enforce have become more stringent, it remains unlikely that the best college athletes will receive even respectable educations. For what has driven collegiate athletics for well over a century has been the players', coaches', and alumni's desire for victory. As Ronald Smith argues persuasively in *Sports and Freedom*, the very people who have been expected to "clean up" college athletics—college presidents—have never had the power to do so. Those who did have the power, those who actually controlled college sports programs—boards of trustees and the alumni—have consistently refused to tamper with big-time college athletics.

Nor has the NCAA ever been powerful enough to ensure the integrity of genuinely amateur sports. Created in the wake of the brutal 1905 football season, it has always been more concerned with upholding a pristine *image* of college sports than with tackling tough issues. Prior to 1940, member colleges kept the organization weak by giving it limited authority over playing rules and national tournaments. Colleges themselves retained control of their recruiting and training practices; so despite moralizing pronouncements from the NCAA on these matters, coaches and athletic directors did whatever they felt necessary to win games. The high-toned declarations met with approval from the press and the public, as fans eagerly sought to eat their cake (swearing allegiance to amateur principles) and have it, too (accumulating victories).

All through the late nineteenth century, college rowing, baseball, and football teams were dogged by struggles over the eligibility and covert payment of their better players. "Tramp athletes" circulated from college to college, in a practice reminiscent of baseball "revolving" in the 1860s. Even players and coaches with national reputations, men whose names now grace field houses, stadiums, and sportsmanship awards, participated fully in the system. Fielding Yost, a talented tackle for West Virginia University, "transferred" to Pennsylvania's Lafayette College in 1896 just in time for its big game with the powerful University of Pennsylvania. In one of the greatest football games of the nineteenth century, Lafayette upset Penn with the assistance of "freshman" Yost. Yost went right back to West Virginia, where he earned a law degree; later, at the University of Michigan, he became a famous and successful football coach and continued to flout regulations in order to produce winning teams. Walter Camp, that rock-ribbed defender of sporting honor, ran a secret fund out of which he paid tutors for Yale athletes. Amos Alonzo Stagg, the YMCA colleague of Luther Gulick and James Naismith at Springfield College in the early 1890s, "bought" athletes with money from a Rockefeller-established trust fund at the University of Chicago.

The culture of college football, in other words, was organized to evade eligibility requirements and strictures against paying athletes. With impressive understatement, the exhaustive study made by the Carnegie Commission and published in 1929 as *American College Athletics* observed: "Apparently the ethical bearing of intercollegiate football contests and their scholastic aspects are of secondary importance to the winning of victories and financial success." By the 1920s, college football had become so popular, and had absorbed the investment of so much money, so much publicity, and so many people, that teams had achieved an existence virtually independent of the "educational" institutions for which they played. Professional coaches became the stars of football programs, receiving, on average, salaries 20 percent higher than those of full professors.

Half a century later, schools such as the University of Nevada at Las Vegas, or the University of Alabama, or the University of Southern California are better known for their football and basketball teams than for scholarly or academic achievement. Bear Bryant, the legendary Alabama football coach during the 1960s and 1970s, wielded far greater power on campus and across his state than the president of the university. In fact, many schools with top-ranked teams provide educational "cover" for an essentially professional endeavor: the recruitment, training, display, and marketing of first-rate athletic performance. Within academia, Oklahoma may have a reputation for a fine university press, or Clemson may be known for its engineering department. But the public, national reputation of these colleges and universities, the reputation that shows up in newspapers and on television and in game-show answers, is built on sports. What Frederick Rudolph observed of colleges in the 1890s—that football had become their major public relations tool—remains even more true a century later. In the mid-1980s, for example, a halftime commercial for the University of Alabama featured thenpresident Joab Thomas holding in his left hand a book and declaring, "At the University of Alabama, we're going to make *this* as important as"—his right hand raised a football—"this."

Baseball had begun to follow the lead of other big-time college sports. Television commentators never quite got over the fact that Ron Darling, a pitcher for the New York Mets, majored in

East Asian studies at Yale. The major leagues certainly include more college graduates now than they did a generation ago, when Jim Bouton observed (with some exaggeration) in *Ball Four* that any ballplayer caught reading a book without pictures was dubbed an intellectual. Still, most professional ballplayers who attend college, especially the southwestern baseball colleges (USC, Arizona State), do so less for academic training than for their top-flight baseball programs.

All college teachers, and many if not most high-school teachers, know the dilemma of having one of the school's better athletes in class. The finer the institution's athletic reputation, the more acute the quandary. Most athletes have difficulty as students because first-rate athletic performance is at least as demanding as first-rate academic performance. Generally, extensive practice time, game time, and time spent on travel to and from games effectively preclude anything more than nominal class participation or preparation during the season. Even out of season, the balance tips in favor of athletics. A 1988 NCAA survey found that year-round college athletes averaged thirty hours per week on their sport and twenty-six hours on schoolwork. Athletes frequently ask for teachers' understanding—which can range from an extended deadline on a paper to a virtual exemption from course work. Especially if the sport is considered to be vital to the school, instructors feel pressure to grant athletes' requests. A particularly flagrant example of this tendency occurred in early 1993, when it was revealed that a paper handed in by a star basketball player at UNLV was partly in the handwriting of his private tutor (who took the blame). But any teacher who breaks the implicit agreement to honor this system is considered to have violated and betrayed an unwritten code.

While it is possible to envision a sports program at a college or university that considered academics as other than an unfortunate hurdle to be overcome, it is not possible to imagine such a program being competitive with more mainstream schools. If students played football and basketball only when their normal studying was done, or, say, two hours each day, they could develop skills, keep in shape, and have some fun. In fact, the athletic programs at today's Ivy League colleges are limited along these lines. As important training grounds for the children of the American upper class, such institutions pay closer attention to the more rounded educations of their students, and they do not generally recruit students purely for their athletic ability. Physical and moral "toughening" are of considerably less importance to elite culture now than they were a century ago. Since upper-class children prepare to win positions of influence and power, they spend less time on sports. As a result, they rarely play and even more rarely win basketball games against opponents who practice three times as much, who pursue a rigorous training regimen, who room together and talk basketball into the night. Students in limited programs would always lose because they could not spend the time practicing or concentrating on the game as the very best players must do.

The point here is not to criticize athletes for the strong commitment they have to their sport. That would be akin to denigrating a concert pianist who spends six or eight hours a day at the keyboard, or a ballet dancer's long and arduous preparation for a performance. All three performers might be open to the criticism of overspecialization, but for most Americans there is little compensation for the achievement that comes from being well rounded. We most value the display of art, dance, music, and sports executed as well as humanly possible. Those who master such disciplines receive some of the most lavish rewards society has to offer: fame, wealth, adulation.

While only a relative handful of colleges and universities are at the pinnacle of college sports, the influence of the big time spreads far beyond their immediate circle. The history of the NCAA in the past fifty years is instructive. The governing body for all college athletics, the NCAA has in fact been dominated by its relationship to the most powerful centers for college sports—the most successful football and basketball schools. During these years, two fundamental issues have helped the NCAA gain power: sports-minded colleges' desire to win the games they play; and those same institutions' interest in profiting from television revenue.

In the years following World War II, colleges scrambled for winning teams with a new intensity, a rush accompanied by recruiting and money violations galore. Occasional scandals surfaced, most significantly at the U.S. Military Academy in 1950 (where most of the varsity football team was expelled for cheating on exams) and in college basketball in 1951, when several dozen players from seven different colleges were charged with point shaving (taking bribes from gamblers to help them predict the size of the victory—and therefore beat the betting odds—in a given game) in that and previous years.

The prevalence of scandal and the lure of television led member colleges by the early 1950s to give the NCAA the authority to discipline particularly egregious violators. It helped, of course, that television was beginning to show its potential impact on college sports, especially football and basketball. Individual colleges at first made their own deals for television broadcasts, and the airwaves were filled with college games. Attendance dropped precipitously. Quickly colleges realized that they needed to handle the broadcasting of their games in a more orderly fashion, and they went to the NCAA. As manager of the college sports cartel, the NCAA did a creditable job, although, according to Benjamin Rader, it was a decade before attendance recovered, and even television revenue climbed slowly at first. The NCAA television contracts reinforced the financial inequality between colleges but did provide an enormous bonanza for the best conferences and programs. In 1983, for example, television networks paid the NCAA nearly $75 million for rights to televise its football games.

Periodically, a distressing scandal comes to light and brings new pressure for reform of big-time college athletics. No reforms can change the fact that college administrations want their teams to win, and the teams themselves want to win, and the home-team fans want them to win. Given that emphasis on winning, a college does stay longer in the public eye if it reaches, for instance, the Final Four in the NCAA basketball tournament. As long as winning is of overwhelming importance, coaches and alumni and administrators will conspire to "buy" great athletes, to evade eligibility regulations, to alter grade point averages, and to persuade professors and registrars to tamper with grades and transcripts.

The Impact of Television

Even if the desire to "play for fun" were to take hold in collegiate athletic programs, the multimillion-dollar investments colleges and their alumni associations have made in facilities, equipment, financial aid, recruitment, and coaching salaries would effectively block any such transformation. This logic does not apply only to the very best college sports teams. Athletic fields and gymnasiums are substantial expenses even for second-, third-, and fourth-rank institutions. A hundred years ago, the stakes were considerably lower, so the early history of football is filled with colleges deciding to pull out of league competition for a year or two. Today, a decision to leave the Division I arena would be considered incomprehensible for economic reasons alone. If college sports' love affair with victory drew them into professionalism, television performed the marriage. Since sports television so often reaches a large national audience, it is particularly attractive to advertisers who have proved willing to pay nearly unimaginable sums of money in order to communicate to this audience.

While television has had a tremendous impact on modern sports, we must beware of idealizing the pre-television age. Network executives are steered by many of the same concerns that have guided sports entrepreneurs for nearly two centuries. For both, the most important objective has always been putting spectators (viewers) in the seats. If altering a game is likely to produce more spectators or a larger audience, those in the business of putting on sports exhibitions are likely to give change a try. Baseball owners have frequently tinkered with the rules of their game. When spitballs were outlawed, for instance, or when dirty baseballs started to be replaced regularly with clean ones, power hitting received a boost; so did attendance. The All-Star Game, now a high point of the baseball season, was introduced in 1933 in order to combat declining attendance during the Great Depression.

It should not be surprising, as Warren I. Susman liked to point out, that sports entrepreneurs, including television networks, have a different approach to games from that of fans. Because television networks make money by, in effect, renting audiences to advertisers, they have considerably less interest in the internal structures, particular histories and traditions, or distinctive rhythms of a given sport—except insofar as they affect the number of viewers.

The history of every sport reveals a constant effort on the part of its businessmen, owners, rule makers, and league officials to adjust the balance between offense and defense to produce the maximum number of spectators. The three-point shot in professional basketball was just such an innovation; so was the splitting of each league into two divisions in major league baseball, which was accompanied by a vertical shrinking of the strike zone and a lowering of the pitcher's mound. Longtime fans tend to glorify the "good old days" when excellent defense and low-scoring games were the rule. Babe Ruth, for example, was widely considered by many fans in the 1920s to have ruined "real baseball." Such longtime fans condescend to the less intense, more casual fans, who generally prefer offense, whether it be base hits, home runs, completed passes, touchdowns, slugging, slam dunks, or three-point shots. There is a tendency among sports commentators, including historians, to demonize television executives, as though selling sports were a relatively new phenomenon. But there is little about Roone Arledge (the man who ran the American Broadcasting Companies' sports division during the 1970s) that Albert G. Spalding would not have understood and appreciated.

Television's arrival happened so quickly that networks and sports organizations took time to grasp its potential. While radio was an important medium from the 1920s on, and had been vital in the national marketing of big prizefights, it never exercised the enormous power that television now has over organized sports. For one thing, the money radio stations and networks paid clubs for broadcast rights, particularly in smaller cities, became substantial only in the television age. Some clubs, fearing that radio broadcasts would cut into attendance, refused to allow their games to be carried on the air. New York's three baseball teams agreed on just such a prohibition in 1934, although it was not to last. When Larry MacPhail, one of baseball's more imaginative businessmen of the 1930s, came to Brooklyn as general manager of the Dodgers in 1938, he promptly sold the team's broadcast rights for the then enormous sum of $70,000 annually. Broadcast revenue for all of major league baseball remained under a million dollars as late as 1946. Six years later, total broadcast income (from radio and television) topped $5 million. Thereafter, broadcast revenue doubled roughly every five to seven years until it reached $40 million in 1971.

Fewer than a million families owned television sets in 1949. Two years later, the figure was 10 million; by 1953, it had reached 20 million. Two years later, two-thirds of American households owned a television set; by 1960, almost 90 percent had a television. Even though networks did not at first invest heavily in sports programming, what broadcasting they did began to change the shape of decades-old habits of sports spectatorship.

The most famous—and dramatic—example of this impact was on minor league baseball. The draw of nationally televised major league games proved nearly fatal to the minor leagues, whose attendance plummeted from 42 million in 1949 to a mere 15 million in 1957. Boxing, too, came under the television spell and experienced a brief Golden Age as Gillette sponsored Friday-night telecasts of Madison Square Garden bouts. But fight fans soon discovered what baseball fans would find a generation later: sponsors wanted to show winning boxers and offense—in this case, tough, dramatic slugging. And since there were not enough boxers with winning records to go around, the quality of the contests deteriorated. At the same time, independent boxing clubs could not compete with TV's Friday-night card. By the late 1950s, in a development paralleling the minor league debacle, more than half the fight clubs in smaller cities had closed their doors. Even in New York, most clubs shut down, and relatively small crowds actually came to Madison Square Garden on Friday nights. Boxing received a final body blow in the late fifties, when organized crime was "discovered" to be deeply involved in the management of the sport.

It took Roone Arledge at ABC to fully realize what television could do for sports. In his greatest achievement, "Monday Night Football," Arledge demonstrated that a complicated professional sport with a grimy, working-class reputation that appealed almost entirely to men could be remade into first-rate and "respectable" family entertainment. His new techniques—the use of multiple cameras, slow-motion replays, close-ups of players and fans, and directional microphones—essentially disassembled a professional football game into its component parts and put it back together so that viewers experienced a brand-new game.

Arledge understood what he was doing. His first "heretical idea," according to Marc Gunther and Bill Carter in *Monday Night Mayhem: The Inside Story of ABC's "Monday Night Football,"* was that sports television did not exist to promote sports and sell tickets. Like the rest of television, it should entertain and hold the audience at home. The show mattered far more than the contest itself. As Arledge himself put it in a planning memo to his boss, *"We are going to add show business to sports!"* Since football had always had a quality of spectacle, it was perhaps most easily married to TV's entertainment ethic.

Football was not the only game that fans learned to perceive differently. The way we *see* a baseball game—rather than the form of the game itself—is probably what has changed most in the past couple of generations. For example, the center-field camera shot of pitcher, batter, and catcher that dominates most televised games was a view largely unavailable to fans before television. Still, neither major league baseball nor football nor basketball has been willing to resist television's interest in restructuring these sports. In baseball, for instance, television has made it very profitable to lengthen the season, invent new championships (the League Championship Series), and then lengthen them (from best of five to best of seven games—and the owners have now approved an additional round of playoffs), all the while dictating the times at which ball games are played.

Like most baseball games, the World Series is now played entirely at night because that is when networks can maximize audiences. Traditionalists lament the loss of the time in which the World Series could actually interrupt the workday, but the truth is that baseball entrepreneurs have always tried to schedule games for the least interference with potential spectators' working times. Even in the game's earliest years, 3:00 p.m. starts were common, after many working-class men had already put in a full day. It would have been self-destructive to do otherwise.

Night baseball made so much economic sense that Negro League teams used to carry around their own lights. Because baseball is play for fans—potentially very serious, emotionally riveting, depressing, or exciting, but play nevertheless—they are frequently pleased when play interrupts the workday. For professional players and sports entrepreneurs, on the other hand, games are work and ought to be producing income. That is why they have struggled, ever since the origins of professional sports, to make the exhibition of games pay. In the 1870s, Harry Wright spent nearly every evening during the baseball season trying to arrange the most remunerative matches he could. When his old friend Nick Young (of the Washington Olympics) complained of being scheduled after Wright's game with the rival Nationals, Wright responded with emotional and business acumen:

> I am very sorry there is so much feeling existing between your two clubs . . . I made the game with the Nationals first, because my experience has taught me that the [Boston] nine play a better game when they play the weaker club first . . . I look on our game with your nine as certain to draw a large crowd if it was the last of half a dozen games . . . Base ball is business now, Nick, and I am trying to arrange our games and make them pay, irrespective of my feelings, and to the best of my ability.

While television has added huge sums of money to professional sports, and has done much to recast sports, in Benjamin Rader's apt phrase, "in its own image," the medium itself has only exaggerated tensions inside sports that have existed for a century and a half. Long before network executives dreamed of wild-card teams, a Sun Belt World Series, and the Battle of the Network Stars, fans appreciated first-rate play and were willing to pay to see it. As a result, sports in general have been played at their best by professionals, whether or not they have been acknowledged as such. While the preponderance of the athletes in the United States remain unpaid and therefore, in strict terms, amateur, our attitudes are shaped more than we know by the heavily subsidized sports we watch on television. The real impact of television lies in its pervasiveness: that there are so few sporting experiences that have not at least been exposed to—and therefore in an important sense measured by—the professional ethos of televised sports.

The Historical Roots of the Drug Problem in Sports

A historical perspective on amateurism and professionalism can help us understand why drugs have become a pervasive problem in modern sports. Recreational drugs that provide highs include alcohol, marijuana, cocaine, and the various stimulants and tranquilizers known as uppers and downers. Some commentators would include tobacco, which is often chewed and smoked by baseball players. Although, under the influence of these substances, athletes may believe that they play better, few would argue that their purpose is to increase physical coordination or strength or skill. There is one argument, however, that might be made, and that is for a drug's ability to provide relaxation. Top-flight athletes perform under conditions of such psychological tension that their culture has always included ways of reducing the pressure and getting them through events.

In the past, professional sports culture was never located very far from the saloon. During the nineteenth century, tavern keepers arranged and promoted prizefights, cockfights, and other blood sports and either ran or housed sports gambling operations.

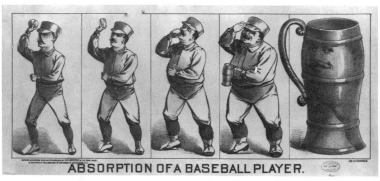

ABSORPTION OF A BASEBALL PLAYER.

There is, as this 1889 lithograph shows, a long history involving sport and drugs. Alcohol has always been an important part of professional baseball culture, among both fans and players. At the same time, moralists and reformers have tried, mostly without success, to purge athletics of its unsavory connection to alcohol and other drugs. "Absorption of a Baseball Player" illustrates how ballplayers, many of them second-generation Irish and German immigrants who spent a good bit of time in saloons, were considered suspect by the guardians of middle-class Victorian morality *(Library of Congress)*

Volunteer fire companies, urban gangs, volunteer militia companies, political factions, and early baseball clubs all made their headquarters in saloons. Heavy drink was basic to the bachelor subculture of antebellum American cities. After the Civil War, too, saloons were the quintessential public spaces and social centers for working-class men, and they have continued to play a fundamental role in all male sporting culture, from the major leagues to municipal softball.

Professional baseball, for instance, has never fully escaped its connection to saloon culture and the sleazier aspects of night life. To take two prominent contemporary examples, one need only think of the late Billy Martin's barroom exploits (spanning three decades), or of Pete Rose's immersion in the world of taverns, bookies, and shady dealings, to see how powerful the connection has remained. Sports teams, professional or amateur, have always traveled, and lodged in hotels. Athletes play games in the late afternoon or evening, and therefore have few responsibilities after work. Like others in the entertainment business, they circulate in the late-night world of cafés and cabarets, nightclubs and hotel bars. Their very domestic rootlessness opens them further to temptation. After all, such entertainers (and those who live in their shadow) have in common enormous amounts of relatively unstructured time, especially when the workaday world is either occupied or asleep. In the past few decades, they have also had much more money than the rest of the population.

That athletes move and live in a different world invites them to think of themselves as living by different rules. From the time that his skill or talent is discovered, a young male athlete is treated differently by teachers, parents, coaches, and fellow students. His athletic accomplishments, while frequently demanding hard work, self-discipline, and self-sacrifice, receive great praise from principals, superintendents, local newspapers, service and booster clubs, politicians, and community leaders. For the attention he brings to his school and community his elders are grateful. His teachers and coaches begin to bend rules to make sure that he is able to excel at what he does best. Fellow students treat him with a mixture of awe and respect, and he finds himself pursued by the most desirable girls in his school. From an early age, the athlete finds that the pleasures of the world are his reward for athletic accomplishment; that he is treated differently from the rest. If he is a well-known champion, a star, people stand in line to do homework for him, businesses eagerly subsidize his no-show weekend job, and shoe manufacturers pay for the right to put their sneakers on his feet. There are obvious consequences to this socialization.

The athlete knows, if only partially, that he does not live like the rest of his peers. On a college campus, he may room in a building set apart for athletes, eat at a training table specially provided for athletes, receive special tutoring, hold nonexistent university "jobs" available only to athletes. At the same time, he knows that this life depends completely on the quality of his athletic performance, which cannot always be at its peak. That knowledge produces a good deal of psychological pressure, pressure that often creates anxiety, typically relieved by men through drink and, in the last fifteen to twenty years, through the use of drugs.

Sports in which there are high stakes, then, are fertile environments for recreational alcohol and drug use. Athletes in these sports tend to think that they can use illegal drugs without fear of punishment because rules have been bent for them all their athletic lives. We should also understand that the release of anxiety accomplished with the help of such drugs is both fun and at least partly felt as therapeutic. These factors would encourage drug use even if there were no substantial financial stakes. But when athletes make large amounts of money, the pressure to perform increases, as does the availability of the drugs that seem to lessen that pressure or enhance the performance that guarantees the income.

A college sophomore on a top-ranked NCAA basketball team is probably already living a more luxurious, if emotionally pressured, life than he has ever experienced. He has begun thinking about a pro career, and his agent may already have been talking to sporting goods companies about endorsement income. The high financial rewards awaiting the successful college basketball player resemble lottery winnings, in that they offer young men ordinarily of modest means the opportunity to become rich. The athletes know, however, that the high-stakes sporting world is callous and unforgiving of failure. They also know that failure is not just an occasional part of sports—it is actually central to the sports experience. The tension produced by such simultaneously grim and exhilarating realities do not make it easier for athletes to forgo recreational or "therapeutic" use of alcohol, cocaine, uppers, downers—whatever substance seems to work.

It is important in this context, then, to understand that in the past generation the single factor raising the financial stakes for athletes the most has been television. In the 1980 NCAA basketball tournament, the Final Four teams earned $1 million each for their colleges—in addition to immense national publicity. Network contracts with athletic organizations, whether "amateur" (like the NCAA and International Olympic Committee) or "professional" (like Major League Baseball, the National Basketball Association, and the National Football League), routinely involve tens of millions of dollars and, in the case of the 1990 CBS multi-year contract to televise major league baseball, can reach the billion-dollar range.

At the same time, professional players have gained a significantly larger portion of the revenues they help generate. In the 1970s, football, baseball, and basketball players all began to receive some benefits from building stronger, more aggressive unions with professional organizers and negotiators. While baseball saw the greatest victories for players—most notably with the 1975 elimination of the reserve clause—salaries climbed for all professional players. Baseball players' salaries simply exploded, from an average of $46,000 per player in 1975, to $433,000 in 1988, to $850,000 in 1991. The following winter the New York Mets signed Bobby Bonilla to a multi-year $29 million contract, then the most lucrative player contract in American sports history. The record did not last, as owners opened their wallets even wider the next season. Barry Bonds signed a six-year contract with the San Francisco Giants worth nearly $44 million, while Kirby Puckett signed for five years and $30 million with the Minnesota Twins.

The lure of these fantastic sums now pulls athletes, schools, and coaches into the financial net of professional sports much earlier than ever before. Athletes, parents, and spectators at very different places in the sporting world cannot but be affected by what appears to be the pot of gold at the end of the rainbow. Top high-school basketball players in New York and Los Angeles are recruited nationwide by basketball colleges (and high schools recruit from junior highs), and many African-American boys see an athletic scholarship as their best chance to get a college degree.

The rewards of making it in college and professional sports are entirely too seductive for anyone to expect adolescent males to resist them. That is why the issue of performance-enhancing drugs is so conceptually straightforward. As long as there remain disproportionately valuable prizes for those who win games, people who play them will break the law and endanger their health. There are simply no effective countervailing influences in the sporting world even to make possible the elimination of, say, anabolic steroids. Taking such drugs is considered a matter of course in college wrestling, weightlifting, and football, and they are used as well by high-school athletes in these sports. Because performance-enhancing drugs contribute substantially to producing physical size and strength, even well-known side effects —impotence, liver damage, emotional instability—deter few athletes.

Winning provides entirely too many rewards in this culture for significant numbers of athletes voluntarily to risk losing. Nothing in the socialization and training of first-rate athletes, nothing in the culture of athletic boosterism encourages honor over victory or rule-following over rule-bending. It's not only that "nice guys finish last," in Leo Durocher's legendary dictum; they also finish out of the money.

The sports where athletes are least likely to use performance-enhancing drugs are precisely those in which the rewards of fame or money are limited: weekend tennis, amateur running, youth soccer, Little League baseball, municipal softball, YMCA basketball, Ping-Pong, recreational cycling, boating, or skiing. These sports have not been integrated into the structure of big-time sports. But if an Olympic medal can be glimpsed in the distance, or a four-year scholarship to a private college, or a television commercial, the calculation changes.

While television cannot be held responsible for creating a drug problem in sports—we have seen how drinking has played a central role in sporting culture for well over a century—it is true that the extraordinary flood of TV dollars into organized sports in the past twenty years has probably made drugs in sports a problem without a solution. Young athletes and their parents cannot help but be mesmerized by million-dollar contracts. As long as professional sports remain one of the very few ways to strike it rich in American society, young men and, increasingly, young women are going to do what they can to enter the charmed and golden circle of winners.

It is worth recalling that when the "championship" entries consisted of just a dozen or so baseball clubs in the New York area in the late 1850s and early 1860s, some clubs paid good players under the table and players jumped from club to club in search of better deals. Fans got into fights, gamblers tried to fix contests, and spectators sometimes interfered bodily in the play of a game. If the history of these matters is any guide, then we know that fine players will be subsidized in some way. To imagine a world in which money would not be offered is to imagine a world in which winning received little attention, in which the skillful performance and display of the sport was its own reward. For as much as television has fueled the professionalization of sports in the United States, long before television and radio, long before the concentration of print media into one or two dailies in each large city (as opposed to five or ten), and long before national broadcast contracts, late-nineteenth-century colleges used "tramp" athletes to win football games and participated proudly in a system in which such practices were an open secret. The desire to win had already undermined official pronouncements about Ivy League "honor."

So today, when a handful of colleges and universities stand to make tens of millions of dollars by means of first-rate athletic teams, and hundreds of other institutions of higher learning reap smaller but still substantial rewards, they can hardly be expected to support regulations that would jeopardize their position, or even to follow stringently already existing rules that might lead to fewer victories. Nor is it likely that individual colleges will adopt policies to eliminate drug abuse among their athletes. They did not create the problem, and they cannot solve it alone. Whatever the heartfelt good intentions of individual coaches and administrators, competitive pressures force them to do little more than give the *impression* of concern for the law, for the health of their athletes, for the integrity of their staffs and institutions. Likewise, professional teams find it difficult to deal with drugs beyond the level of image and marketing. The need to win, to avoid scandals, and to keep the fans interested in watching the games places a premium on public relations "solutions," such as announcements of new rules, "programs" for athletes, and largely ineffective drug testing.

Finally, the abuse of drugs by athletes is part of a larger problem of suspect medical practices in sports. On the one hand, sports medicine has expanded our knowledge of athletic injuries and their remedies. But on the other, because of the pressure to win, athletes, coaches, and even team doctors are constantly tempted to get hurt players back into the game as rapidly as possible. The problem goes beyond the willingness of athletes to play injured, or of trainers to use painkillers as a quick fix. The whole ethos of modern sports dictates that the body can be manipulated to achieve rationalized goals. The use of drugs—recreational drugs to alter moods, performance-enhancing drugs to increase strength and endurance, analgesics to enable pain to be endured—grows out of the larger assumption that our bodies can be objectified in the most extreme ways in order to attain the desired end, victory over an opponent.

George Allen, head coach of the Los Angeles Rams and the Washington Redskins, once said that "winning isn't everything—it's the only thing." Allen spoke to more than his own personal obsession. Indeed, he summarized the worldview of big-time American athletics. Sports contain many cultural messages, but always there is competition, winning and losing. Since the late nineteenth century, sports have been more than games; they have been businesses. From that point on, victory was no longer just a personal desire but an organizational necessity. Among professionals, athletes and owners of winning teams make money. For college and even high-school programs, winning keeps athletes' chances for professional dollars alive, allows coaches and administrators to improve their status, and maintains the flow of alumni dollars.

Attaching the cultural desire for victory to the capitalist imperative of making money has had inescapable consequences during the twentieth century. Sports have become valuable entertainment goods, and new mass media, particularly radio and television, have at once sold and shaped those goods. The financial opportunities opened up by the marketing of sports have enticed the most talented people onto our playing fields, have encouraged new ways to develop that talent, and have given us ever-improving, often astonishing displays of physical excellence. But because businesses desire to keep their profits flowing, because institutions such as major league teams and university athletic programs resist outside regulation, and because athletes do not wish to have their privacy invaded—all of which reasons are perfectly understandable—problems such as drug abuse are all but impossible to solve.

So the same combination of forces leads us to modern sports' simultaneous triumph and corruption. Even as our athletes soar to unheard-of heights, we are in danger of losing sight of all values beyond winning. In the worst case, we become complicit in a system that makes money its god; we find ourselves watching televised spectacles that bury athletic competition with commentators' babble, with advertisers' useless products, with a cult of fame and glamour; and we ignore the destruction of our most physically gifted young people's bodies through drugs pushed by a systemic compulsion to win at all costs.

Young men in groups (with an occasional woman) have always given the baseball stadium most of its cultural flavor and tone. These fans are at New York's Polo Grounds, April 12, 1911 *(Library of Congress)*

Epilogue

Field of dreams, arena of conflict, playground of God and the Devil—sport has been all of these. A critical study of sports history teaches Americans about who we have been and who we would like to be, about worlds we have lost and opportunities we have gained, about how we have worked and played. In this book, we have sought to identify important ongoing issues in American sports history rather than compile a comprehensive narrative. If we cannot provide a grand conclusion, at least we may allude to some main themes.

While sports have grown enormously in variety, pervasiveness, and economic impact, there have always been on the sidelines—or, more precisely in churches, universities, newspaper offices, or other bastions of "culture"—segments of American society that have denounced the goings on in our stadiums and arenas. A powerful Manichaean strain in American public morality has often branded activities as indelibly good or evil, and recreations have not escaped such moral absolutism. Sports have been repeatedly condemned as sins against God and the Sabbath, sins against society, sins against the body and spirit, sins against manhood and womanhood.

But even when pastimes were under official or unofficial bans—indeed, often because of those bans—they have found articulate supporters. Sports advocates defended their turf with a variety of cultural claims: the godliness of exercise, the social utility of allowing the poor to blow off steam, the need to defend masculine honor against effeminacy, the necessity of toughening the ruling elite in a Darwinian world. While sports proponents usually acknowledged and sometimes emphasized that sports were also fun, joyousness was nearly always a distinctly minor concern. Participants and spectators might think in terms of fun, but those involved in organizing, promoting, or planning emphasized that sports were above all useful in one way or another. If anything, this trend grew stronger as increasing numbers of people made their living from sports spectacles.

Both the interdictions against sports and the earnest pleas made in their defense shared a common source: the undeniable reality that sports never were and never will be models of purity. Players, promoters, and spectators have always had some connection to less than savory realms of human behavior, including the culture of the streets and saloons, of brothels and gambling houses. From the passionate carousing of sixteenth-century England to Babe Ruth's legendary appetites; from the college basketball point-shaving scandals of 1950 and 1951 to Wilt Chamberlain's arithmetically remarkable sexual exploits, sports have consistently declared their refusal to be completely absorbed into a respectable way of life.

Even more disturbing for many fans, to the extent that sports succeed as businesses—providing profits for owners and high salaries for players—feelings of loyalty to communities, schools, or cities seem to erode. But fans have always complained that "greed has ruined our games," or that "players used to be grateful for the chance to play," or that "men were tougher back then." The history of American sports reveals that motives were never pure; there were no "good old days" when people played only for the honor of their town or the love of the game.

This is not to say that all is right with the sporting world, as our brief history clearly reveals. But despite the problems, Americans over the years have expanded their chances to express themselves through watching and playing sports. Opportunities have never been equitably distributed, but some groups—most recently African Americans and women—have made significant gains by asserting their rights. Indeed, the history of American sports has been, in important ways, the history of excluded groups insisting on equality, despite the barriers of race, class, or gender. Pious Victorian women who were scandalized by the crudity of baseball players found their daughters playing on teams at Vassar or Mount Holyoke; descendants of slaves earned their livings playing sports from which their ancestors had been banned.

The pattern was an old one: immigrant children played baseball in the streets when they had no access to ball parks; men braved employers, police, and public disapprobation to attend prizefights (and their pleasure was all the sweeter when champions of their own ethnic group carried the day); even rich young men risked life and limb as they tested themselves on collegiate gridirons, often in violation of genteel strictures. Though the scale of organized athletics has grown to proportions unimaginable a century ago, we may still recognize the ways in which sports meet and address people's desires for play, especially in the face of an increasingly routinized workaday world.

So we are left today ambivalent about our sporting heritage. For example, the spread of humanitarian sentiments has rendered blood sports—in which fans cheered wildly as animals clawed or bit each other to death—beyond the pale of modern sensibilities, and certainly less common than in the nineteenth century. Yet millions of us watch boxers punch each other unconscious under the genteel Queensberry rules, and millions more watch football players inflict lifelong disabilities on their opponents. Some of the old machismo of the rural gentry and the urban bachelor subculture has declined along with sports such as bare-knuckle prizefighting and violent quarter-horse races. Yet sports are still dominated by men, and they have remained a source of male privilege and power, of masculine language, metaphor, and memory. Moreover, sports that officially banned black players not half a century ago now routinely offer them million-dollar contracts. Those same sports, however, generally keep the doors to management and ownership closed to minorities. So it is fair to say that sports have given voice to the hopes of particular groups for equality, and dramatized their efforts to attain it; but the history of sports also contains overwhelming evidence of the persistence of inequality.

Having said all of this, having noted the history of racial and class prejudice, the vagaries of religious beliefs and their impact on sports, the hypocrisy of the amateur ideal, the violence and sexism of our sporting history, the dilemmas of sport as big business, the corruptions of commercialization, and countless other historical issues, we are still, as fans, left with moments of joy from our own personal pasts. For each of us, intertwined with intimate memories of family and community are images shared by millions of others: of Muhammad Ali regaining his title, a vindication it seemed, for his stand against the Vietnam War; of Sandy Koufax pitching a perfect—*perfect*—game; of Joe Namath dismantling the unbeatable Baltimore Colts in the third Super Bowl; of Reggie Jackson hitting three consecutive home runs in the 1978 World Series; of Julius Erving scoring baskets no human being should make; of Kirk Gibson pinch-hitting a home run, then hobbling around the bases as the life seeped out of the 1988 Oakland Athletics. No doubt other moments have been as vivid to other individuals. What they all have in common is the feeling of transcendence, the sense of limitless possibility that sports can give us. Arousing deep longings for beauty, for awe, for shared community, such moments give us glimpses of a better world and nourish our hopes for much that is noble in humankind.

Bobby Thomson of the New York Giants immediately following one of the most spectacular hits in baseball history—his winning home run in the ninth and final inning of the last game of the three-game playoffs against the Brooklyn Dodgers, which sent the Giants to the 1951 World Series *(Library of Congress)*

Bibliographic Essay

While there is considerable popular writing on sports history, this bibliographic essay samples the scholarly literature. We include here works that we have found particularly interesting and useful. For more comprehensive listings, consult the fine bibliographies published regularly in the *Journal of Sport History*.

GENERAL WORKS
Scholarly writing on sports history has ranged from national and even international surveys to finely focused case studies. Beginning with the former, Allen Guttmann has written some of the most thoughtful works on sport as an international phenomenon. See his *From Ritual to Record: The Nature of Modern Sports* (New York, 1978); *Sports Spectators* (New York, 1986); *The Games Must Go On: Avery Brundage and the Olympic Movement* (New York, 1984); and *Women's Sports: A History* (New York, 1991). For an overview of sports history worldwide, see

257

Richard D. Mandell, *Sport: A Cultural History* (New York, 1984). On the history of early recreations in Europe, try Peter Burke, *Popular Culture in Early Modern Europe* (New York, 1978), and for English pastimes, see Dennis Brailsford, *Sport and Society: Elizabeth to Anne* (London, 1969), and Robert W. Malcolmson, *Popular Recreations in English Society, 1700–1850* (Cambridge, 1973). A thoughtful interpretation of the development of English sports is provided by Eric Dunning and Kenneth Sheard in *Barbarians, Gentlemen, and Players* (Oxford, 1979). For an interesting sociological analysis, see Norbert Elias and Eric Dunning, *The Quest for Excitement: Sport and Leisure in the Civilizing Process* (Oxford, 1986).

Several overviews of American sports history exist, and they provide outstanding sources of detail. See Foster Rhea Dulles, *A History of Recreation: America Learns to Play* (New York, 1965); John A. Lucas and Ronald A. Smith, *The Saga of American Sport* (Philadelphia, 1978); John Rickard Betts, *America's Sporting Heritage, 1850–1950* (Reading, Mass., 1974); and the most intellectually sophisticated of these works, Benjamin G. Rader, *American Sports: From the Age of Folk Games to the Age of Spectators* (Englewood Cliffs, N.J., second ed., 1990). For a collection of essays and documents, see Steven A. Riess, ed., *The American Sporting Experience* (West Point, N.Y., 1984). A series of interesting essays spanning American history can be found in Allen Guttmann's *A Whole New Ball Game: An Interpretation of American Sports* (Chapel Hill, N.C., 1988). For a collection of fascinating essays on the history of physical culture, try Katheryn Grover, ed., *Fitness in American Culture: Images of Health, Sport and the Body, 1830–1940* (Amherst, Mass., 1989). Scholarly articles appear regularly in the *Journal of Sport History* (hereafter *JSH*), the *Canadian Journal of Sport History*, and the *International Journal of the History of Sport*. There are now some fine historical studies of sport in American literature; see Christian Karl Messenger, *Sport and the Spirit of Play in American Fiction: Hawthorne to Faulkner* (New York, 1981); Michael Oriard, *Dreaming of Heroes: American Sports Fiction, 1868–1980* (Chicago, 1982); and especially Oriard, *Sporting with the Gods: The Rhetoric of Play and Game in American Culture* (New York, 1991).

Among the most interesting works in sports history have been those that focus on particular cities, such as Dale Somers, *The Rise of Sport in New Orleans, 1850–1900* (Baton Rouge, La., 1972); Stephen Hardy, *How Boston Played: Sport, Recreation and Community, 1865–1915* (Boston, 1982); and especially Melvin Adelman's impressive work on the cradle of American sports, *A Sporting Time: New York City and the Rise of Modern Athletics, 1820–1870* (Urbana, Ill., 1986). For a fine discussion of sport history and urbanization, see Steven A. Riess, *City Games: The Evolution of American Urban Society and the Rise of Sports* (Urbana, Ill., 1989).

THE COLONIAL ERA

American sports through the eighteenth century have received remarkably little attention. For a sampling of Indian recreations, see Stewart Culin, *Games of the North American Indians* (Washington, D.C., 1907); for a single in-depth study, try Kendall Blanchard, *The Mississippi Choctaws at Play* (Urbana, Ill., 1981); for a brief survey, see Michael A. Salter, "Play in Ritual: An Ethnohistorical Overview of Native North America," *Stadion* 3 (1977): 230–43, or Guttmann, *A Whole New Ball Game*, chapter 2. Among the best works on colonial New England are Hans Peter Wagner, *Puritan Attitudes Toward Recreation in Early Seventeenth-Century New England* (Frankfurt, Germany, 1982), and Nancy Struna, "Puritans and Sport," *JSH* 4 (1977): 1–21. On Pennsylvania, see J. Thomas Jable, "Pennsylvania's Blue Laws: A Quaker Experiment in the Suppression of Sport and Amusements, 1682–1740," *JSH* 1 (1974): 107–21, and Stephen Brobeck, "Revolutionary Change in Colonial Philadelphia: The Brief Life of the Proprietary Gentry," *William and Mary Quarterly* 33 (1976): 410–34. For Northern cities in the colonial era, try Carl Bridenbaugh, *Cities in the Wilderness: The First Century of Urban Life in America* (New York, 1938). Rural life in the eighteenth century is discussed in James T. Lemon, *The Best*

Poor Man's Country (Baltimore, 1972); David Hackett Fischer, *Albion's Seed: Four British Folkways in America* (New York, 1989); and especially Christopher Clark, *The Roots of Rural Capitalism: Western Massachusetts, 1780–1860* (Ithaca, N.Y., 1990).

Early Virginia receives detailed discussion in Jane Carson, *Colonial Virginians at Play* (Charlottesville, Va., 1965). Rhys Isaac presents fine examples and a provocative interpretation in *The Transformation of Virginia, 1740–1790* (Chapel Hill, N.C., 1982). For a brilliant essay on the social and cultural context of horse racing, see Timothy H. Breen's "Horses and Gentlemen: The Cult of Gambling among the Gentry of Virginia," *William and Mary Quarterly* 34 (1977): 239–57. On fighting along the Southern frontier, see Elliott J. Gorn, " 'Gouge and Bite, Pull Hair and Scratch': The Social Significance of Fighting in the Southern Backcountry," *American Historical Review* 90 (1985): 18–43. Nancy Struna has written extensively and well on sport in the Southern colonies; see especially "The Formalizing of Sport and the Formation of an Elite: The Chesapeake Gentry, 1650–1720," *JSH* 13 (1986): 212–34, and "Gender and Sporting Practice in Early America, 1750–1810," *JSH* 18 (1991): 10–30. While there are few available studies specifically about African-American pastimes during the colonial era, some information comes from Peter Wood, *Black Majority: Negroes in Colonial South Carolina from 1670 through the Stono Rebellion* (New York, 1974), and David K. Wiggins, "Good Times on the Old Plantation: Popular Recreations of the Black Slaves in the Antebellum South, 1810–1860," *JSH* 4 (1977); 260–84. C. Vann Woodward's essay "The Southern Ethic in a Puritan World" in his *American Counterpoint* (Boston, 1971) provides a provocative look at the contrasting cultures of Virginia and New England.

THE EARLY REPUBLIC THROUGH THE CIVIL WAR

There is now an extensive literature on sports in the nineteenth century. Early boxing is covered in Elliott J. Gorn, *The Manly Art: Bare-Knuckle Prize Fighting in America* (Ithaca, N.Y.,

1986). Baseball's first decades are chronicled and analyzed in Warren Goldstein, *Playing for Keeps: A History of Early Baseball* (Ithaca, N.Y., 1989). For a biography of the most prominent sporting journalist before the late nineteenth century, see Norris W. Yates, *William T. Porter and the Spirit of the Times* (Baton Rouge, La., 1957). Health and fitness are discussed in Harvey Green, *Fit for America: Health, Fitness, Sport and American Society* (Baltimore, 1988), and James Whorton, *Crusaders for Fitness: The History of American Health Reformers* (Princeton, N.J., 1982). George B. Kirsch, *The Creation of American Team Sports: Baseball and Cricket, 1838–1872* (Urbana, Ill., 1989), discusses the parallel histories of baseball and cricket. Gerald Redmond, *The Caledonian Games in Nineteenth Century America* (Rutherford, N.J., 1971), details an important ethnic sporting tradition. The relationship between athleticism, gambling, and the spirit of play is the subject of John Dizikes, *Sportsmen and Gamesmen* (Boston, 1981).

An important sign of sport history's health is a flourishing literature of scholarly essays. Important articles for the antebellum era include George Moss, "The Long Distance Runners of Ante-Bellum America," *Journal of Popular Culture* 8 (1977): 370–82; Elliott J. Gorn, " 'Good-Bye Boys, I Die a True American': Homicide, Nativism, and Working-Class Culture in Antebellum New York City," *Journal of American History* 74 (1987): 388–410; Nancy Struna, "The North-South Races: American Thoroughbred Racing in Transition, 1823–1950," *JSH* 8 (1981): 28–57; R. M. Lewis, "American Croquet in the 1860's: Playing the Game and Winning,' *JSH* 18 (1991): 365–86; Peter Levine, "The Promise of Sport in Antebellum America," *Journal of American Culture* 2 (1980): 623–34; Benjamin G. Rader, "The Quest for Subcommunities and the Rise of American Sports," *American Quarterly* 29 (1977): 355–69; William G. Durick, "The Gentlemen's Race: An Examination of the 1869 Harvard-Oxford Boat Race," *JSH* 15 (1988): 41–63; Roberta J. Park, "The Attitudes of Leading New England Transcendentalists Toward Healthful Exercise, Active Recreations, and Proper Care of the Body, 1830–1860," *JSH* 4 (1971): 34–50; Soren S. Brynn,

"Some Sports in Pittsburgh During the National Period," *Western Pennsylvania Historical Magazine* pt. 1, 51 (1968): 345–64, pt. 2, 52 (1969): 57–104; Roberta J. Park, " 'Embodied Selves': The Rise and Development of Concern for Physical Education, Active Games and Recreation among American Women, 1776–1865," *JSH* 5 (1978): 5–41; William R. Hogan, "Sin and Sports," in Ralph Slovenko and James A. Knight, eds., *Motivation in Play, Games, and Sport* (Springfield, Ill., 1967).

THE GILDED AGE THROUGH THE TWENTIETH CENTURY
Many of the works mentioned above go beyond the antebellum era and well into the late nineteenth century. The following is a sampling of the available works on sport and leisure for the Gilded Age through the twentieth century. On the play movement, see David Nasaw, *Children of the City: At Work and at Play* (New York, 1985), and Stephen Hardy and Alan G. Ingham, "Games, Structures, and Agencies: Historians on the American Play Movement," *Journal of Social History* 17 (1983): 285–301. For a sophisticated discussion of sports and intellectual history, try Donald J. Mrozek, *Sport and American Mentality, 1880–1910* (Knoxville, Tenn., 1983). On religion and sports, see Guy Lewis, "The Muscular Christianity Movement," *Journal of Health, Physical Education, and Recreation* 5 (1966): 27–42, and Richard A. Swanson, "The Acceptance and Influence of Play in American Protestantism," *Quest* 11 (1968): 58–70. Case studies of sport and business can be found in Peter Levine, *A. G. Spalding and the Rise of Baseball: The Promise of American Sport* (New York: 1985), and Steven M. Gelber, " 'Their Hands Are All Out Playing': Business and Amateur Baseball, 1845–1917," *JSH* 11 (1984): 5–27. For a discussion of Richard Kyle Fox, see Elliott J. Gorn, "The Wicked World: The *National Police Gazette* and Gilded Age America," *Media Studies Journal* 6 (1992): 1–15. On the bicycle craze, see Richard Hammond, "Progress and Flight: An Interpretation of the American Cycle Craze of the 1890's," *JSH* 5 (1971): 235–57. For a case study of sport and medical controversy, see James C. Whorton, "Athlete's Heart: The Med-

ical Debate over Athleticism, 1870–1920," *JSH* 9 (1982): 30–52. An examination of sport and middle-class life appears in Glenn Uminowicz, "Sport in a Middle-Class Utopia: Asbury Park, New Jersey, 1871–1895," *JSH* 11 (1984): 51–73. The best overview of the recent history of big-time sports is Randy Roberts and James Olson, *Winning Is the Only Thing: Sports in America Since 1945* (Baltimore, 1989). On performance-enhancing drugs, try Terry Todd, "Anabolic Steroids: The Gremlins of Sport," *JSH* 14 (1987): 87–107. The issues of sports, money, and television are closely linked, even if they have received little academic attention. The principal work here is Benjamin G. Rader, *In Its Own Image: How Television Has Transformed Sports* (New York, 1984). See also William O. Johnson, Jr., *The Super Spectator and the Electric Lilliputians* (Boston, 1971). On television networks and sports broadcasting, see also Randolph Sugar, *"The Thrill of Victory": The Inside Story of ABC Sports* (New York, 1978); Ron Powers, *Supertube: The Rise of Television Sports* (New York, 1984); and Jim Spense, *Up Close & Personal: The Inside Story of Network Television Sports* (New York, 1988). Still useful are Roger Noll, ed., *Government and the Sports Business* (Washington, D.C., 1974); Joseph Durso, *The All-American Dollar: The Big Business of Sports* (Boston, 1971); and Robert Lipsyte, *SportsWorld: An American Dreamland* (New York, 1975). Also see Marc Gunther and Bill Carter, *Monday Night Mayhem: The Inside Story of ABC's "Monday Night Football"* (New York, 1988), a lively account of the most influential program in the history of sports broadcasting. For the views of an on-air sports broadcaster of the seventies and early eighties, see Howard Cosell, *Cosell* (New York, 1974), *Like It Is* (New York, 1974), and *I Never Played the Game* (New York, 1985). On the connections between drugs, sports, money, and television, see Arthur Kempton's extraordinary essay "Native Sons" in *The New York Review of Books* 38 (April 11, 1991): 55–61. For the association of sports with consumer culture, see Mark Dyreson, "The Emergence of Consumer Culture and the Transformation of Physical Culture: American Sport in the 1920's," *JSH* 16 (1989): 261–81. On the rise of athleticism over the past generation, see Benjamin G. Rader, "The Quest for Self-Sufficiency and the New Strenuosity: Reflections on the Strenuous Life of the 1970s and 1980s," *JSH* 18 (1991): 255–66.

BASEBALL

Several sports have developed extensive bibliographies of their own, and baseball is by far the most written-about American sport. The best basic chronological account of baseball history through the early twentieth century remains Harold Seymour's two volumes *Baseball: The Early Years* (New York, 1960) and *Baseball: The Golden Years* (New York, 1971). Also useful are David Quentin Voigt, *American Baseball: From Gentleman's Sport to the Commissioner System* (Norman, Okla., 1966), and *American Baseball: From the Commissioners to Continental Expansion* (Norman, Okla., 1970). *The Bill James Historical Baseball Abstract*, 2nd ed. (New York, 1988), though not an academic survey, is an indispensable and thoroughly enjoyable aid to understanding how and by whom the game was played, decade by decade, since the 1870s. For a fine history in one volume, see Benjamin G. Rader, *Baseball: A History of America's Game* (Urbana, Ill., 1992).

Few baseball histories make any genuine attempt to connect sporting developments to patterns in the larger culture. Exceptions include Warren Goldstein's *Playing for Keeps* (cited above), an in-depth cultural history of the game prior to the founding of the National League; Jules Tygiel's superb *Baseball's Great Experiment: Jackie Robinson and His Legacy* (New York, 1983); and Bruce Kuklick's *To Every Thing a Season: Shibe Park and Urban Philadelphia, 1909–1976* (Princeton, N.J., 1991). Harold Seymour's final volume, *Baseball: The People's Game* (New York, 1990), demonstrates just how much about the national pastime still remains to be mined out of local and regional sources. For a remarkable piece of speculation about baseball's popularity in the late nineteenth century, see Ronald Story, "In the Country of the Young," in Alvin L. Hall, ed., *Cooperstown*

Symposium on Baseball and the American Culture (1989) (Westport, Conn., 1991).

For other interesting discussions of the meaning of the national
pastime, see Leverett T. Smith, Jr., *The American Dream and
the National Game* (Bowling Green, Ohio, 1975); Tristram Pot-
ter Coffin, *The Old Ball Game: Baseball in Folklore and Fiction*
(New York, 1971); and Richard C. Crepeau, *Baseball's Diamond
Mind* (Orlando, Fla., 1979). The reserve clause and baseball's
labor struggles still await a full social history, but much of the
story may be found in Seymour and in Lee Lowenfish and Tony
Lupien, *The Imperfect Diamond: The Story of Baseball's Reserve
System and the Men Who Fought to Change It* (New York,
1980). One player's struggle against the reserve clause is available
in Curt Flood with Richard Carter, *The Way It Is* (New York,
1970). For an example of the kind of work that can be done with
local sources, see Robert Weir, "Take Me Out to the Brawl Game:
Sports and Workers in Gilded Age Massachusetts," in Ronald
Story, ed., *Sports in Massachusetts: Historical Essays* (West-
field, Mass., 1991).

The best demographic research into nineteenth- and early-
twentieth-century baseball players has been done by Steven A.
Riess in *Touching Base: Professional Baseball and American
Culture in the Progressive Era* (Westport, Conn., 1980); by Melvin L. Adelman in *A Sporting Time*; and by George B. Kirsch,
in *The Creation of American Team Sports*. On spectatorship, in
addition to Allen Guttmann, *Sports Spectators*, see Dean Sullivan, "Faces in the Crowd: A Statistical Portrait of Baseball Spectators in Cincinnati, 1886–1888," *JSH* 17 (1990). Otherwise the
history of the sport can be followed through biographies, auto-
biographies, and oral histories of outstanding players and managers. The best of these include Robert Creamer's *Babe: The
Legend Come to Life* (New York, 1974) and Charles C. Alexander's *Ty Cobb* (New York, 1984) and *John McGraw* (New York,
1988). Also see such elegiac classics as Lawrence S. Ritter, *The
Glory of Their Times: The Story of the Early Days of Baseball
Told by the Men Who Played It* (New York, 1966); Roger Kahn,
The Boys of Summer (New York, 1973); and Donald Honig,

Baseball When the Grass Was Real (New York, 1975). See also Peter Levine, *A. G. Spalding and the Rise of Baseball*; Christy Mathewson, *Pitching in a Pinch* (New York, 1912); Anthony J. O'Connor, *Baseball for the Love of It: Hall of Famers Tell It Like It Was* (New York, 1982).

The business side of baseball has also received increased attention in recent years. The classic *No Joy in Mudville: The Dilemma of Major League Baseball*, by Ralph Andreano (Cambridge, Mass., 1965), may now be supplemented by James Edward Miller, *The Baseball Business: Pursuing Pennants and Profits in Baltimore* (Chapel Hill, N.C., 1990); and Andrew Zimbalist, *Baseball and Billions: A Probing Look Inside the Big Business of Our National Pastime* (New York, 1992).

BOXING

After baseball, boxing has been the sport most chronicled by historians, writers, and scholars. Dennis Brailsford, in *Bareknuckles: A Social History of Prize Fighting* (Cambridge, 1988), and John Ford, *Prize Fighting: The Age of Regency Boximania* (South Brunswick, N.J., 1971), tell the story of the English origins of the ring. For early fighting on the frontier, see Elliott J. Gorn, "Gouge and Bite," and for the American bareknucklers, Elliott J. Gorn, *The Manly Art*. For a fine overall treatment of the sport in the twentieth century, try Jeffrey Sammons, *Beyond the Ring: The Role of Boxing in American Society* (Urbana, Ill., 1988). Boxing's heroic, elemental qualities make it a natural for biographies. See Michael T. Isenberg's *John L. Sullivan and His America* (Urbana, Ill., 1988). Randy Roberts has written beautifully on boxing and American culture in *Jack Dempsey: The Manassa Mauler* (Baton Rouge, La., 1979) and *Papa Jack: Jack Johnson and the Era of White Hopes* (New York, 1983). For a slightly different view of Dempsey, see Elliott J. Gorn, " 'The Manassa Mauler and the Fighting Marine': An Interpretation of the Dempsey-Tunney Fights," *Journal of American Studies* 19 (1985): 27–47. For Joe Louis, see Chris Mead, *Champion: Joe Louis in White America* (New York,

1985): For a moving account of "the Greatest," see Thomas Hauser, *Muhammad Ali: His Life and Times* (New York, 1991).

BASKETBALL AND FOOTBALL

Neither basketball nor football, alas, has a literature comparable to those of baseball and boxing. Both sports still await a full historical treatment, though Robert W. Peterson, *Cages to Jump Shots: Pro Basketball's Early Years* (New York, 1990), is a start for basketball. In the absence of a scholarly biography of James Naismith, there is Bernice Larson Webb, *The Basketball Man: James Naismith* (Lawrence, Kans., 1973). Leonard Koppett, *24 Seconds to Shoot* (New York, 1968), has good material on the organized game's early years, and Stanley Cohen, *The Game They Played* (New York, 1977), focuses on the scandals in college basketball during 1950 and 1951, as does Charles Rosen, *The Scandals of '51: How Gamblers Almost Killed College Basketball* (New York, 1978). See also Neil D. Isaacs, *All the Moves: A History of College Basketball* (Philadelphia, 1975); Lewis Cole, *A Loose Game: The Sport and Business of Basketball* (New York, 1978); and Alexander Weyand, *The Cavalcade of Basketball* (New York, 1960). Fine contemporary accounts include Pete Axthelm, *The City Game: Basketball, from the Playground to Madison Square Garden* (New York, 1970), and David Halberstam, *The Breaks of the Game* (New York, 1981). Finally, Ted Vincent, *Mudville's Revenge: The Rise and Fall of American Sport* (New York, 1981), has provocative material on basketball and other sports. The following works also contain useful information: David S. Neft, *The Sports Encyclopedia: Pro Basketball* (New York, 1975); Larry Fox, *Illustrated History of Basketball* (New York, 1974); Dave Anderson, *The Story of Basketball* (New York, 1988); and William S. Jarrett, *Timetables of Sports History: Basketball* (New York, 1990).

Football, too, has attracted more contemporary than historical attention. Easily the most ambitious and sophisticated work is Michael Oriard's *Reading Football: Sport, Popular Journalism, and American Culture, 1876–1913* (Chapel Hill, N.C., 1993).

Walter Camp's papers are voluminous and accessible, yet he still has no modern biographer. Of some use is Harford Powel, Jr., *Walter Camp: The Father of American Football* (Boston, 1926), but also see Walter Camp, *The Book of Football* (New York, 1910). Football's earliest years are ably analyzed in Ronald A. Smith's *Sports and Freedom: The Rise of Big-Time College Athletics* (New York, 1988), which is the best general work on early college sports. While Oriard and Smith have begun the long-overdue research into the social and cultural history of football, the professional game's business history may be followed in David Harris, *The League: The Rise and Decline of the NFL* (New York, 1986).

There are countless team histories and popular chronicles of the game, but few scholarly works. Some of the more useful popular accounts include Harold Classen, *The History of Professional Football* (New York, 1963); Christy Walsh, ed., *Intercollegiate Football: A Complete Pictorial and Statistical Review from 1869 to 1934* (New York, 1934); Harold Classen, *Encyclopedia of Football* (New York, 1961); Cliff Christl, *Sleepers, Busts and Franchise-makers: The Behind-the-Scenes Story of the Pro Football Draft* (Seattle, 1983). On the connections between football and college life in the late nineteenth and early twentieth centuries, see Frederick Rudolph, *The American College and University* (New York, 1962). For relations between faculty and students and the growth of the extracurriculum, see Laurence R. Veysey, *The Emergence of the American University* (Chicago, 1965). The most ambitious effort to place football in the social and cultural context of upper-class revitalization in the late nineteenth and early twentieth centuries remains Christopher Lasch's seminal essay "The Moral and Intellectual Rehabilitation of the Ruling Class," in *The World of Nations* (New York, 1973). Some of the same themes are carried forward into the twentieth century in Lasch's chapter "The Degradation of Sport," in *The Culture of Narcissism: American Life in an Age of Diminishing Expectations* (New York, 1978). The game's crisis during Theodore Roosevelt's Presidency is ably discussed in Roberta J. Park, "From Football to Rugby—and Back, 1906–1919: The University of

California–Stanford University Response to the Football Crisis of 1905," *JSH* 11 (1984): 5–40.

AMATEUR SPORTS

The substantial literature on amateur sports in America consists almost entirely of laments about their decline and efforts to document abuses; but a few works go beyond that formula. Ronald A. Smith, *Sports and Freedom*, is the best account of the origins of amateur college sports. Donald J. Mrozek, *Sport and American Mentality*, offers useful analyses of changes in the intellectual and cultural attitudes toward sports in the late nineteenth through early twentieth centuries. Robert Lipsyte's classic article "Varsity Syndrome: The Unkindest Cut," is most readily available in Peter Levine, *American Sport: A Documentary History* (Englewood Cliffs, N.J., 1989). A comprehensive history of the NCAA would be an important contribution to the field. In the meantime, there is Joseph Durso, *The Sports Factory: An Investigation into College Sports* (New York, 1975); Dan Jenkins, *Saturday's America* (Boston, 1970); Neil Amdur, *The Fifth Down: Democracy and the Football Revolution* (New York, 1971); John J. Rooney, *The Recruiting Game: Toward a New System of Intercollegiate Athletics* (Lincoln, Neb., 1980); Robert H. Atwell et al., *The Money Game: Financing College Athletics* (Washington, D.C., 1980); Jim Benagh, *Making It to #1: How College Football and Basketball Teams Get There* (New York, 1976); and Willie Morris, *The Recruiting of Marcus Dupree* (Garden City, N.Y., 1983). Scandals past are readily traced in back issues of *The New York Times* and in more depth in the *Chronicle of Higher Education*.

On the playground movement, see Dominick Cavallo, *Muscles and Morals: Organized Playgrounds and Urban Reform* (Philadelphia, 1981); Cary Goodman, *Choosing Sides: Playground and Street Life on the Lower East Side* (New York, 1979); David Nasaw, *Children of the City: At Work and at Play*; and the essay by Stephen Hardy and Alan G. Ingham, "Games, Structures, and Agencies: Historians on the American Play

Movement." For the cultural struggles over recreation in late-nineteenth- and early-twentieth-century cities, see Roy Rosenzweig, *Eight Hours for What We Will: Workers and Leisure in an Industrial City, 1870–1920* (New York, 1983), and Stephen Hardy, *How Boston Played.* Also of interest is Timothy P. O'Hanlon, "School Sports as Social Training: The Case of Athletics and the Crisis of World War I," *JSH* 9 (1982): 5–29. For a detailed discussion of one particular ethnic group in sports history, see Peter Levine's *Ellis Island to Ebbets Field: Sport and the American Jewish Experience* (New York, 1992). A smaller-scale ethnic case study is provided by Gary Ross Mormino, "The Playing Fields of St. Louis: Italian Immigrants and Sports, 1925–1941," *JSH* 9 (1982): 5–19.

AFRICAN AMERICANS AND SPORTS

There is a growing literature on African Americans in sports. Harry Edwards, *The Revolt of the Black Athlete* (New York, 1969), was an early salvo in the battle for black athletes' rights on and off the playing field. Also see Jack Olson, *The Black Athlete: A Shameful Story* (New York, 1968). Arthur Ashe's three-volume history of African Americans in sport, *A Hard Road to Glory: A History of the African American Athlete, 1619–1918* (New York, 1988), is a major achievement. For a fine study of one city, try Rob Ruck, *Sandlot Seasons: Sport in Black Pittsburgh* (Urbana, Ill., 1987). See also Arthur Ashe and Neil Amdur, *Off the Court* (New York, 1981). For a study of college campuses and integration, see David K. Wiggins, "The Future of College Athletics Is at Stake: Black Athletes and Racial Turmoil on Three Predominantly White University Campuses, 1968–1972," *JSH* 15 (1988): 304–33. For other accounts of famous African-American athletes, see Al-Tony Gilmore, *Bad Nigger: The National Impact of Jack Johnson* (Port Washington, N.Y., 1975); Jackie Robinson and Alfred Duckett, *I Never Had It Made* (New York, 1974); William Baker, *Jesse Owens: An American Life* (New York, 1986); Curt Flood with Richard Carter, *The Way It Is* (New York, 1970); and Bill Russell and Taylor Branch,

Second Wind: Memoirs of an Opinionated Man (New York, 1979). On the most famous African-American sports figure of the twentieth century, see Thomas Hauser, *Muhammad Ali*.

The literature on blacks in baseball has been particularly rich. For the all-black leagues, see Harold W. Peterson, *Only the Ball Was White: A History of Legendary Black Players and All-Black Professional Teams* (New York, 1970), and Donn Rogosin, *Invisible Men: Life in Baseball's Negro Leagues* (New York, 1983). Also important are John Holway, *Voices from the Great Negro Baseball Leagues* (New York, 1975) and *Black Diamonds: Life in the Negro Leagues from the Men Who Lived It* (Westport, Conn., 1989); William Brashler, *Josh Gibson: A Life in the Negro Leagues* (New York: 1978); and Phil Dixon and Patrick J. Hannigan, *The Negro Baseball Leagues: A Photographic History* (Mattituck, N.Y., 1992). Jules Tygiel's *Baseball's Great Experiment: Jackie Robinson and His Legacy* is indispensable to understanding the reintegration of the game, but also see Harvey Frommer, *Rickey and Robinson: The Men Who Broke Baseball's Color Barrier* (New York, 1982); Jackie Robinson and Alfred Duckett, *I Never Had It Made*; and Murray Polner, *Branch Rickey: A Biography* (New York, 1982). For other memoirs of black ballplayers, see Roy Campanella, *It's Good to Be Alive* (New York, 1974); Willie Mays and Charles Einstein, *Willie Mays: My Life In and Out of Baseball* (New York, 1972); Leroy "Satchel" Paige and David Lipman, *Maybe I'll Pitch Forever* (New York, 1962); and Quincy Trouppe, *20 Years Too Soon* (Los Angeles, 1977). For an excellent discussion of the connections between racial discrimination and baseball in the Dominican Republic, see Rob Ruck, *The Tropic of Baseball: Baseball in the Dominican Republic* (Westport, Conn., 1991).

WOMEN AND SPORTS
The literature on women's sports is growing rapidly, mostly in the *Journal of Sports History* (which devoted an entire issue to the subject in Spring 1991, edited by Roberta J. Park), but also in scholarly and popular books. See Stephanie Twin, ed., *Out of*

the Bleachers: Writings on Women and Sport (Old Westbury, N.Y., 1979); the excellent collection edited by James A. Mangan and Roberta J. Park, *From "Fair Sex" to Feminism: Sport and the Socialization of Women in the Industrial and Post-Industrial Eras* (London, 1987); Allen Guttmann, *Women's Sports: A History* (New York, 1991); and Martha H. Verbrugge, *Able-Bodied Womanhood: Personal Health and Social Change in Nineteenth Century Boston* (New York, 1988). Lois Brown adds to our understanding of women's baseball in *The Girls of Summer* (New York, 1992). Important memoirs and biographies include Billie Jean King and Kim Chapin, *Billie Jean* (New York, 1974); and William Oscar Johnson and Nancy P. Williamson, *"Whatta-Gal": The Babe Didrickson Story* (Boston, 1977).

GENERAL WORKS IN SOCIAL AND CULTURAL HISTORY
The transformation of nineteenth-century American culture and society has been the subject of countless works. We have found the following books particularly useful. For labor and working-class life, try Herbert Gutman, *Work, Culture, and Society in Industrializing America* (New York, 1976); Daniel T. Rodgers, *The Work Ethic in Industrial America, 1850–1920* (Chicago, 1978); Paul Faler, *Mechanics and Manufacturers in the Early Industrial Revolution, Lynn, Massachusetts, 1760–1860* (Albany, N.Y., 1981); Bruce Laurie, *Artisans into Workers: Labor in Nineteenth Century America* (New York, 1989); Sean Wilentz, *Chants Democratic: New York City and the Rise of the American Working Class, 1788–1850* (New York, 1984); Richard B. Stott, *Workers in the Metropolis: Class, Ethnicity, and Youth in Antebellum New York City* (Ithaca, N.Y., 1990); Allen F. Davis and Mark H. Haller, *The Peoples of Philadelphia: A History of Ethnic Groups and Lower Class Life, 1790–1940* (Philadelphia, 1973).

More generally, recent years have seen an explosion of interest in social and cultural history. Among the more exciting works that have important things to say about the nineteenth century are Lawrence Levine, *Highbrow/Lowbrow: The Emergence of*

Cultural Hierarchy in America (Cambridge, Mass., 1988) and *Black Culture and Black Consciousness* (New York, 1977); Timothy J. Gilfoyle, *City of Eros: New York City, Prostitution, and the Commercialization of Sex, 1790–1920* (New York, 1992); Roy Rosenzweig and Elizabeth Blackmar, *The Park and the People: A History of Central Park* (Ithaca, N.Y., 1992); Paul E. Johnson, *A Shopkeeper's Millennium* (New York, 1978); Karen Halttunen, *Confidence Men and Painted Women: A Study of Middle-Class Culture in America, 1830–1870* (New Haven, Conn., 1982); Susan G. Davis, *Parades and Power: Street Theater in Nineteenth Century Philadelphia* (Berkeley, Calif., 1986); Daniel Walker Howe, ed., *Victorian America* (Philadelphia, 1976); Richard D. Brown, *Modernization: The Transformation of American Life, 1600–1865* (New York, 1976); Ann Fabian, *Card Sharps, Dream Books, and Bucket Shops: Gambling in 19th Century America* (Ithaca, N.Y., 1990); Mary P. Ryan, *Cradle of the Middle Class: The Family in Oneida County, New York, 1790–1865* (Cambridge, England, 1981); George Fredrickson, *The Inner Civil War* (New York, 1965); Bruce Levine, *Half Slave and Half Free: The Roots of Civil War* (New York, 1992).

Works that are particularly useful to the study of gender and masculinity include Peter Stearns, *Be a Man: Males in Modern Society* (New York, 1979); E. Anthony Rotundo, *American Manhood: Transformation in Masculinity from the Revolution to the Modern Era* (New York, 1993); Joseph Pleck, *The Myth of Masculinity* (Cambridge, Mass., 1981); Joseph and Elizabeth Pleck, eds., *The American Man* (Englewood Cliffs, N.J., 1980); David Leverenz, *Manhood and the American Renaissance* (Ithaca, N.Y. 1989); Ann Douglass, *The Feminization of American Culture* (New York, 1977); Joseph F. Kett, *Rites of Passage: Adolescence in America, 1790 to the Present* (New York, 1977); Barbara Clark Smith and Kathy Peiss, *Men and Women: A History of Costume, Gender, and Power* (Washington, D.C., 1989); Christine Stansell, *City of Women: Sex and Class in New York, 1789–1869* (New York, 1986); David MacLeod, *Building Character in the American Boy: The Boy Scouts, YMCA, and Their Forerunners, 1870–1920* (Madison, Wis., 1983); Mary

Ann Clawson, *Constructing Brotherhood: Class, Gender, and Fraternalism* (Princeton, N.J., 1989); and Mark C. Carnes and Clyde Griffen, eds., *Meanings for Manhood: Constructions of Masculinity in Victorian America* (Chicago, 1990).

Recent years have brought a flowering of the study of American culture at the end of the nineteenth century. For an interpretive overview see Alan Trachtenberg, *The Incorporation of America: Culture and Society in the Gilded Age* (New York, 1982). Kathy Peiss, *Cheap Amusements: Working Women and Leisure in Turn of the Century New York* (Philadelphia, 1986), is a fine study of working-class women and recreation. On the growing importance of cabaret life, see Lewis A. Erenberg, *Steppin' Out: New York Nightlife and the Transformation of American Culture, 1890–1930* (Westport, Conn., 1981). For labor and culture, try Roy Rosenzweig, *Eight Hours for What We Will;* Michael H. Frisch and Daniel J. Walkowitz, eds., *Working Class America: Essays on Labor, Community and American Society* (Urbana, Ill., 1983); and Herbert Gutman et al., *Who Built America*, vol. 2. (New York, 1992). John Kasson has done as much as any other historian to help us understand the cultural life of the nineteenth century; see his *Civilizing the Machine: Technology and Republican Values in America, 1776–1990* (New York, 1976); *Amusing the Million: Coney Island at the Turn of the Century* (New York, 1978); and *Rudeness and Civility: Manners in Nineteenth-Century Urban America* (New York, 1990).

The pioneering essays of Warren Susman in American cultural history are collected in *Culture as History: The Transformation of American Society in the Twentieth Century* (New York, 1984). For the bourgeois cult of the strenuous life, see T. J. Jackson Lears, *No Place of Grace: Antimodernism and the Transformation of American Culture, 1880–1920* (New York, 1981). A classic statement of the changes America underwent at the turn of the century is to be found in John Higham, "The Reorientation of American Culture in the 1890's," in John Weiss, ed., *The Origins of Modern Consciousness* (Detroit, 1965). Social Darwinism is discussed in Richard Hofstadter's *Social Darwinism in American Thought, 1860–1915* (Philadelphia, 1944), and nativism is the subject of John Higham's enduring *Strangers in the Land: Patterns of American Nativism, 1860–1925* (New York, 1970). For gender and masculinity across classes, see Estelle Freedman and John D'Emilio, *Intimate Matters: A History of Sexuality in America* (New York, 1988); Mark C. Carnes, *Secret Ritual and Manhood in Victorian America* (New Haven, Conn., 1989); and Michael Denning, *Mechanic Accents: Dime Novels, and Working Class Culture in America* (London, 1987).

Other works added immensely to our understanding of twentieth-century American culture and society. Among the more important ones were Gunther Barth, *City People: The Rise of Modern City Culture in Nineteenth-Century America* (New York, 1980); David Montgomery, *The Fall of the House of Labor: The Workplace, the State, and American Labor Activism, 1865–1925* (New York, 1988) and *Workers' Control in America: Studies in History of Work, Technology, and Labor Struggles* (New York, 1979); Sara M. Evans, *Born for Liberty: A History of Women in America* (New York, 1989) and *Personal Politics: The Roots of Women's Liberation in the Civil Rights Movement and the New Left* (New York, 1979); Andrew Bergman, *We're in the Money: Depression America and Its Films* (New York, 1971); Kenneth T. Jackson, *Crabgrass Frontier: The Suburbanization of America* (New York, 1985); Paul Carter, *The Twenties in America* (New York, 1968); Charles Forcey, *The Crossroads of Liberalism: Croly, Weyl, Lippman, and the Progressive Era, 1900–1925* (New York, 1961); Irving Howe, *World of Our Fathers* (New York, 1976); William Chafe, *The Unfinished Journey: America Since World War II* (New York, 1986); Godfrey Hodgson, *America in Our Time* (Garden City, N.Y., 1976); Robert S. and Helen M. Lynd, *Middletown: A Study in Contemporary American Culture* (New York, 1929); Roderick Nash, *The Nervous Generation: American Thought, 1917–1930* (Chicago, 1970); Taylor Branch, *Parting the Waters: America in the King Years, 1954–1963* (New York, 1988); Harvard Sitkoff, *The Struggle for Black Equality, 1954–1992*, rev. ed. (New York, 1993); Richard Sennett, *The Fall of Public Man: On the Social Psychology of Capitalism* (New York, 1977); Warren Susman, ed.,

Culture and Commitment, 1929–1945 (New York, 1973); William Chafe, *The American Woman: Her Changing Social, Economic, and Political Roles, 1920–1970* (New York, 1972); Loren Baritz, ed., *The Culture of the Twenties* (New York, 1970); and Elaine Tyler May, *Great Expectations: Marriage and Divorce in Post Victorian America* (Chicago, 1980) and *Homeward Bound: American Families in the Cold War Era* (New York, 1988).

The twentieth century cannot be understood apart from popular culture, media, and the advertising industry. We have found particularly useful Stuart Ewen, *Captains of Consciousness: Advertising and the Social Roots of the Consumer Culture* (New York, 1976); Stuart and Elizabeth Ewen, *Channels of Desire: Mass Images and the Shaping of American Consciousness*, 2nd ed. (Minneapolis, 1982); Marshall McLuhan, *The Mechanical Bride: Folklore of Industrial Man* (Boston, 1951); George Lipsitz, *Time Passages: Collective Memory and American Popular Culture* (Minneapolis, 1990); Roland Marchand, *Advertising the American Dream: Making Way for Modernity, 1920–1940* (Berkeley, Calif., 1985); Neil Postman, *Amusing Ourselves to Death* (New York, 1985); James Weinstein, *The Corporate Ideal in the Liberal State: 1900–1918* (Boston, 1968); Paul Buhle, *Popular Culture in America* (Minneapolis, 1987); Robert Sklar, *Movie-Made America: A Cultural History of American Movies* (New York, 1975); Lary May, *Screening Out the Past: The Birth of Mass Culture and the Motion Picture Industry* (New York, 1980); Thomas S. W. Lewis, *Empire of the Air: The Men Who Made Radio* (New York, 1991); Leo Lowenthal, *Literature, Popular Culture and Society* (Englewood Cliffs, N.J., 1961); and Richard Wightman Fox and T. J. Jackson Lears, eds., *The Culture of Consumption; Critical Essays in American History, 1880–1980* (New York: 1983).

Index

277